Warman's®
Depression
Glass

FIELD GUIDE
5th Edition

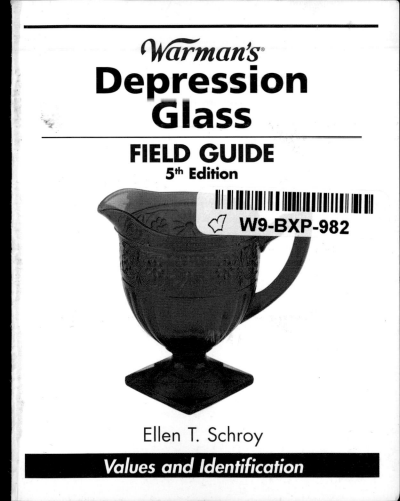

Ellen T. Schroy

Values and Identification

Published by

700 East State Street • Iola, WI 54990-0001
715-445-2214 • 888-457-2873
www.krausebooks.com

To order books or other products call toll-free 1-800-258-0929
or visit us online at www.krausebooks.com

ISBN-13: 978-1-4402-3456-9
ISBN-10: 1-4402-3456-6

Cover Designed by Kevin Ulrich
Interior Designed by Jana Tappa
Edited by Mary Sieber

Printed in China

ACKNOWLEDGMENTS

Many thanks to the following people, without whom I could not have created this book:

PATTERN SILHOUETTES OF DEPRESSION GLASS PATTERNS

Jerry O'Brien

PHOTOGRAPHY

Ron and Julie Madlung
Frank and Caren Reed
Donna Chiarelli
Kris Kandler

Thanks also to the collectors, dealers, and auctioneers who let us photograph their Depression glass over the past several editions.

CONTENTS

PATTERNS

INTRODUCTION

Depression glass is called such because collectors generally associate mass-produced glassware found in pink, yellow, crystal, or green with the years surrounding the Great Depression in America.

The housewives of the Depression-era were able to enjoy the wonderful colors offered in this new inexpensive glass dinnerware because they received pieces of their favorite patterns packed in boxes of soap, or as premiums given at "dish night" at the local movie theater. Merchandisers, such as Sears & Roebuck and F. W. Woolworth, enticed young brides with the colorful wares that they could afford even when economic times were harsh.

Because of advancements in glassware technology, Depression-era patterns were mass-produced and could be purchased for a fraction of what cut glass or lead crystal cost. As one manufacturer found a pattern that was pleasing to the buying public, other companies soon followed with their adaptation of a similar design. Patterns included several design motifs, such as florals, geometrics, and even patterns that looked back to Early American patterns like Sandwich glass.

As America emerged from the Great Depression and life

became more leisure-oriented again, new glassware patterns were created to reflect the new tastes of this generation. More elegant shapes and forms were designed, leading to what is sometimes called "Elegant Glass." Today's collectors often include these more elegant patterns when they talk about Depression-era glassware.

A time line that highlights the beginnings, major events, and endings of American glassware manufacturers is included in this edition to show the scope of the companies that helped produce glassware in this era. Also included in this edition is a section of pattern sihouette sketches that will help you identify which patterns you have or want to add to your collection.

Depression-era glassware is one of the best-researched collecting areas available to the American marketplace. This is due in large part to the careful research of several people, including Hazel Marie Weatherman, Gene Florence, Barbara Mauzy, Carl F. Luckey, and Kent Washburn. Their books are held in high regard by researchers and collectors today.

Regarding values for Depression glass, rarity does not always equate to a high dollar amount. Some more readily found items command lofty prices because of high demand or other factors, not because they are necessarily rare. As collectors' tastes range from the simple patterns to the more elaborate patterns, so does the ability of their budget to invest in inexpensive patterns to multi-hundreds of dollars per form patterns. Condition and color clarity are even more important to present day collectors. A premium price is commanded when a piece of Depression glass has its original paper label fully intact, and many can still be found today.

To maintain the fine tradition of extensive descriptions typically found in Warman's price guides, as much information as possible has been included as far as sizes, shapes, colors, etc. Whenever possible, the original manufacturer's language was maintained. As the patterns evolved, sometimes other usage names were assigned to pieces. Color names are also given as the manufacturers originally named them.

The Depression-era glassware researchers have many accurate sources, including company records, catalogs, magazine advertisements, oral and written histories from sales staff, factory workers, etc. The dates included in the introductions are approximate as are some of the factory locations. When companies had more than one factory, usually only the main office or factory is listed.

COMPANY TIME LINE

19th C   Ohio Flint Glass founded, later becomes part of National Glass Company conglomerate.

Indiana Glass Company established in 1907.

Bottle plant at Jeannette, Pennsylvania becomes Jeannette Glass Company.

1853   McKee and Brothers founded in Pittsburgh.

1887   Fostoria Glass Company founded in Fostoria, Ohio, but moves to Moundsville, West Virginia when fuel supply is depleted.

1888   McKee moves to Jeannette, Pennsylvania.

1890   Westmoreland Specialty Company is established in Grapeville, Pennsylvania. Early manufacture includes bottles and food containers. During World War I, glass candy containers are made. The plant continues on to make colored and opaque glassware in both Depression glass patterns and later a giftware line.

1891   U. S. Glass Company organizes by combining 18 different glass houses located in Pennsylvania, Ohio, and West Virginia. The main offices are in Pittsburgh, as well as some manufacturing.

1899   Macbeth merges with Evans, creating Macbeth-Evans. Main factory located in Charleroi, Pennsylvania, with others located in Marion, Bethevan, and Elwood, Indiana, as well as Toledo.

1900   Federal Glass Company opens Columbus, Ohio, plant. First wares are crystal with needle etching, various decorations, and crackle finish. After switching to automation, the company soon begins production of tumblers and many Depression-era patterns, as well as restaurant wares, all at an economical price.

1901   Imperial Glass Company organizes. Produces first glass at Bellaire, Ohio, plant in 1904.

Morgantown Glass Works begins production in Morgantown, West Virginia.

New Martinsville Glass Manufacturing Company is established at New Martinsville, West Virginia.

1902   Hazel Atlas Glass Company established in Washington, Pennsylvania, a result of the merger of the Hazel Glass Company and its neighboring factory, Atlas Glass and Metal Company. Corporate offices are later established at Wheeling, West Virginia.

1903   Morgantown Glass Works reorganizes as Economy Tumbler Company and operates using that name.

Liberty Cut Glass Works established in Egg Harbor, New Jersey. Primarily a cutting house for years, pressed glass is also made.

McKee Brothers reorganizes into McKee Glass Company and continues until 1951.

1905   Hocking Glass Company established in Lancaster, Ohio. Well known by the mid-1920s for their tumbler and tableware production.

1906   Fenton Art Glass Company built a new factory in Williamstown, West Virginia. While their giftware lines are well known, some Depression-era glassware was produced.

1907   Indiana Glass Company established at Dunkirk, Indiana. Early production is hand pressed. Assembly line patterns evolve during the 1920s, although some still require handwork. Later produce automobile glassware items and becomes a subsidiary of Lancaster Colony.

1908   Lancaster Glass Company, Lancaster, Ohio, built by first president of Fostoria.

1911   L. E. Smith begins in the glass trade. A lot of the production of this company is utilitarian in nature. Also makes lenses for automobiles.

1916   Paden City Glass Manufacturing Company is established at Paden City, West Virginia. Production includes some Depression-era patterns, but company is better known for its elegant lines, vases, lamps, and restaurant wares.

1923 Economy Tumbler Company changes name to Economy Glass Company.

1924 Fostoria introduces color and starts national magazine advertising campaign.

Jeannette toted by trade as "one of the most complete automatic factories in the country."

Lancaster becomes subsidiary of Hocking Glass Company. Continues to make kitchenware, cut and decorated tableware under the Lancaster name until 1937. Also makes colored blanks for Standard Glass Company, another Hocking subsidiary, where the glass is etched and cut. Known as Plant #2 to Anchor Hocking.

1927 Jeannette management ceases all hand operations.

1928 Jeannette makes green and pink glass automatically in a continuous tank, a first!

Trade journals proclaim Clarksburg, West Virginia, Hazel-Atlas factory as "World's Largest Tumbler Factory," which accurately describes the fully automated factory.

1929 Economy Glass Company changes name back to Morgantown Glass Works, Inc.

1932   Liberty Cut Glass Works destroyed by fire, never to rebuild.

1937   Corning Glass Works purchases Macbeth-Evans.

Hocking Glass Company merges with Anchor Cap and Closure Corp., Long Island City, New York, creating the huge Anchor Hocking Glass Corp., which has continued to have a major impact on the glassware industry.

Morgantown Glass Works, Inc., closes.

1938   U. S. Glass moves main offices to Tiffin, Ohio, and production decreases.

1939   Morgantown Glassware Guild organizes and reopens factory.

1944   New Martinsville sold and reorganizes as Viking Glass Company.

1949   Westmoreland Glass Company begins to use impressed intertwined "W" and "G" mark.

1951   The only operating company of the former U. S. Glass is Tiffin. The rest have all closed.

McKee sold to Thatcher Manufacturing Company.

1952   Fire destroys Belmont plant, Bellaire, Ohio, destroying records.

1955   Duncan and Miller molds are acquired by Tiffin, which begins to produce colors and crystal wares with these molds.

1956   Continental Can purchases Hazel-Atlas and continues to sell tableware under name "Hazelware."

1958   Federal Glass becomes a division of Federal Paper Board Company and continues glassware production.

1961   Jeannette buys old McKee factory in Jeannette and moves there to continue production.

1964   Brockway Glass Company buys out Continental Can's interest in Hazel-Atlas and begins operation.

1965   Fostoria Glass Company purchases Morgantown Glassware Guild.

1966   Continental Can takes over operation of Tiffin until 1969, with glass production continuing.

1971   Glass production is terminated at Fostoria's Morgantown facility, ending the Morgantown Glassware Guild.

1973   Imperial Glass Company sold to Lenox, Inc.

1980   Tiffin Glass discontinues operation.

1982   Westmoreland Glass Company closes factory in May. Reorganizes in July.

1983   Lancaster Glass purchases Fostoria.

Westmoreland begins to use full name as imprinted mark.

Westmoreland Glass Company again closes Grapeville plant.

1999   L. G. Wright discontinues operation. Molds, factory equipment liquidated at public auction in May.

2000   Indiana Glass goes out of business in November.

2004   L. E. Smith ceases production in June but manages to reorganize, and limited production later resumes.

2005   L. E. Smith acquired by Willman Kelman.

2007   Fenton Art Glass discontinues production of all but a few lines.

2011   Fenton ceases production.

PATTERN SILHOUETTE IDENTIFICATION GUIDE

For more listings, photos, and pattern silhouettes, consult *Warman's Depression Glass*, 5th edition, which can be purchased at your local bookstore or directly from the publisher online at www.krausebooks.com or by phone at (800) 258-0929.

ART DECO	BASKETS	BEADED EDGES

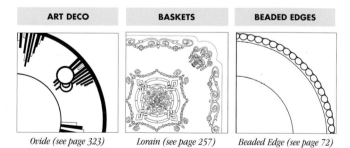

Ovide (see page 323)   *Lorain (see page 257)*   *Beaded Edge (see page 72)*

BIRDS

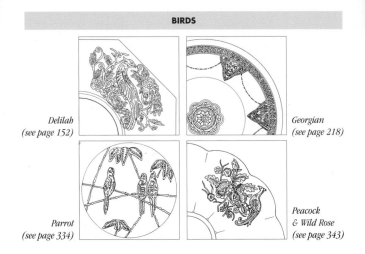

Delilah
(see page 152)

Georgian
(see page 218)

Parrot
(see page 334)

Peacock
& Wild Rose
(see page 343)

BLOCKS

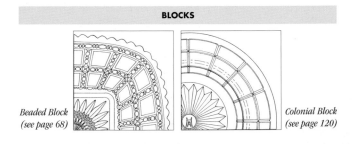

Beaded Block
(see page 68)

Colonial Block
(see page 120)

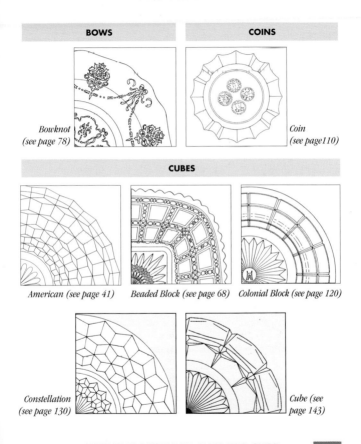

BOWS

Bowknot
(see page 78)

COINS

Coin
(see page110)

CUBES

American (see page 41)

Beaded Block (see page 68)

Colonial Block (see page 120)

Constellation
(see page 130)

Cube (see
page 143)

DIAMONDS

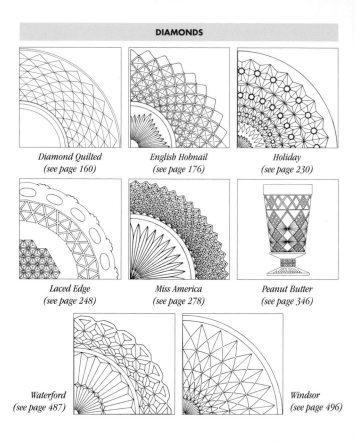

Diamond Quilted
(see page 160)

English Hobnail
(see page 176)

Holiday
(see page 230)

Laced Edge
(see page 248)

Miss America
(see page 278)

Peanut Butter
(see page 346)

Waterford
(see page 487)

Windsor
(see page 496)

ELLIPSES

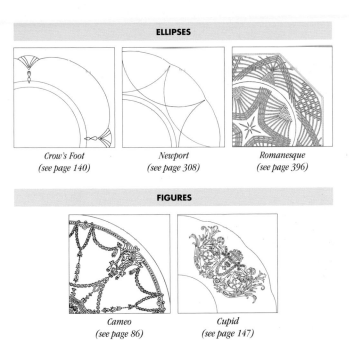

Crow's Foot
(see page 140)

Newport
(see page 308)

Romanesque
(see page 396)

FIGURES

Cameo
(see page 86)

Cupid
(see page 147)

FLORALS

Alice (see page 40)

Cherry Blossom (see page 95)

Cloverleaf (see page 107)

Daisy (see page 149)

Dogwood (see page 166)

Doric (see page 168)

Doric & Pansy (see page 170)

Floragold (see page 189)

Floral (see page 192)

FLORALS

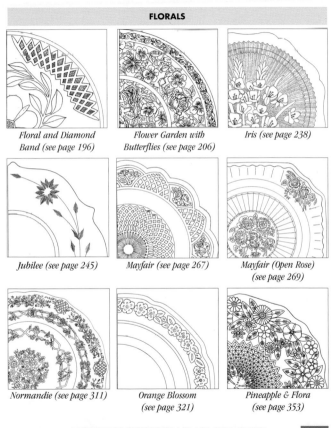

Floral and Diamond Band (see page 196)

Flower Garden with Butterflies (see page 206)

Iris (see page 238)

Jubilee (see page 245)

Mayfair (see page 267)

Mayfair (Open Rose) (see page 269)

Normandie (see page 311)

Orange Blossom (see page 321)

Pineapple & Flora (see page 353)

FLORALS

Primrose (see page 364)

Rose Cameo (see page 398)

Rosemary(see page 400)

Royal Lace (see page 407)

Seville (see page 433)

Sharon (see page 437)

Sunflower (see page 452)

Thistle (see page 465)

Tulip (see page 470)

FRUITS

Avocado (see page 66)

Cherryberry (see page 99)

Della Robbia (see page 154)

Fruits (see page 216)

Paneled Grape (see page 327)

Strawberry (see page 447)

GEOMETRIC AND LINE DESIGNS

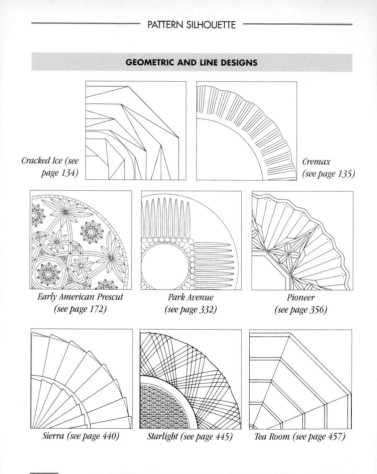

Cracked Ice (see page 134)

Cremax (see page 135)

Early American Prescut (see page 172)

Park Avenue (see page 332)

Pioneer (see page 356)

Sierra (see page 440)

Starlight (see page 445)

Tea Room (see page 457)

HONEYCOMB

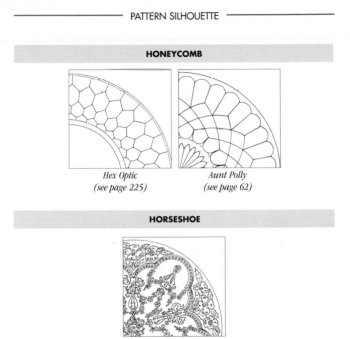

Hex Optic
(see page 225)

Aunt Polly
(see page 62)

HORSESHOE

Horseshoe
(see page 235)

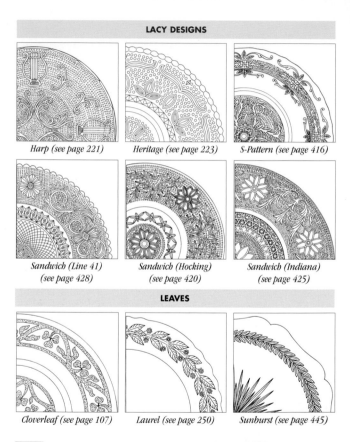

LACY DESIGNS

Harp (see page 221)

Heritage (see page 223)

S-Pattern (see page 416)

Sandwich (Line 41)
(see page 428)

Sandwich (Hocking)
(see page 420)

Sandwich (Indiana)
(see page 425)

LEAVES

Cloverleaf (see page 107)

Laurel (see page 250)

Sunburst (see page 445)

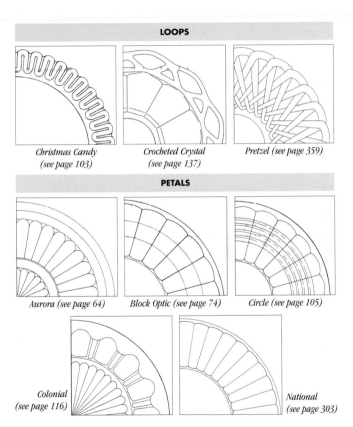

LOOPS

Christmas Candy
(see page 103)

Crocheted Crystal
(see page 137)

Pretzel (see page 359)

PETALS

Aurora (see page 64)

Block Optic (see page 74)

Circle (see page 105)

Colonial
(see page 116)

National
(see page 303)

PETALS

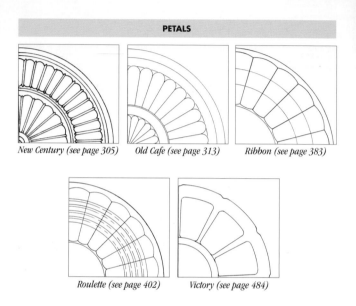

New Century (see page 305) *Old Cafe (see page 313)* *Ribbon (see page 383)*

Roulette (see page 402) *Victory (see page 484)*

PETALS OR RIDGES WITH DIAMOND ACCENTS

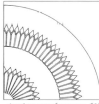

Anniversary (see page 60)

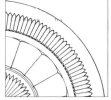

Coronation (see page 132)

Fortune (see page 214)

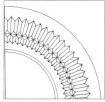

Lincoln Inn (see page 253)

Petalware (see page 347)

Queen Mary (see page 372)

PLAIN

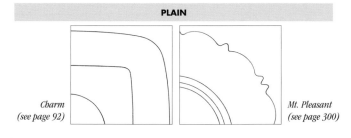

*Charm
(see page 92)*

*Mt. Pleasant
(see page 300)*

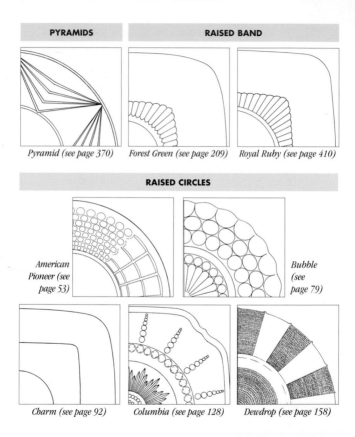

PYRAMIDS

RAISED BAND

Pyramid (see page 370)

Forest Green (see page 209)

Royal Ruby (see page 410)

RAISED CIRCLES

American Pioneer (see page 53)

Bubble (see page 79)

Charm (see page 92)

Columbia (see page 128)

Dewdrop (see page 158)

RAISED CIRCLES

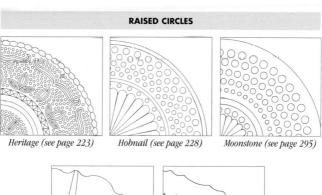

Heritage (see page 223)   *Hobnail (see page 228)*   *Moonstone (see page 295)*

Oyster & Pearl (see page 325)   *Radiance (see page 376)*

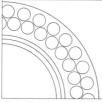  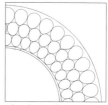

Raindrops (see page 381)   *Teardrop (see page 460)*   *Thumbprint (see page 467)*

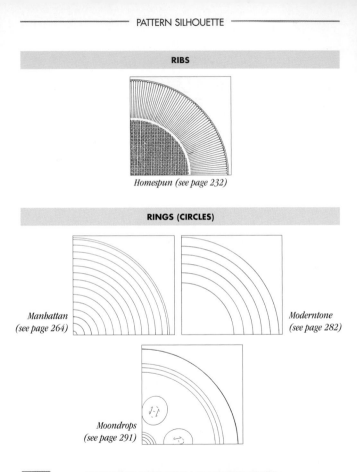

RIBS

Homespun (see page 232)

RINGS (CIRCLES)

Manhattan (see page 264)

Moderntone (see page 282)

Moondrops (see page 291)

RINGS (CIRCLES)

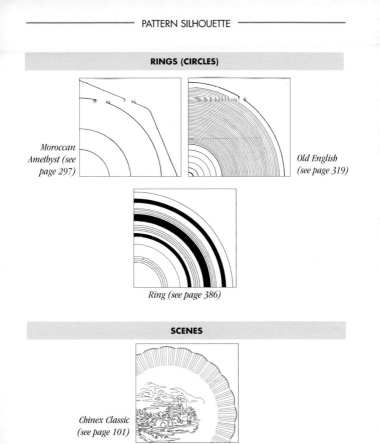

Moroccan Amethyst (see page 297)

Old English (see page 319)

Ring (see page 386)

SCENES

Chinex Classic (see page 101)

SCROLLING DESIGNS

Adam (see page 37)

American Sweetheart (see page 56)

Florentine No. 1 (see page 198)

Florentine No. 2 (see page 201)

Madrid (see page 260)

Patrick (see page 341)

Philbe (see page 350)

Primo (see page 362)

Princess (see page 366)

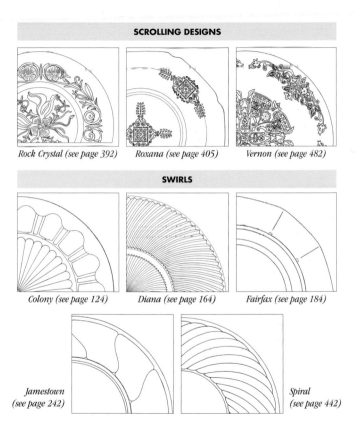

SCROLLING DESIGNS

Rock Crystal (see page 392)

Roxana (see page 405)

Vernon (see page 482)

SWIRLS

Colony (see page 124)

Diana (see page 164)

Fairfax (see page 184)

Jamestown (see page 242)

Spiral (see page 442)

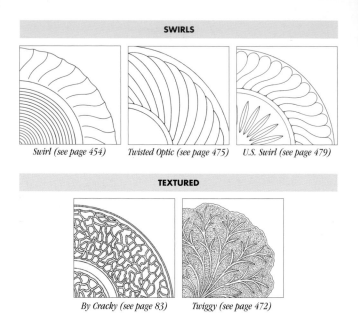

SWIRLS

Swirl (see page 454)   *Twisted Optic (see page 475)*   *U.S. Swirl (see page 479)*

TEXTURED

By Cracky (see page 83)   *Twiggy (see page 472)*

ADAM

Manufactured by Jeannette Glass Company, Jeannette, Pennsylvania, from 1932 to 1934.

Pieces were made in crystal, Delphite blue, green, pink, some topaz, and yellow. Delphite 4-inch high candlesticks are valued at $250 a pair. A yellow cup and saucer are valued at $200, and a 7-3/4" diameter yellow plate is valued at $115. Production in topaz and yellow was limited. Crystal prices are approximately 50 percent of the prices listed for green.

Reproductions: † Butter dish in pink and green.

ITEM	GREEN	PINK
Ashtray, 4-1/2" d	28.00	32.00
Berry bowl, small	20.00	18.50
Bowl, 9" d, cov	95.00	80.00
Bowl, 9" d, open	45.00	30.00
Bowl, 10" l, oval	40.00	40.00
Butter dish, cov †	325.00	100.00
Cake plate, 10" d, ftd	38.00	35.00
Candlesticks, pr, 4" h	125.00	80.00
Candy jar, cov, 2-1/2" h	125.00	95.00
Casserole, cov	95.00	80.00
Cereal bowl, 5-3/4" d	50.00	48.00
Coaster, 3-1/4" d	25.00	35.00

ITEM	GREEN	PINK
Creamer	28.00	30.00
Cup	28.00	30.00
Dessert bowl, 4-3/4" d	25.00	25.00
Iced tea tumbler, 5-1/2" h	70.00	75.00
Lamp	500.00	500.00
Pitcher, 32 oz, round base	—	125.00
Pitcher, 32 oz, 8" h	48.00	65.00
Plate, 6" d, sherbet	12.00	10.00
Plate, 7-3/4" d, salad, sq	15.00	16.00
Plate, 9" d, dinner, sq	30.00	35.00

Adam, green ashtray, $28; pink pitcher, $65.

ITEM	GREEN	PINK
Plate, 9" d, grill	32.00	37.50
Platter, 11-3/4" l, rect	30.00	35.00
Relish dish, 8" l, divided	27.00	20.00
Salt and pepper shakers, pr, 4" h	120.00	90.00
Saucer, 6" sq	10.00	6.00
Sherbet, 3"	40.00	35.00
Sugar, cov	42.00	35.00
Tumbler, 4-1/2" h	35.00	40.00
Vase, 7-1/2" h	150.00	220.00
Vegetable bowl, 7-3/4" d	30.00	40.00

Adam, pink 10" oval bowl, $40.

ALICE

Manufactured by Anchor-Hocking Glass Corp. under its Fire King trademark in the early 1940s. Pieces were made in Jade-ite, white with blue trim, and white with red trim.

ITEM	JADE-ITE	WHITE, BLUE TRIM	WHITE, RED TRIM
Cup	8.00	12.00	15.00
Cup and saucer	20.00	20.00	20.00
Plate, 9-1/2" d	40.00	28.00	30.00
Saucer	8.00	7.50	8.00

Fire King Alice, Jade-ite cup and saucer, $20.

AMERICAN
LINE NO. 2056

Manufactured by Fostoria Glass Company, Moundsville, Virginia, from 1915 to 1986.

Pieces were made in crystal, some amber, blue, green, yellow, pink, pink tinting to purple in the late 1920s and white and red in the 1980s. Pieces are currently being produced in red and crystal for Lancaster Colony by Dalzell Viking. Prices for colors fluctuate greatly.

ITEM	CRYSTAL
Almond bowl, 3-3/4" l, oval	18.00
Appetizer insert, 3-1/4"	30.00
Appetizer tray, 10-1/2" l, 6 inserts	250.00
Ashtray, 2-7/8" w, sq	7.00
Ashtray, 3-7/8" l, oval	25.00
Ashtray, 5" w, sq	35.00
Ashtray, 5-1/2" l, oval	18.00
Basket, open handle	125.00
Basket, 7" x 9", reeded handle	95.00
Basket, 10", c1988	40.00
Beer mug, 4-1/2" h, 12 oz	60.00

ITEM	CRYSTAL
Bitter bottles, 5-3/4" h, 4-1/2 oz, 2 pc set	270.00
Boat, 8-1/2" d	15.00
Boat, 9" d, two parts	12.00
Boat, 12" l	17.50
Bonbon, 6" d, 7" d, 8" d, 3 ftd	20.00
Bowl, 4-1/2" d, 1 handle	15.00
Bowl, 5" d, handle, tricorner	15.00
Bowl, 7" d, 4-1/2" h, cupped	85.00
Bowl, 8" d, deep	50.00
Bowl, 8" d, ftd	55.00
Bowl, 8-1/2" d, 2 handles	60.00
Bowl, 9" l, oval, #4836	60.00
Bowl, 9-1/2" d, 6" w, three parts	40.00
Bowl, 10" d, deep	48.00
Bowl, 10" d, 14" d liner	50.00
Bowl, 11-1/2" d rolled edge	75.00
Bowl, 11-3/4" l, oval, deep	40.00
Box, cov, 4-1/2" x 4-1/2"	200.00
Brush tray	50.00
Bud vase, 6" h, flared or ftd *	25.00
Bud vase, 8-1/2" h, cupped or flared	20.00
Butter dish, cov, 1/4 lb	30.00
Butter dish, cov, 7-1/4" d, round plate	120.00
Cake plate, 10" d, 2 handles	24.00
Cake plate, 12" d, 3 ftd	55.00
Cake stand, 10" round, pedestal foot	165.00
Cake stand, 10" sq, pedestal foot	165.00
Cake stand, 11" d, round, pedestal foot	195.00
Cake tray, 10-1/2" d, crook-shaped handle	45.00
Candelabrum, 6-1/2", two-light, bell base, bobeche, pr	125.00
Candle lamp, 8-1/2" h, chimney, candle part, 3-1/2"	170.00

ITEM	CRYSTAL
Candlestick, 2", chamber, finger hold	60.00
Candlesticks, pr, 3", round, ftd	30.00
Candlesticks, pr, 4-3/8", two-light, round foot	90.00
Candlesticks, pr, 6", octagon foot	60.00
Candlesticks, pr, 6-1/2", two-light, bell base	265.00

American, crystal bowl, flared, $75.

ITEM	CRYSTAL
Candlesticks, pr, 6-1/4", round foot	360.00
Candlesticks, pr, 7", sq, column	225.00
Candlesticks, pr, 7-1/4", Eiffel Tower	375.00
Candy box, cov, three parts, triangular	95.00
Catsup bottle	145.00
Celery tray, 10" l, oblong	35.00
Centerpiece bowl, 9-1/2" d	45.00
Centerpiece bowl, 11" d	45.00
Centerpiece bowl, 11" d, tricorner	45.00
Centerpiece bowl, 15" d, hat-shape	165.00
Cheese and cracker, 5-3/4" comport, 11-1/2" d plate	125.00
Cigarette box, cov, 4-3/4"	80.00
Claret, 4-5/8" h, 3-1/2 oz, plain bowl, #5056	65.00
Claret, 4-7/8" h, 7 oz, #2056	75.00
Coaster, 3-3/4" d	20.00
Cocktail, 2-7/8" h, cone, ftd, 3 oz, #2506	15.00
Cocktail, 4" h, 3-1/2 oz, plain bowl, #5056	18.00
Cologne bottle, orig stopper, 5-3/4" h, 6 oz	95.00
Cologne bottle, orig stopper, 7-1/4" h, 8 oz or 9 oz	90.00
Comport, 5" d, covered	25.00
Comport, 8-1/2" d, 4" h	45.00
Comport, 9-1/2" d, #3237	75.00
Condiment bottle	115.00
Condiment set, 2 oils, 2 shakers, mustard, tray	325.00
Condiment tray, clover leaf	375.00
Cordial, 3-1/8" h, 1 oz, plain bowl, #5056	25.00
Cordial bottle, 7-1/4" h, 9 oz	95.00
Cream soup bowl, 5" d, two handles	45.00
Cream soup liner	20.00
Creamer and sugar tray, 6-3/4" l, handle	15.00
Creamer, 3 oz, 2-3/8" h, tea size	15.00

ITEM	CRYSTAL
Creamer, 4-3/4 oz, individual size	12.50
Creamer, 9-1/2 oz	25.00
Cruet, orig stopper, 5 oz or 7 oz	45.00
Crushed fruit, cov, spoon, 10" h	1,225.00
Cup, flat	8.50
Cup, ftd, 7 oz	7.50
Decanter, stopper, 24 oz, 9-1/4" h	150.00
Dresser tray, 11"	450.00
Finger bowl, 4-1/2" d, underplate	110.00
Float bowl, 10" d or 11-1/2" d	45.00
Float bowl, 10" l or 11-1/2" l, oval	55.00
Fruit bowl, 10-1/2" d, 3 ftd	40.00
Fruit bowl, 11-1/2" d, 2-3/4" h, rolled edge	45.00
Fruit bowl, 13" d, shallow	65.00
Fruit bowl, 4-3/4" d, flared	18.00
Fruit bowl, 16" d, pedestal foot	250.00
Fruit cocktail, 4-3/4" h, 4-1/2 oz, hex foot, #2506	40.00
Glove box, cov, 9-1/2 x 3-1/2"	325.00
Goblet, 9 oz, 4-3/8" h, low foot, #2056	12.00
Goblet, 10 oz, 6-1/8" h, plain bowl, #5056	12.50
Goblet, 10 oz, 6-7/8" h, hex foot, #2056	14.00
Hat, 2-1/8"	30.00
Hat, 3" h or 4"h	40.00
Hat, western style	200.00
Honey jar, metal lid	450.00
Hurricane lamp, 12" h, complete	425.00
Ice bucket, tongs	90.00
Ice cream saucer, two styles	55.00
Ice cream tray, 13-1/2" l, oval	600.00
Ice dish for 4-oz crab or 5-oz tomato liner	65.00
Ice dish insert	18.00

ITEM	CRYSTAL
Ice tub, with liner, 5-3/8"	75.00
Ice tub, with liner, 6-1/2"	80.00
Iced tea tumbler, handle	215.00
Iced tea tumbler, 12 oz, 5-3/4" h, 12 oz, low foot, #2056	20.00

American, crystal 10" bowl, $48.

ITEM	CRYSTAL
Jam pot, cov	60.00
Jelly bowl, 4-1/4" d, 4-1/4" h	25.00
Jelly bowl, cov, 4-1/2" d, 6-3/4" h	28.00
Jelly comport, 4-1/2" d	25.00
Jelly comport, 5" d, flared	70.00
Jelly comport, cov, 6-3/4" d	30.00
Jewel box, cov, 5-1/4 x 2-1/4"	325.00
Juice tumbler, 5 oz, straight sides, #2056-1/2, flat	12.00
Juice tumbler, 4-1/8" h, 5 oz, ftd, plain bowl	15.00
Juice tumbler, 4-3/4" h, 5 oz, ftd, #2056	12.00
Lemonade tumbler, 11 oz, 5-3/4" h, ftd	500.00
Lemon bowl, cov, 5-1/2" d	28.00
Lily pond bowl, 12" d	100.00
Marmalade, cov, chrome spoon	125.00
Mayonnaise, divided	25.00
Mayonnaise, ladle, pedestal foot	45.00
Mayonnaise, liner, ladle	55.00
Molasses can, 11 oz, 6-3/4" h, one handle	950.00
Muffin tray, 10" l, two upturned sides	35.00
Mustard, cov	45.00
Napkin ring	45.00
Nappy, 4-1/2"	24.00
Nappy, 5" d	24.00
Nappy, 5" d, cov	45.00
Nappy, 6" d	24.00
Nappy, 7" d	17.50
Nappy, 8" d	20.00
Old-fashioned tumbler, 3-3/8" h, 6 oz, flat	10.00
Olive, 6" l, oblong	22.00
Oyster cocktail, 3-1/2" h, 4-1/2 oz, #2056	17.50
Oyster cocktail, 3-1/2" h, 4 oz, plain bowl, #5056	16.00

ITEM	CRYSTAL
Pastry server, orig spoon, orig box	45.00
Perfume bottle, orig stopper **	100.00
Pickle jar, pointed cov, 6" h	650.00
Pickle, 8" l, oblong	25.00
Picture frame	40.00
Pin tray, oval, 5-1/2" x 4-1/2"	120.00
Pitcher, 1 pt, 5-3/8" h, flat	35.00
Pitcher, 1 qt, flat	40.00
Pitcher, 1/2 gal, 8", ftd	90.00
Pitcher, 1/2 gal, ice lip, 8-1/4", flat bottom	165.00
Pitcher, 1/2 gal, without ice lip	265.00
Pitcher, 2 pt, 7-1/4" h, ftd	70.00
Pitcher, 3 pt, 8", ftd	65.00
Pitcher, 3 pt, ice lip, 6-1/2", ftd, fat	65.00
Plate, 6" d, bread and butter	8.00
Plate, 7" d, salad	15.00
Plate, 7-1/2 x 4-3/8", crescent salad	45.00
Plate, 8" d, sauce liner, oval	28.00
Plate, 8-1/2" d, luncheon	18.00
Plate, 9-1/2" d, dinner	20.00
Platter, 10-1/2" l, oval	40.00
Platter, 12" l, oval	48.00
Pomade box, 2" sq	365.00
Preserve bowl, cov, 5-1/2" d, two handles	95.00
Punch bowl, 14" d, high foot, base, two gallon	250.00
Punch bowl, 14" d, low foot, base	275.00
Punch bowl, 18" d, low, 3-3/4 gallon	300.00
Punch cup, flared rim	12.50
Punch cup, straight edge	12.50
Relish boat, 12" l, two parts	16.50
Relish tray, 6-1/2" x 9", four parts	42.00

*American, crystal relish, **$16.50**; luncheon plate, **$18**; footed tumbler, **$12**.*

ITEM	CRYSTAL
Relish/celery, 11" l, three parts	40.00
Rose bowl, 3-1/2" d	24.00
Rose bowl, 5" d	30.00
Salt and pepper shakers, pr, individual, tray, 2" h	24.00
Salt shaker, 3" h	10.00
Salt shaker, 3-1/2" h	7.50
Salt shaker, 3-1/4" h	9.50
Salt, individual	12.00
Sandwich plate, 9" d, small center	20.00
Sandwich plate, 10-1/2" d, small center	22.00
Sandwich plate, 11-1/2" d, small center	40.00
Sandwich tray, 12" d, center handle	35.00
Sauce boat with underplate	50.00
Saucer	3.25
Service tray, 9-1/2", two handles	32.00
Sherbet, 4-1/2 oz, 3-1/2" h, handle	95.00
Sherbet, 4-1/2 oz, 4-3/8" h, flared, #2056	10.00
Sherbet, 4-1/2 oz, 4-1/2" h, #2056-1/2	7.50
Sherbet, 5 oz, 3-1/2" h, low, #2056-1/2	12.00
Sherbet, 5-1/2 oz, 4-1/8" h, plain bowl, #5056	8.50
Shrimp bowl, 12-1/4" d	395.00
Spooner, 3-3/4" h	60.00
Straw holder, 10" h, cov	325.00
Sugar shaker	50.00
Sugar, cov, two handles	22.00
Sugar, cov, 6-1/4" h	65.00
Sugar cube holder	200.00
Sugar, handle, 3-1/4" h	15.00
Sugar, tea, 2-1/4" h	15.00
Sundae, 3-1/8" h, 6 oz, low foot, #2056	12.50
Sweet pea vase, 4-1/2" h	75.00

ITEM	CRYSTAL
Syrup, drip-proof top	75.00
Syrup, 6 oz, non-pour screw top, 5-1/2" h	200.00
Syrup, 6-1/2 oz, Sanl-cut server, #2056-1/2	175.00
Syrup, 10 oz, glass cov, 6" liner plate	145.00
Tea tumbler, 5" h, 12 oz, straight sides, #2056-1/2	17.50
Tea tumbler, 5-1/2" h, plain bowl, #5056	15.00
Tea tumbler, 5-1/4" h, 12 oz, flat, flared	17.50
Tidbit tray, metal crook-shaped handle	30.00
Toddler set, baby tumbler, bowl	85.00
Tom and Jerry mug, 3-1/4" h, 5-1/2 oz	42.00
Tom and Jerry, 12" d, small punch bowl, pedestal foot	225.00
Toothpick holder	25.00
Torte plate, 13-1/2" d, oval	65.00
Torte plate, 14" d	90.00
Torte plate, 18" d	150.00
Torte plate, 20" d	250.00
Torte plate, 24" d	275.00
Tray, cloverleaf	250.00
Tray, 5" x 2-1/2", rect	80.00
Tray, 6", oval, handle	45.00
Tray, 10" w, sq	115.00
Tray, 10" w, sq, four parts	85.00
Tray, 10-1/2" x 5", oval, handle	48.00
Tray, 10-1/2" x 7-1/2", rect	75.00
Tray, 10-3/4" sq, four parts	95.00
Tray, 12" d, round	185.00
Tray, 14-1/8", 5 part ***	160.00
Trifle bowl, 8" d, 4" h	300.00
Trophy cup, 8" d, ftd, two handles	145.00
Tumbler, 3-7/8" h, straight sides, #2056-1/2	17.50
Tumbler, 4-1/8" h, 8 oz, flat, flared	10.00

ITEM	CRYSTAL
Tumbler, 4-7/8" h, 9 oz, ftd	12.00
Urn, 6" h, sq, pedestal foot	32.00
Urn, 7-1/2" sq, pedestal foot	75.00
Vase, 6" h, straight side	38.00
Vase, 6-1/2" h, flared rim	18.00
Vase, 7" h, flared	80.00
Vase, 8" h, flared	85.00
Vase, 8" h, porch, 5" d	315.00
Vase, 8" h, straight side	45.00
Vase, 9" h, sq pedestal foot	125.00
Vase, 9-1/2" h, swung	300.00
Vase, 10" h, cupped top	250.00
Vase, 10" h, flared	95.00
Vase, 10" h, straight side	95.00
Vase, 10" h, swung	295.00
Vase, 12" h, straight side	125.00
Vase, 12" h, swung	295.00
Vase, 14" h, swung	310.00
Vase, 20" h, swung	395.00
Vegetable bowl, 9" l, oval	32.00
Vegetable bowl, 10" l, oval, two parts	35.00
Wedding bowl, cov, 6-1/2" w, 5-1/4" h, sq, pedestal	90.00
Whiskey, 2 oz	12.00
Whiskey, 2-1/4" h, 6 oz, #2056	10.00
Wine, 4-3/8" h, 2-1/2 oz, hex foot, #2056	15.00

* Bud vase, 6" h, flared, in ruby red is valued at $95.
** Perfume bottle, orig stopper, 5-1/2" h, in amber is valued at $425.
*** Tray, 14-1/8" d, five parts, in blue is valued at $185.

AMERICAN PIONEER

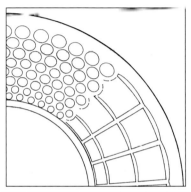

Manufactured by Liberty Works, Egg Harbor, New Jersey, from 1931 to 1934.

Pieces were made in amber, crystal, green, and pink.

ITEM	AMBER	CRYSTAL	GREEN	PINK
Bowl, 5" d, handle	45.00	24.00	27.50	24.00
Bowl, 8-3/4" d, cov	—	115.00	125.00	115.00
Bowl, 9" d, handle	—	24.00	30.00	24.00
Bowl, 9-1/4" d, cov	—	120.00	150.00	120.00
Bowl, 10" d	—	50.00	70.00	60.00
Candlesticks, pr, 6-1/2" h	—	75.00	95.00	75.00
Candy jar, cov, 1 pound	—	100.00	115.00	110.00
Candy jar, cov, 1-1/2 pound	—	75.00	125.00	95.00
Cheese and cracker set, indented plate and compote	—	50.00	65.00	55.00
Coaster, 3-1/2" d	—	30.00	35.00	32.00
Cocktail, 3 oz, 3-13/16" h	45.00	—	—	—
Cocktail, 3-1/2 oz, 3-15/16" h	45.00	—	—	—

ITEM	AMBER	CRYSTAL	GREEN	PINK
Console bowl, 10-3/4" d	—	50.00	75.00	60.00
Creamer, 2-3/4" h	—	20.00	22.00	25.00
Creamer, 3-1/2" h	60.00	30.00	32.00	30.00
Cup	24.00	10.00	15.00	10.00

American Pioneer, green 8" plate, $12; cup, $15; saucer, $5.

ITEM	AMBER	CRYSTAL	GREEN	PINK
Dresser set, two cologne bottles, powder jar, 7-1/2" tray	—	300.00	345.00	365.00
Goblet, 8 oz, 6" h, water	—	40.00	45.00	40.00
Ice bucket, 6" h	—	50.00	80.00	65.00
Juice tumbler, 5 oz	—	40.00	45.00	40.00
Lamp, 1-3/4", metal pole, 9-1/2"	—	—	85.00	—
Lamp, 5-1/2" round, ball shape	175.00	—	—	70.00
Lamp, 8-1/2" h	—	90.00	115.00	110.00
Mayonnaise, 4-1/4"	—	60.00	90.00	60.00
Pilsner, 5-3/4" h, 11 oz	—	100.00	110.00	100.00
Pitcher, cov, 5" h	295.00	150.00	225.00	165.00
Pitcher, cov, 7" h	325.00	175.00	250.00	195.00
Plate, 6" d	—	12.50	17.50	12.50
Plate, 6" d, handle	15.00	12.50	17.50	12.50
Plate, 8" d	20.00	8.00	12.00	10.00
Plate, 11-1/2" d, handle	40.00	20.00	24.00	20.00
Rose bowl, 4-1/4" d, ftd	—	40.00	50.00	45.00
Saucer, 6" sq	10.00	4.00	5.00	5.50
Sherbet, 3-1/2" h	—	18.00	22.00	20.00
Sherbet, 4-3/4" h	12.00	15.50	35.00	25.00
Sugar, 2-3/4" h	—	20.00	27.50	25.00
Sugar, 3-1/2" h	30.00	20.00	27.50	25.00
Tumbler, 8 oz, 4" h	—	32.00	55.00	35.00
Tumbler, 12 oz, 5" h	—	40.00	55.00	40.00
Vase, 7" h, 4 styles	—	115.00	145.00	115.00
Vase, 9" h, round	—	—	245.00	—
Whiskey, 2 oz, 2-1/4" h	—	50.00	100.00	50.00

AMERICAN SWEETHEART

Manufactured by MacBeth-Evans Glass Company, Charleroi, Pennsylvania, from 1930 to 1936. Some forms, like sherbets, were packed in Wonder Ware Oats.

Pieces were made in blue, Monax, pink, and red. There was a limited production in Cremax and color-trimmed Monax.

ITEM	BLUE	CREMAX	MONAX
Berry bowl, 3-1/4" d, flat	—	—	—
Berry bowl, 9" d	—	120.00	65.00
Cereal bowl, 6" d	—	9.50	10.00
Chop plate, 11" d	—	—	25.00
Cream soup bowl, 4-1/2" d	—	—	115.00
Creamer, ftd	195.00	—	12.00
Cup	140.00	—	6.00
Lamp shade	—	450.00	995.00
Pitcher, 60 oz, 7-1/2" h	—	—	—
Pitcher, 80 oz, 8" h	—	—	—
Plate, 6" d, bread and butter	—	—	6.50
Plate, 8" d, salad	135.00	—	10.00

American Sweetheart, pink cup, $18.

ITEM	MONAX WITH COLOR- TRIM	PINK	RED
Berry bowl, 3-1/4" d, flat	—	95.00	—
Berry bowl, 9" d	180.00	65.00	—
Cereal bowl, 6" d	25.00	14.00	—
Chop plate, 11" d	—	—	—
Cream soup bowl, 4-1/2" d	—	100.00	—
Creamer, ftd	110.00	20.00	175.00
Cup	90.00	18.00	90.00
Lamp shade	—	—	—
Pitcher, 60 oz, 7-1/2" h	—	995.00	—
Pitcher, 80 oz, 8" h	—	795.00	—
Plate, 6" d, bread and butter	24.00	10.00	—
Plate, 8" d, salad	30.00	15.00	145.00

ITEM	BLUE	CREMAX	MONAX
Plate, 9" d, luncheon	—	—	12.50
Plate, 9-3/4" d, dinner	—	—	28.00
Plate, 10-1/4" d, dinner	—	—	30.00
Platter, 13" l, oval	—	—	85.00
Salt and pepper shakers, pr, ftd	—	—	395.00
Salver plate, 12" d	250.00	—	25.00
Saucer	25.00	—	3.00
Serving plate, 15-1/2" d	450.00	—	250.00
Sherbet, 3-3/4" h, ftd	—	—	25.00
Sherbet, 4-1/4" h, ftd	—	—	22.00
Soup bowl, flat, 9-1/2" d	—	—	75.00
Sugar lid	—	—	300.00
Sugar, open, ftd	195.00	—	10.00
Tidbit, two-tier	250.00	—	85.00
Tidbit, three-tier	650.00	—	175.00
Tumbler, 5 oz, 3-1/2" h	—	—	—
Tumbler, 9 oz, 4-1/4" h	—	—	—
Tumbler, 10 oz, 4-3/4" h	—	—	—
Vegetable bowl, 11"	—	—	90.00

American Sweetheart, Monax open sugar, $10; creamer $12.

ITEM	MONAX WITH COLOR-TRIM	PINK	RED
Plate, 9" d, luncheon	40.00	—	—
Plate, 9-3/4" d, dinner	60.00	45.00	—
Plate, 10-1/4" d, dinner	—	40.00	—
Platter, 13" l, oval	225.00	65.00	—
Salt and pepper shakers, pr, ftd	—	500.00	—
Salver plate, 12" d	—	25.00	190.00
Saucer	18.00	7.50	45.00
Serving plate, 15-1/2" d	—	—	350.00
Sherbet, 3-3/4" h, ftd	—	18.00	—
Sherbet, 4-1/4" h, ftd	90.00	22.00	—
Soup bowl, flat, 9-1/2" d	140.00	50.00	—
Sugar lid	—	—	—
Sugar, open, ftd	110.00	22.00	175.00
Tidbit, two-tier	—	—	200.00
Tidbit, three-tier	—	—	500.00
Tumbler, 5 oz, 3-1/2" h	—	95.00	—
Tumbler, 9 oz, 4-1/4" h	—	75.00	—
Tumbler, 10 oz, 4-3/4" h	—	165.00	—
Vegetable bowl, 11"	—	80.00	—

American Sweetheart, pink soup bowl, $50.

ANNIVERSARY

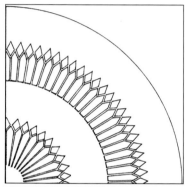

Manufactured by Jeannette Glass Company, Jeannette, Pennsylvania, from 1947 to 1949 and from the late 1960s to the mid-1970s.

Pieces were made in crystal, iridescent, and pink.

ITEM	CRYSTAL	IRIDESCENT	PINK
Berry bowl, 4-7/8" d	6.50	5.50	12.00
Butter dish, cov	25.00	—	50.00
Cake plate, 12-3/8" w, square	7.00	—	16.50
Cake plate, 12-1/2" d, round	10.00	—	18.50
Cake plate, metal cover	15.00	—	—
Candlesticks, pr, 4-7/8" h	20.00	25.00	—
Candy jar, cov	24.00	—	45.00
Chip & dip set, MIB	20.00	—	—
Comport, open, three legs	5.00	5.00	16.00
Comport, ruffled, three legs	14.50	—	—
Creamer, ftd	6.00	6.50	12.50
Cup	5.00	4.00	9.00
Fruit bowl, 9" d	15.00	14.50	32.50

ITEM	CRYSTAL	IRIDESCENT	PINK
Pickle dish 9" d	5.50	7.50	12.00
Plate, 6-1/4" d, sherbet	2.00	3.50	4.00
Plate, 9" d, dinner	8.00	8.50	18.00
Plate, 10" d, dinner	15.00	—	—
Relish dish, 8" d	10.00	12.50	16.00
Sandwich server, 12-1/2" d	6.50	10.00	20.00
Saucer	1.00	1.50	6.00
Sherbet, ftd	10.00	—	12.00
Soup bowl, 7-3/8" d	9.00	7.50	18.00
Sugar, cov	12.00	15.00	20.00
Sugar, open, gold trim	4.50	—	—
Tidbit, metal handle	14.00	—	—
Vase, 6-1/2" h	20.00	—	30.00
Wall pocket	65.00	—	90.00
Wine, 2-1/2 oz	12.00	—	20.00

*Anniversary,
iridescent dinner
plate, $8.50.*

AUNT POLLY

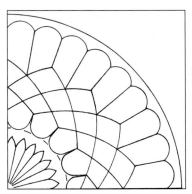

Manufactured by U. S. Glass Company, Pittsburgh, Pennsylvania, in the late 1920s.

Pieces were made in blue, green, and iridescent.

ITEM	BLUE	GREEN	IRIDESCENT
Berry bowl, 4-3/4" d, individual	20.00	15.00	15.00
Berry bowl, 7-1/8" d, master	45.00	22.00	22.00
Bowl, 4-3/4" d, 2" h	—	15.00	15.00
Bowl, 5-1/2" d, one handle	25.00	15.00	15.00
Bowl, 8-3/8" l, oval	80.00	42.00	42.00
Butter dish, cov	200.00	200.00	170.00
Candy jar, cov, two handles	50.00	30.00	30.00
Candy jar, ftd, two handles	—	27.50	27.50
Creamer	60.00	32.00	32.00
Pickle, 7-1/4" l, oval, handle	45.00	20.00	20.00
Pitcher, 48 oz, 8" h	175.00	—	—
Plate, 6" d, sherbet	16.00	6.00	6.00

ITEM	BLUE	GREEN	IRIDESCENT
Plate, 8" d, luncheon	20.00	—	—
Salt and pepper shakers, pr	200.00	—	—
Sherbet	16.00	12.00	12.00
Sugar	175.00	95.00	95.00
Tumbler, 8 oz, 3-5/8" h	30.00	—	—
Vase, 6-1/2" h, ftd	40.00	35.00	30.00

Aunt Polly, blue sherbet, $16.

Aunt Polly, blue 6-1/2" h vase, $40.

AURORA

Manufactured by Hazel Atlas Glass Company, Clarksburg, West Virginia, and Zanesville, Ohio, in the late 1930s.

Pieces were made in cobalt (Ritz) blue, crystal, green, and pink.

Aurora, cobalt blue cereal bowl, $14; 4-1/2" d bowl, $50; milk pitcher, $30.

ITEM	COBALT BLUE	CRYSTAL	GREEN	PINK
Bowl, 4-1/2" d	50.00	—	—	75.00
Breakfast set, 24 pcs, service for four	420.00	—	—	—
Cereal bowl, 5-3/8" d	14.00	12.00	9.50	15.00
Cup	15.00	8.00	10.00	15.00
Milk pitcher	30.00	—	—	25.00
Plate, 6-1/2" d	15.00	—	—	12.50
Saucer	7.50	2.00	3.00	6.00
Tumbler, 10 oz, 4-3/4" h	25.00	—	—	30.00

*Aurora,
cobalt blue
tumbler,
$25.*

AVOCADO
NO. 601

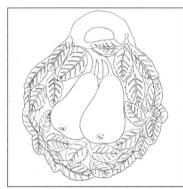

Manufactured by Indiana Glass Company, Dunkirk, Indiana, from 1923 to 1933.

Pieces were made in crystal, green, pink, and white.

Reproductions: † Creamer, 8-inch pickle, 64-ounce pitcher, plates, sherbet, sugar, and tumblers. Reproductions can be found in amethyst, blue, dark green, frosted green, frosted pink, pink, red, and yellow, representing several colors not made originally.

Avocado, green sugar, $35; creamer, $35.

ITEM	CRYSTAL	GREEN	PINK	WHITE
Bowl, 5-1/4" d, 2 handles	12.00	38.00	27.50	—
Bowl, 8" d, two handles, oval	17.50	30.00	25.00	—
Bowl, 8-1/2" d	20.00	60.00	50.00	—
Bowl, 9-1/2" d, 3-1/4" deep	35.00	160.00	150.00	—
Cake plate, 10-1/4" d, two handles	22.50	60.00	40.00	—
Creamer, ftd †	17.50	35.00	35.00	—
Cup, ftd	—	36.00	30.00	—
Pickle bowl, 8" d, two handles, oval †	17.50	30.00	25.00	—
Pitcher, 64 oz †	385.00	1,100.00	900.00	425.00
Plate, 6-3/8" d, sherbet †	6.00	18.00	20.00	—
Plate, 8-1/4" d, luncheon †	7.50	25.00	20.00	—
Preserve bowl, 7" l, handle	10.00	32.00	28.00	—
Relish, 6" d, ftd	10.00	30.00	25.00	—
Salad bowl, 7-1/2" d	9.00	65.00	37.50	—
Saucer	6.00	24.00	15.00	—
Sherbet, ftd †	—	55.00	55.00	—
Sugar, ftd †	17.50	35.00	35.00	—
Tumbler †	25.00	250.00	150.00	35.00

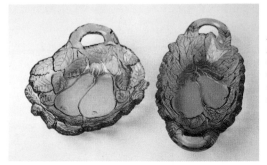

Avocado, green preserve bowl with handle, $32; bowl with two handles, $38.

BEADED BLOCK

Manufactured by Imperial Glass Company, Bellaire, Ohio, from 1927 to the 1930s.

Pieces were made in amber, crystal, green, ice blue, iridescent, milk white (1950s), opalescent, pink, red, and vaseline. Some pieces are still being made in pink and are embossed with the "IG" trademark.

The only form known in red is the 4-1/2-inch lily bowl valued at $300. The secondary market for milk white is still being established.

ITEM	AMBER	CRYSTAL	GREEN	ICE BLUE
Bowl, 4-1/2" d, lily	20.00	24.00	22.00	24.00
Bowl, 4-1/2" d, two handles	18.00	10.00	22.00	28.00
Bowl, 5-1/2" sq	18.00	8.00	20.00	12.00
Bowl, 5-1/2" d, one handle	18.00	8.00	20.00	12.00
Bowl, 6" deep	24.00	20.00	24.00	85.00
Bowl, 6-1/4" d	24.00	8.50	20.00	12.00
Bowl, 6-1/2" d, two handles	24.00	8.50	20.00	12.00
Bowl, 6-3/4" d	28.00	12.00	28.00	14.00
Bowl, 7-1/4" d, flared	30.00	12.00	28.00	14.00
Bowl, 7-1/2" d, fluted	30.00	22.00	30.00	24.00
Bowl, 7-1/2" plain	30.00	20.00	40.00	22.00
Candy dish, cov, pear- shaped	425.00	—	395.00	—
Celery, 8-1/4" d	35.00	24.00	55.00	20.00

*Beaded Block, opalescent 4-1/2" d lily bowl, **$60**;*
*opalescent vase with two handles, **$110**.*

ITEM	IRIDESCENT	OPAL	PINK	VASELINE
Bowl, 4-1/2" d, lily	18.00	60.00	18.00	50.00
Bowl, 4-1/2" d, two handles	20.00	30.00	35.00	35.00
Bowl, 5-1/2" sq	10.00	15.00	30.00	12.00
Bowl, 5-1/2" d, one handle	10.00	15.00	30.00	12.00
Bowl, 6" deep	12.00	24.00	35.00	15.00
Bowl, 6-1/4" d	12.00	18.00	10.00	12.00
Bowl, 6-1/2" d, two handles	52.00	18.00	28.00	12.00
Bowl, 6-3/4" d	15.00	20.00	14.00	14.00
Bowl, 7-1/4" d, flared	15.00	20.00	14.00	14.00
Bowl, 7-1/2" d, fluted	20.00	24.00	24.00	24.00
Bowl, 7-1/2" plain	24.00	24.00	20.00	22.00
Candy dish, cov, pear- shaped	—	—	—	650.00
Celery, 8-1/4" d	28.00	30.00	26.50	28.00

ITEM	AMBER	CRYSTAL	GREEN	ICE BLUE
Creamer, ftd	25.00	25.00	25.00	24.00
Jelly, 4-1/2" h, stemmed	20.00	25.00	30.00	32.00
Jelly, 4-1/2" h, stemmed, flared lid	24.00	30.00	35.00	40.00
Pitcher, one- pt, 5-1/4" h	95.00	75.00	150.00	115.00
Plate, 7-3/4" sq	40.00	7.50	30.00	20.00
Plate, 8-3/4"	20.00	24.00	30.00	30.00
Sugar, ftd	25.00	24.00	30.00	30.00
Syrup	—	—	—	—
Vase, 6" h, ftd	215.00	20.00	35.00	85.00

Beaded Block, ice blue vase, $85; crystal jelly, stemmed, $25.

ITEM	IRIDESCENT	OPAL	PINK	VASELINE
Creamer, ftd	24.00	30.00	30.00	28.00
Jelly, 4-1/2" h, stemmed	20.00	25.00	32.00	32.00
Jelly, 4-1/2" h, stemmed, flared lid	35.00	28.00	40.00	22.00
Pitcher, one- pt, 5-1/4" h	115.00	125.00	195.00	115.00
Plate, 7-3/4" sq	20.00	15.00	38.00	50.00
Plate, 8-3/4"	20.00	24.00	20.00	20.00
Sugar, ftd	20.00	60.00	30.00	20.00
Syrup	—	—	—	165.00
Vase, 6" h, ftd	25.00	110.00	40.00	90.00

Beaded Block, Vaseline square plate, $50; iridescent round plate, $20.

BEADED EDGE

PATTERN #22 MILK GLASS

Made by Westmoreland Glass Company from the late 1930s to the 1950s.

Pieces were made in white milk glass. Painted decorations add interesting variety to this pattern. Collectors can find eight different fruit patterns and eight different floral patterns. Other designs include birds and Christmas designs. Another variation incorporates a red edge or band into the design.

ITEM	DECORATED	PLAIN	RED EDGE
Bowl	18.00	5.00	9.50
Creamer, cov, ftd	30.00	20.00	25.00
Creamer, open, ftd	18.00	10.00	14.00
Cup	12.00	5.00	6.50
Goblet	18.00	8.50	12.00
Nappy, 5" d	16.00	4.50	10.00
Nappy, 6" d, crimped	22.00	7.50	12.00
Plate, 6" d, bread and butter	9.00	5.00	7.00
Plate, 7" d, salad	14.00	6.00	8.00
Plate, 7-1/2" d, coupe	15.00	10.00	12.00
Plate, 8-1/2" d, luncheon	20.00	6.50	9.00
Plate, 10-1/2" d, dinner	35.00	12.00	20.00

Beaded Edge, white luncheon plate, $6.50.

Beaded Edge, decorated 6" crimped nappy, $22; decorated 5" nappy, $16.

ITEM	DECORATED	PLAIN	RED EDGE
Platter, 12" l, tab handles	90.00	75.00	45.00
Relish, 3-part	90.00	25.00	50.00
Salt and pepper shakers, pr	75.00	30.00	35.00
Saucer	5.00	2.00	2.50
Sherbet, ftd	18.00	8.50	12.00
Sugar, cov, ftd	30.00	20.00	25.00
Sugar, open, ftd	18.00	10.00	14.00
Torte plate, 15" d	70.00	25.00	40.00
Tumbler, ftd, 8 oz	18.00	8.50	12.00

BLOCK OPTIC
BLOCK

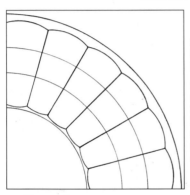

Manufactured by Hocking Glass Company, Lancaster, Ohio, from 1929 to 1933.

Pieces were made in amber, crystal, green, pink, and yellow. Production in amber was very limited. An 11-3/4-inch diameter console bowl is valued at $50, and a pair of matching 1-3/4-inch candlesticks is valued at $110.

ITEM	CRYSTAL	GREEN	PINK	YELLOW
Berry bowl, 8-1/2" d	20.00	30.00	40.00	—
Bowl, 4-1/4" d, 1-3/8" h	64.00	15.00	10.00	—
Bowl, 4-1/2" d, 1-1/2" h	—	28.00	—	—
Bowl, 8-5/8" d, low, ruffled	—	150.00	—	—
Butter dish, cov	—	50.00	—	—
Cake plate, 10" d, ftd	18.00	—	—	—
Candlesticks, pr, 1-3/4" h	—	100.00	70.00	—
Candy jar, cov, 2-1/4" h	30.00	60.00	55.00	75.00
Candy jar, cov, 6-1/4" h	40.00	70.00	60.00	—
Cereal bowl, 5-1/2" d	—	15.00	25.00	—
Champagne, 4-3/4" h	10.00	27.50	16.50	20.00

Block Optic, green cup, $8.

ITEM	CRYSTAL	GREEN	PINK	YELLOW
Cocktail, 4" h	—	35.00	35.00	—
Comport, 4" wide	—	36.00	70.00	—
Console bowl, 11-3/4" d, rolled edge	55.00	75.00	65.00	—
Creamer*	12.00	19.50	20.00	20.00
Cup*	7.50	8.00	7.00	10.00
Goblet, 9 oz, 5-3/4" h	12.00	40.00	48.00	
Goblet, 9 oz, 7-1/2" h, thin	15.00	—	35.00	30.00
Ice bucket	—	40.00	48.00	—
Ice tub, open	—	60.00		—
Mug	—	35.00		—
Pitcher, 54 oz, 7-5/8" h, bulbous	—	85.00	85.00	—

ITEM	CRYSTAL	GREEN	PINK	YELLOW
Pitcher, 54 oz, 8-1/2" h	—	42.00	40.00	—
Pitcher, 80 oz, 8" h	—	90.00	85.00	—
Plate, 6" d, sherbet	1.50	5.00	5.00	6.50
Plate, 8" d, luncheon	3.50	8.000	7.50	8.50
Plate, 9" d, dinner	11.00	32.50	35.00	45.00
Plate, 9" d, dinner, snowflake center	—	16.50	—	—
Plate, 9" d, grill	15.00	27.50	30.00	60.00
Salad bowl, 7-1/4" d	—	118.00	—	—

Block Optic, pink 4-3/4" footed sherbet, $17.50.

Block Optic, green 4-3/4" cone-shaped footed tumbler, $28.

ITEM	CRYSTAL	GREEN	PINK	YELLOW
Salt and pepper shakers, pr, ftd	—	42.00	90.00	75.00
Salt and pepper shakers, pr, squatty	—	100.00	—	—
Sandwich plate, 10-1/4" d	—	27.50	30.00	—
Sandwich server, center handle	—	65.00	70.00	—
Saucer, 5-3/4" d	—	5.00	10.00	—
Saucer, 6-1/8" d	2.00	10.00	7.00	3.50
Sherbet, cone	—	12.00	6.00	—
Sherbet, 5-1/2 oz, 3-1/4" h	3.00	12.00	9.50	7.50
Sherbet, 6 oz, 4-3/4" h	7.00	28.00	17.50	18.00
Sugar, cone	—	20.00	12.00	12.00
Sugar, flat	—	10.00	10.00	—
Sugar, round, ftd	10.00	12.00	18.00	—
Tumbler, 3 oz, 2-5/8" h	—	30.00	28.00	—
Tumbler, 3 oz, 3-1/4" h, ftd	—	27.50	25.00	—
Tumbler, 5 oz, 3-1/2" h, flat	—	18.00	19.50	—
Tumbler, 5-3/8" h, ftd	—	—	24.00	18.00
Tumbler, 9" h, ftd	—	—	17.50	22.00
Tumbler, 9-1/2 oz, 3-13/16" h, flat	—	17.50	15.00	—
Tumbler, 10 oz, 6" h, ftd	12.00	—	—	—
Tumbler, 10 or 11 oz, 5" h, flat	—	30.00	20.00	—
Tumbler, 12 oz, 4-7/8" h, flat	—	35.50	30.00	—
Tumbler, 15 oz, 5-1/4" h, flat	18.00	32.50	55.00	—
Tumble-up, 3" h tumbler and bottle	—	90.00	75.00	—
Vase, 5-3/4" h, blown	—	350.00	—	—
Whiskey, 1 oz, 1-5/8" h	20.00	40.00	45.00	—
Whiskey, 2 oz, 2-1/4" h	15.00	35.00	30.00	—
Wine, 4-1/2" h	15.00	32.00	30.00	—

* There are five styles of creamers and four styles of cups; each has a relative value.

BOWKNOT

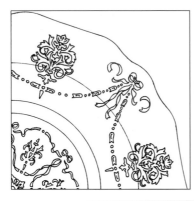

Unknown maker, late 1920s.

Pieces were made in green.

ITEM	GREEN
Berry bowl, 4-1/2" d	28.00
Cereal bowl, 5-1/2" d	30.00
Cup	12.00
Plate, 7" d, salad	16.00
Sherbet, low, ftd	25.00
Tumbler, 10 oz, 5" h, flat	20.00
Tumbler, 10 oz, 5" h, ftd	20.00

Bowknot, green tumbler, $20; footed berry bowl, $28.

BUBBLE

BULLSEYE, PROVINCIAL

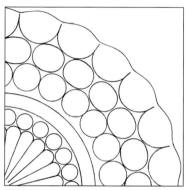

Manufactured originally by Hocking Glass Company, and followed by Anchor Hocking Glass Corp., Lancaster, Ohio, from 1937 to 1965.

Pieces were made in crystal (1937), forest green (1937), pink, Royal Ruby (1963), and sapphire blue (1937). Production in pink was limited. The current value for a pink cup and saucer is $175.

ITEM	CRYSTAL	FOREST GREEN	ROYAL RUBY	SAPPHIRE BLUE
Berry bowl, 4" d	5.00	—	10.00	12.00
Berry bowl, 8-3/4" d	12.00	15.00	38.00	18.00
Bowl, 9" d, flanged	8.00	—	—	335.00
Candlesticks, pr	18.00	40.00	—	—
Cereal bowl, 5-1/4" d	8.00	20.00	—	12.50
Cocktail, 3-1/2 oz	4.50	10.00	10.00	—
Cocktail, 4-1/2 oz	4.50	12.50	12.50	—
Creamer	7.50	18.00	18.00	25.00
Cup	4.50	10.00	12.50	15.00
Fruit bowl, 4-1/2" d	5.00	11.00	9.00	12.00

ITEM	CRYSTAL	FOREST GREEN	ROYAL RUBY	SAPPHIRE BLUE
Goblet, 9 oz, stem, 5-1/2" h	7.50	15.00	15.00	—
Goblet, 9-1/2 oz, stem	7.50	15.00	15.00	—
Iced tea goblet, 14 oz	8.00	17.50	—	—
Iced tea tumbler, 12 oz, 4-1/2" h	10.00	—	15.00	—
Juice goblet, 4 oz	3.00	16.00	—	—
Juice goblet, 5-1/2 oz	5.00	12.50	12.50	—
Juice tumbler, 6 oz, ftd	4.00	12.00	12.00	—
Lamp, three styles	42.00	—	—	—
Lemonade tumbler, 16 oz, 5-7/8" h	16.00	—	19.00	—

Bubble, sapphire blue grill plate, $22; platter, $22; soup bowl, $20; 4" d berry bowl, $12.

Bubble, forest green sugar, $18.50.

ITEM	CRYSTAL	FOREST GREEN	ROYAL RUBY	SAPPHIRE BLUE
Old fashioned tumbler, 8 oz, 3-1/4" h	7.50	16.50	12.00	—
Pitcher, 64 oz, ice lip	60.00	—	60.00	—
Plate, 6-3/4" d, bread and butter	5.00	14.50	—	3.25
Plate, 9-3/8" d, dinner	7.50	28.00	30.00	9.00
Plate, 9-3/8" d, grill	—	20.00	—	22.00
Platter, 12" l, oval	10.00	—	—	22.00
Sandwich plate, 9-1/2" d	7.50	25.00	22.00	8.00
Saucer	1.00	5.00	5.00	1.50
Sherbet, 6 oz	4.50	9.50	12.00	—
Soup bowl, flat, 7-3/4" d	10.00	—	—	20.00
Sugar	8.00	18.50	—	27.50
Tidbit, two-tier	—	—	35.00	—
Tumbler, 9 oz, water	6.00	—	10.00	—
Vegetable bowl, 8" d, 2-3/4" h	20.00	35.00	45.00	30.00

Bubble, royal ruby 3" old fashioned glass, $12.

BY CRACKY

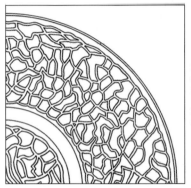

Manufactured by L. E. Smith Glass Company, Mount Pleasant, Pennsylvania, in the late 1920s.

Pieces were made in amber, canary, crystal, and green.

ITEMS	AMBER	CANARY	CRYSTAL	GREEN
Cake plate, ftd	35.00	40.00	30.00	30.00
Candleholder, octagonal base	7.50	10.00	5.00	5.00
Candleholder, round base	5.00	7.50	5.00	5.00
Candy box, cov	17.50	20.00	15.00	17.50
Candy jar, cov	20.00	25.00	17.50	17.50
Center bowl, 10-3/4" d	15.00	17.50	12.00	15.00
Center bowl, 12", octagonal	15.00	17.50	12.00	15.00
Cup	5.00	5.00	5.00	5.00
Flower block, 3"	15.00	17.50	7.50	10.00
Goblet	12.00	14.00	8.00	10.00
Pitcher, cone shape	25.00	30.00	15.00	20.00
Plate, 8", octagonal	15.00	16.50	7.50	10.00

ITEMS	AMBER	CANARY	CRYSTAL	GREEN
Plate, 8-1/2", grill	18.50	22.00	12.00	17.50
Plate, 9", dinner	17.50	20.00	9.50	15.00
Saucer	3.00	5.00	2.00	2.00
Sherbet	7.50	10.00	5.00	5.00
Sherbet plate	12.00	15.00	5.00	7.50
Vase, fan shape	20.00	25.00	15.00	15.00
Violet bowl	20.00	25.00	15.00	15.00

By Cracky, green cup, $5; cone-shaped pitcher, $20.

*By Cracky,
green
sherbet, $5.*

*By Cracky,
green cup,
$5.*

CAMEO

BALLERINA, DANCING GIRL

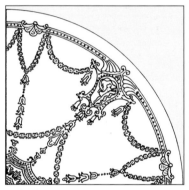

Manufactured by Hocking Glass Company, Lancaster, Ohio, from 1930 to 1934.

Pieces were made in crystal, green, pink, and yellow. Only the crystal has a platinum rim.

Reproductions: † Salt shakers made in blue, green, and pink. Children's dishes have been made in green and pink but were never part of the original pattern. A squatty candy dish in cobalt blue has also been made. Again, this was not an original color.

ITEM	CRYSTAL	GREEN	PINK	YELLOW
Berry bowl, 4-1/4" d	15.00	—	—	—
Berry bowl, 8-1/4" d	—	45.00	175.00	—
Butter dish, cov	—	175.00	—	1,200.00
Cake plate, 10" d, three legs	—	28.00	—	—
Cake plate, 10-1/2" d, flat	—	120.00	165.00	—
Candlesticks, pr, 4" h	—	110.00	—	—
Candy jar, cov, 4" h	—	90.00	495.00	125.00
Candy jar, cov, 6-1/2" h	—	195.00	—	—
Cereal bowl, 5-1/2" d	8.50	30.00	160.00	35.00
Cocktail shaker	600.00	—	—	—
Comport, 5" w	—	70.00	200.00	—

ITEM	CRYSTAL	GREEN	PINK	YELLOW
Console bowl, three legs, 11" d	—	85.00	45.00	125.00
Cookie jar, cov	—	55.00	—	—
Cream soup bowl, 4-3/4" d	—	195.00	—	—
Creamer, 3-1/4" h	—	30.00	110.00	25.00
Creamer, 4-1/4" h	—	32.00	115.00	—
Cup	10.00	20.00	85.00	10.00
Decanter, 10" h	225.00	185.00	—	—
Domino tray, 7" l	150.00	175.00	200.00	—
Goblet, 6" h, water	—	75.00	145.00	—
Ice bowl, 3" h, 5-1/2" d	265.00	150.00	550.00	—
Jam jar, cov, 2" h	175.00	225.00	—	—
Juice pitcher, 6" h, 36 oz	—	110.00	—	—
Juice tumbler, 3 oz, ftd	—	65.00	80.00	—
Juice tumbler, 5 oz, 3-3/4" h	—	35.00	—	—
Pitcher, 8-1/2" h, 56 oz	550.00	80.00	1,150.00	—
Plate, 6" d, sherbet	6.00	10.00	90.00	4.00
Plate, 7" d, salad	12.00	13.50	—	—
Plate, 8" d, luncheon	8.00	12.00	36.00	12.50
Plate, 9-1/2" d, dinner	—	18.00	85.00	12.00
Plate, 10-1/2" d, dinner, rimmed	—	115.00	175.00	—
Plate, 10-1/2" d, grill	—	20.00	50.00	15.00
Platter, 12" l	—	30.00	—	42.00
Relish, 7-1/2" l, ftd, three parts	175.00	25.00	—	—
Salad bowl, 7-1/4" d	—	70.00	—	—
Salt and pepper shakers, pr, ftd †	—	95.00	900.00	—
Sandwich plate, 10" d	—	18.00	45.00	—
Saucer	4.00	4.00	90.00	4.50
Sherbet, 3-1/8" h, blown	—	18.00	75.00	—
Sherbet, 3-1/8" h, molded	—	18.00	75.00	40.00
Sherbet, 4-7/8" h	—	40.00	100.00	45.00
Soup bowl, rimmed, 9" d	—	80.00	125.00	75.00
Sugar, 3-1/4" h	—	24.00	—	28.00

ITEM	CRYSTAL	GREEN	PINK	YELLOW
Sugar, 4-1/4" h	—	32.50	125.00	
Syrup pitcher, 20 oz, 5-3/4" h	—	250.00	—	2,000.00
Tumbler, 9 oz, 4" h, 9 oz	16.00	30.00	80.00	—
Tumbler, 9 oz, 5"h, ftd	—	30.00	115.00	15.00
Tumbler, 10 oz, 4-3/4" h, flat	—	30.00	95.00	
Tumbler, 11 oz, 5" h, flat	—	30.00	90.00	60.00
Tumbler, 11 oz, 5-3/4" h, ftd	—	75.00	135.00	—
Tumbler, 15 oz, 5-1/4" h	—	80.00	145.00	—
Tumbler, 15 oz, 6-3/8" h, ftd	—	495.00	—	—
Vase, 5-3/4" h	—	195.00	—	—
Vase, 8" h	—	65.00	—	—
Vegetable, oval, 10" l	—	35.00	—	45.00
Wine, 3-1/2" h	—	900.00	650.00	—
Wine, 4" h	—	80.00	250.00	—

Cameo, yellow 3-1/4" creamer, $25.

Cameo, green vegetable bowl, $35.

CAPRI
ALPINE, COLONIAL, DOTS, SEASHELL, COLONY SWIRL, TULIP

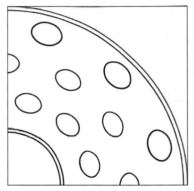

Manufactured by Hazel Ware, a division of Continental Can, in the 1960s. Collectors are starting to divide these wares into several distinct patterns based on the shape. All are the same pretty azure blue color and have the same market value. Original "Capri" paper labels are found on most of the styles.

Pieces were made in azure blue.

ITEM	AZURE BLUE
Ashtray, 3-1/2" sq, emb flower center	15.00
Ashtray, 3-1/4" w, triangular or round	5.00
Ashtray, 5" d, round	7.50
Ashtray, 6-7/8" w, triangular	10.00
Bowl, 4-3/4" d, octagonal or swirled	6.75
Bowl, 4-7/8" d, round, Dots	7.50
Bowl, 5-3/4" w, sq	9.50
Bowl, 5-5/8", Colony Swirl	8.50
Bowl, 6" d, Dots, Colony Swirl	8.00

ITEM	AZURE BLUE
Bowl, 6" d, Tulip	12.00
Bowl, 7-3/4" l, oval	12.00
Bowl, 8-3/4" d, swirled	19.00
Bowl, 9-1/2" l, 4-1/4" w, 1-1/2" h, rect	12.00
Candleholders, pr	28.00
Candy jar, cov, ftd	30.00
Chip and dip set, metal rack	30.00
Creamer	12.00
Cup, octagonal	6.50
Cup, round	5.00
Iced tea tumbler, 5" h, 12 oz	10.00
Old fashioned tumbler, 3-5/8" h, Dots	8.00
Plate, 5-3/4" d, bread and butter	5.00
Plate, 7" d, salad	7.50
Plate, 8" w, sq	7.50
Plate, 9-3/4", dinner	10.00
Relish dish, 9-1/2", rect, metal handle	12.00
Salad bowl, 5-3/8" d	7.50
Saucer, round, sq, or octagonal	1.50

Capri, azure blue 6" d bowl, $8.

Capri, Dots, azure blue saucer, $1.50.

ITEM	AZURE BLUE
Sherbet, Dots	8.00
Snack plate, fan shape	10.00
Snack plate, round	6.50
Sugar, cov	20.00
Tidbit, two bowl tiers, Colony Swirl	45.00
Tidbit, three plate tiers	20.00
Tumbler, 2-3/4" h, Colony Swirl	7.50
Tumbler, 3" h, Dots	5.50
Tumbler, 3-1/16", Colony, Colony Swirl	8.50
Tumbler, 5-1/4" h, Dots	12.50
Vase, 8" h, Dots	30.00
Vase, 8-1/2" h, ruffled rim	30.00

Capri, azure blue 7-3/4" l candy dish with metal handle, $12.

Capri, azure blue covered candy, $30.

CHARM

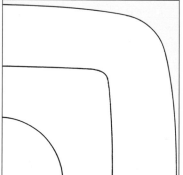

Manufactured by Anchor-Hocking Glass Corp. under its Fire King trademark. Pieces were made in Azur-ite and Jade-ite from 1950-1954, and Forest Green and Ruby Red from 1940-1960. Crystal items are currently being made.

ITEM	AZUR-ITE	FOREST GREEN	JADE-ITE	RUBY RED
Creamer	19.50	10.00	22.00	10.00
Cup	8.50	6.00	15.00	7.00
Dessert bowl, 4-3/4"	8.00	8.00	15.00	8.00
Plate, 6-5/8", salad	12.00	15.00	8.00	15.00
Plate, 8-3/4", luncheon	14.00	10.00	12.00	12.00
Plate, 9-1/2", dinner	40.00	20.00	35.00	20.00
Platter, 11" x 8"	25.00	40.00	32.00	40.00
Salad bowl, 7-3/8"	55.00	22.00	40.00	45.00
Saucer, 5-3/8"	3.50	2.00	6.50	3.00
Soup bowl, 6"	45.00	17.50	70.00	17.50
Sugar	19.50	10.00	22.00	10.00

Fire King Charm, Azur-ite cup, $8.50, and saucer, $3.50.

Fire King Charm, Azur-ite dinner plate, $40; cup, $8.50; saucer, $3.50.

CHERRY BLOSSOM

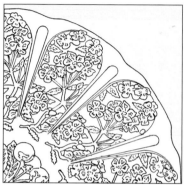

Manufactured by Jeannette Glass Company, Jeannette, Pennsylvania, from 1930 to 1939. Pieces were made in crystal, Delphite, green, jadeite, pink, and red. Production was very limited in crystal, jadeite, and red.

Reproductions: † Reproductions include: small berry bowl, 8-1/2-inch diameter bowl, covered butter dish, cake plate, cereal bowl, cup, pitcher, 6- and 9-inch plates, divided 13-inch platter, salt shaker, sandwich tray, saucer, and 3-3/4- and 4-1/2-inch high footed tumblers. Reproductions have been made in cobalt blue, Delphite, green, pink, and red. A children's butter dish has also been made but was never included in the original production.

ITEM	DELPHITE	GREEN	PINK
Berry bowl, 4-3/4" d †	15.00	25.00	18.00
Berry bowl, 8-1/2" d †	55.00	48.00	65.00
Bowl, 9" d, two handles	20.00	70.00	35.00
Butter dish, cov †	—	115.00	110.00
Cake plate, 10-1/4" d, three legs †	—	38.00	30.00
Cereal bowl, 5-3/4" d †	—	35.00	38.00
Coaster	—	12.50	15.00
Creamer	30.00	28.00	35.00
Cup †	28.00	25.00	28.00

*Cherry Blossom, Delphite 4-3/4" d berry bowls, each **$15.***

ITEM	DELPHITE	GREEN	PINK
Fruit bowl, 10-1/2" d	32.00	90.00	80.00
Iced tea tumbler, 12 oz, flat	—	—	80.00
Juice tumbler, 1 oz, 3-1/2"	25.00	30.00	18.00
Mug, 7 oz	—	175.00	250.00
Pitcher, 36 oz, 6-3/4" h, 36 oz †	95.00	60.00	70.00
Pitcher, 36 oz, 8", PAT, ftd	—	85.00	65.00
Pitcher, 42 oz, 8", PAT, flat	—	75.00	60.00
Plate, 6" d, sherbet †	12.50	12.00	12.00
Plate, 7" d, salad	—	24.50	20.00
Plate, 9" d, dinner †	15.00	28.00	19.00
Plate, 9" d, grill	—	35.00	27.50
Plate, 10" d, grill	—	32.50	35.00

Cherry Blossom, green 11" d two-handled bowl, $70.

ITEM	DELPHITE	GREEN	PINK
Platter, 11" l, oval	40.00	48.00	40.00
Platter, 13" d	—	68.00	80.00
Platter, 13" divided †	—	72.00	75.00
Salt and pepper shakers, pr, scalloped base †	—	995.00	1,250.00
Sandwich tray, 10-1/2" d †	35.00	30.00	32.00
Saucer †	6.00	7.50	6.00
Sherbet	18.00	24.00	17.50
Soup, flat, 7-3/4" d	—	105.00	115.00
Sugar, cov	24.00	35.00	35.00
Tumbler, 3-3/4" h, AOP, ftd †	—	22.00	24.00
Tumbler, 5" h	20.00	70.00	72.00

ITEM	DELPHITE	GREEN	PINK
Tumbler, 8 oz, 4-1/2" h, scalloped ftd base, AOP	—	40.00	38.00
Tumbler, 9 oz, 4-1/4" h	—	20.00	18.00
Tumbler, 9 oz, 4-1/2" h †	18.50	30.00	30.00
Vegetable bowl, 9" l, oval	45.00	50.00	55.00

CHILDREN'S

ITEM	DELPHITE	PINK
Creamer	50.00	37.50
Cup †	24.00	24.00
Plate, 6" d	15.00	15.00
Saucer	5.00	5.00
Sugar	50.00	50.00

Cherry Blossom, pink cup, $28.

CHERRYBERRY

Manufactured by U. S. Glass Company, Pittsburgh, Pennsylvania, in the early 1930s.

Pieces were made in crystal, green, iridescent, and pink.

ITEM	CRYSTAL	GREEN	IRIDESCENT	PINK
Berry bowl, 4" d	7.00	8.75	7.00	8.75
Berry bowl, 7-1/2" d, deep	17.50	20.00	20.00	20.00
Bowl, 6-1/4" d, 2" deep	50.00	55.00	40.00	55.00
Butter dish, cov	150.00	175.00	150.00	175.00
Comport, 5-3/4"	17.50	25.00	17.50	25.00
Creamer, large, 4-5/8"	40.00	45.00	40.00	45.00
Creamer, small	15.00	20.00	15.00	20.00
Olive dish, 5" l, one handle	10.00	15.00	10.00	15.00
Pickle dish, 8-1/4" l, oval	10.00	15.00	10.00	15.00
Pitcher, 7-3/4" h	165.00	175.00	165.00	175.00
Plate, 6" d, sherbet	6.50	11.00	6.50	11.00
Plate, 7-1/2" d, salad	8.50	15.00	9.00	15.00

ITEM	CRYSTAL	GREEN	IRIDESCENT	PINK
Salad bowl, 6-1/2" d, deep	17.50	22.00	17.50	22.00
Sherbet	10.00	12.00	12.00	14.00
Sugar, large, cov	45.00	75.00	45.00	75.00
Sugar, small, open	15.00	20.00	15.00	20.00
Tumbler, 9 oz, 3-5/8" h	20.00	35.00	20.00	35.00

Cherryberry, crystal 7-1/2" d deep bowl, $17.50.

CHINEX CLASSIC

Manufactured by MacBeth-Evans Division of Corning Glass Works, from the late 1930s to early 1940s.

Made in Chinex (ivory) and Chinex with Classic Bouquet or Classic Castle decorations.

ITEM	CHINEX	CHINEX, CLASSIC BOUQUET DECAL	CHINEX, CLASSIC CASTLE DECAL
Bowl, 11" d	20.00	36.00	48.00
Butter dish, cov	55.00	80.00	135.00
Cake plate, 11-1/2" d	8.00	12.00	20.00
Cereal bowl, 5--3/4" d	6.00	8.50	13.50
Creamer	12.50	12.00	20.00
Cup	6.00	9.50	14.50
Plate, 6-1/4" d, sherbet	8.00	6.50	8.00
Plate, 9-3/4" d, dinner	8.00	10.00	16.00
Sandwich plate, 11-1/2" d	8.00	15.00	25.00
Saucer	2.00	4.00	3.00
Sherbet, low, ftd	7.50	10.00	22.00

ITEM	CHINEX	CHINEX, CLASSIC BOUQUET DECAL	CHINEX, CLASSIC CASTLE DECAL
Soup bowl, 7-3/4" d	14.00	25.00	30.00
Sugar, open	12.50	12.50	20.00
Vegetable bowl, 7" d	15.00	25.00	35.00
Vegetable bowl, 9" d	15.00	20.00	40.00

Chinex Classic, dinner plate with castle decal, $16.

CHRISTMAS CANDY

NO. 624

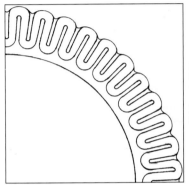

Manufactured by Indiana Glass Company, Dunkirk, Indiana, in the 1950s.

Pieces were made in crystal and Terrace Green (teal).

ITEM	CRYSTAL	TERRACE GREEN
Bowl, 5-3/4" d	6.50	—
Creamer	8.00	30.00
Cup	8.00	40.00
Mayonnaise, ladle, liner	24.00	—
Plate, 6" d, bread and butter	6.00	20.00
Plate, 8-1/4" d, luncheon	8.00	28.00
Plate, 9-5/8" d, dinner	12.00	36.00
Sandwich plate, 11-1/4" d	24.00	65.00

ITEM	CRYSTAL	TERRACE GREEN
Saucer	5.00	20.00
Soup bowl, 7-3/8" d	12.00	75.00
Sugar	8.00	35.00
Tidbit, two tiers	20.00	—
Vegetable bowl, 9-1/2" d	—	235.00

Christmas Candy, crystal sugar, $8; creamer, $8.

CIRCLE

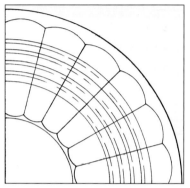

Manufactured by Hocking Glass Company, Lancaster, Ohio, in the 1930s.

Pieces were made in crystal, green, and pink. Crystal is listed in the original catalogs, but few pieces have surfaced to date. A 3-1/8-inch diameter sherbet is known and valued at $4.

ITEM	GREEN	PINK
Bowl, 4-1/2" d	15.00	15.00
Bowl, 5-1/2" d, flared	17.50	17.50
Bowl, 8" d	16.00	16.00
Bowl, 9-3/8" d	18.50	18.50
Creamer, ftd	9.00	16.00
Cup	5.00	6.00
Goblet, 8 oz, 5-3/4" h	16.50	15.00
Iced tea tumbler, 10 oz	17.50	17.50
Juice tumbler, 4 oz	9.50	9.00
Pitcher, 60 oz	35.00	35.00
Pitcher, 80 oz	30.00	32.00
Plate, 6" d, sherbet	3.00	5.00
Plate, 8-1/4" d, luncheon	11.00	11.00

ITEM	GREEN	PINK
Plate, 9-1/2" d, dinner	12.00	12.00
Salt shaker	95.00	95.00
Sandwich plate, 10" d	15.00	17.50
Saucer, 6" d	2.50	2.50
Sherbet, 3-1/8"	5.00	5.00
Sherbet, 4-3/4"	6.00	12.00
Sugar, ftd	12.00	16.00
Tumbler, 8 oz	10.00	10.00
Tumbler, 15 oz, flat	17.50	17.50
Wine, 4-1/2" h	10.00	15.00

Circle, green sugar, footed, $12.

Circle, green pitcher, 80 oz, $30.

CLOVERLEAF

Manufactured by Hazel Atlas Glass Company, Clarksburg, West Virginia, and Zanesville, Ohio, from 1930 to 1936.

Pieces were made in black, crystal, green, pink, and yellow. Collector interest in crystal is minimal; prices are about 50 percent of those listed for green.

ITEM	BLACK	GREEN	PINK	YELLOW
Ashtray, match holder in center, 4" d	65.00	—	—	—
Ashtray, match holder in center, 5-3/4" d	90.00	—	—	—
Bowl, 8" d	—	80.00	—	—
Candy dish, cov	—	65.00	—	130.00
Cereal bowl, 5" d	—	50.00	—	55.00
Creamer, 3-5/8" h, ftd	18.00	12.00	—	24.00
Cup	15.00	10.00	9.00	10.00
Dessert bowl, 4" d	—	30.00	35.00	45.00
Plate, 6" d, sherbet	40.00	7.50	—	10.00
Plate, 8" d, luncheon	14.00	10.00	12.00	15.00
Plate, 10-1/4" d, grill	—	25.00	—	40.00

ITEM	BLACK	GREEN	PINK	YELLOW
Salad bowl, 7" d	—	80.00	—	65.00
Salt and pepper shakers, pr	120.00	70.00	—	24.00
Saucer	3.00	6.00	6.00	2.00
Sherbet, 3" h, ftd	22.00	15.00	10.00	10.00
Sugar, 3-5/8" h, ftd	18.00	12.00	—	24.00
Tumbler, 9 oz, 4" h, flat	—	65.00	26.50	35.00
Tumbler, 10 oz, 3-3/4" h, flat	—	50.00	30.00	—
Tumbler, 10 oz, 5-3/4" h, ftd	—	30.00	—	45.00

Cloverleaf, green saucer, $6; pink plate, $12; pink cup, $9.

Cloverleaf, green sherbet, $15.

COIN
LINE #1372

Manufactured by Fostoria Glass Company, Moundsville, West Virginia, from 1958 to 1982.

Pieces were made in amber, blue, crystal, emerald green, olive green, and red.

Reproductions: † Reproductions have been made in colors similar to the original colors by Lancaster Colony, using original Fostoria molds.

ITEM	AMBER	BLUE	CRYSTAL
Ashtray, #110, cov, 3"	20.00	24.00	24.00
Ashtray, #114, 8" d	25.00	32.00	24.00
Ashtray, #115, 3" x 4" oblong	25.00	22.00	12.00
Ashtray, #119, 7-1/2" d, coin center	20.00	—	15.00
Ashtray, #123, 5" d	25.00	22.50	20.00
Ashtray, #124, 10" d	35.00	30.00	40.00
Bowl, #179, 7-1/2" d	40.00	80.00	20.00
Bowl, #189, 9" d, oval †	55.00	65.00	20.00
Bowl, #199, 8-1/2" d, ftd	75.00	125.00	75.00
Bowl, cov, #212, 8-1/2" d, ftd	225.00	425.00	95.00
Bud vase, #799, 8" h	30.00	70.00	25.00

Coin, red candy jar with cover, $120.

ITEM	EMERALD GREEN	OLIVE GREEN	RED
Ashtray, #110, cov, 3"	30.00	—	—
Ashtray, #114, 8" d	42.00	30.00	35.00
Ashtray, #115, 3" x 4" oblong	25.00	25.00	—
Ashtray, #119, 7-1/2" d, coin center	75.00	20.00	25.00
Ashtray, #123, 5" d	60.00	20.00	25.00
Ashtray, #124, 10" d	65.00	35.00	—
Bowl, #179, 7-1/2" d	95.00	40.00	70.00
Bowl, #189, 9" d, oval †	95.00	30.00	55.00
Bowl, #199, 8-1/2" d, ftd	125.00	65.00	85.00
Bowl, cov, #212, 8-1/2" d, ftd	225.00	—	—
Bud vase, #799, 8" h	125.00	30.00	60.00

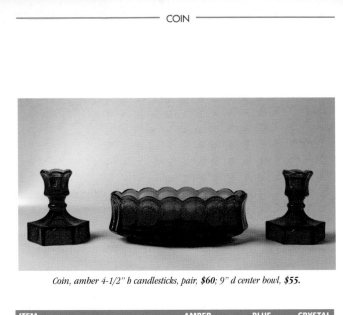

Coin, amber 4-1/2" h candlesticks, pair, $60; 9" d center bowl, $55.

ITEM	AMBER	BLUE	CRYSTAL
Cake salver, #630, ftd †	115.00	295.00	115.00
Candlesticks, pr, #316, 4-1/2" h	60.00	50.00	30.00
Candlesticks, pr, #326, 8" h	115.00	—	150.00
Candy box, cov, 4-1/8", #354	45.00	65.00	40.00
Candy jar, cov, #347, 6-1/2" †	50.00	90.00	40.00
Cigarette box, cov, #374 †	125.00	90.00	75.00
Cigarette holder, ashtray cover, #372	195.00	75.00	40.00
Cigarette urn, 3-1/2", #381	30.00	35.00	30.00
Condiment set, #737, salt & pepper, cruet, tray	225.00	300.00	175.00

Coin, olive green 12-3/4" h covered urn, $75.

ITEM	EMERALD GREEN	OLIVE GREEN	RED
Cake salver, #630, ftd †	275.00	135.00	—
Candlesticks, pr, #316, 4-1/2" h	95.00	35.00	75.00
Candlesticks, pr, #326, 8" h	—	95.00	110.00
Candy box, cov, 4-1/8", #354	165.00	75.00	70.00
Candy jar, cov, #347, 6-1/2" †	95.00	60.00	120.00
Cigarette box, cov, #374 †	195.00	—	—
Cigarette holder, ashtray cover, #372	85.00	—	—
Cigarette urn, 3-1/2", #381	90.00	25.00	60.00
Condiment set, #737, salt & pepper, cruet, tray	—	215.00	—

ITEM	AMBER	BLUE	CRYSTAL
Creamer, #680 †	20.00	25.00	20.00
Cruet, os, #531	55.00	150.00	95.00
Decanter, os, #400, pint †	175.00	265.00	100.00
Goblet, water, #2, 6-1/2", 10-1/2" h	—	—	40.00
Iced tea tumbler, #58, 14 oz	—	—	40.00
Iced tea tumbler, #64, 12 oz	—	—	45.00
Jelly compote, #448 †	48.00	75.00	55.50
Juice tumbler, #81, 9 oz	—	—	40.00
Lamp chimney, #461, patio	50.00	60.00	40.00
Lamp chimney, #292, courting	48.00	65.00	—
Lamp, #310, courting, 9-3/4" h, oil, handle	125.00	310.00	—
Lamp, #311, courting, 10-3/4" h, electric	135.00	315.00	—
Lamp, #320, coach, 13-1/2" h, oil	165.00	355.00	100.00
Lamp, #321, coach, 13-1/2" h, electric	175.00	365.00	100.00
Lamp, #459, patio, 16-1/2", electric	155.00	300.00	145.00
Lamp, #466, patio, 16-1/2" h, oil	195.00	390.00	145.00
Nappy, #495, 4-1/2" d	—	—	55.00
Nappy, handle, #499, 5-3/8" †	27.50	50.00	25.00
Old fashioned tumbler, #23, 10 oz	—	—	45.00
Pitcher, #453, one- qt	25.00	125.00	65.00
Plate, 8" d, #550	—	—	45.00
Salt and pepper shakers, pr, #652	65.00	75.00	25.00
Sherbet, #7, 9 oz	—	—	25.00
Sugar, cov, #673 †	30.00	45.00	30.00
Tumbler, #73, 9 oz, water	—	—	45.00
Urn, cov, #829, 12-3/4" h †	95.00	80.00	60.00
Vase, #818, 10" h, ftd	—	—	125.00
Wedding bowl, cov, #162, 8-1/4" d †	80.00	85.00	65.00
Wine, #26, 5 oz	—	—	60.00

ITEM	EMERALD GREEN	OLIVE GREEN	RED
Creamer, #680 †	25.00	20.00	25.00
Cruet, os, #531	200.00	65.00	—
Decanter, os, #400, pint †	350.00	175.00	—
Goblet, water, #2, 6-1/2", 10-1/2" h	—	65.00	145.00
Iced tea tumbler, #58, 14 oz	—	—	—
Iced tea tumbler, #64, 12 oz	—	35.00	—
Jelly compote, #448 †	65.00	20.00	30.00
Juice tumbler, #81, 9 oz	—	—	—
Lamp chimney, #461, patio	—	—	—
Lamp chimney, #292, courting	—	—	—
Lamp, #310, courting, 9-3/4" h, oil, handle	—	—	—
Lamp, #311, courting, 10-3/4" h, electric	—	—	—
Lamp, #320, coach, 13-1/2" h, oil	—	—	—
Lamp, #321, coach, 13-1/2" h, electric	—	—	—
Lamp, #459, patio, 16-1/2", electric	—	—	—
Lamp, #466, patio, 16-1/2" h, oil	—	—	—
Nappy, #495, 4-1/2" d	—	—	—
Nappy, handle, #499, 5-3/8" †	65.00	25.00	40.00
Old fashioned tumbler, #23, 10 oz	—	—	—
Pitcher, #453, one- qt	200.00	95.00	195.00
Plate, 8" d, #550	—	—	—
Salt and pepper shakers, pr, #652	195.00	65.00	90.00
Sherbet, #7, 9 oz	—	85.00	75.00
Sugar, cov, #673 †	40.00	35.00	40.00
Tumbler, #73, 9 oz, water	—	—	—
Urn, cov, #829, 12-3/4" h †	195.00	75.00	150.00
Vase, #818, 10" h, ftd	—	—	—
Wedding bowl, cov, #162, 8-1/4" d †	135.00	65.00	95.00
Wine, #26, 5 oz	—	45.00	95.00

COLONIAL
KNIFE AND FORK

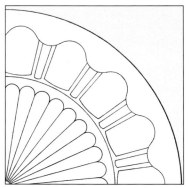

Manufactured by Hocking Glass Company, Lancaster, Ohio, from 1934 to 1938.

Pieces were made in crystal, green, and pink with limited production in opaque white.

ITEM	CRYSTAL	GREEN	PINK
Berry bowl, 3-3/4" d	—	—	60.00
Berry bowl, 4-1/2"	12.00	22.00	18.00
Berry bowl, 9" d	24.00	35.00	30.00
Butter dish, cov	25.00	45.00	—
Cereal bowl, 5-1/2" d	32.00	85.00	60.00
Claret, 4 oz, 5-1/4" h,	20.00	25.00	—
Cocktail, 3 oz, 4" h	18.00	25.00	—
Cordial, 1 oz, 3-3/4" h	18.00	30.00	—
Cream soup, 4-1/2" d	70.00	85.00	72.00
Creamer, 8 oz, 5" h	25.00	25.00	65.00
Cup	8.00	15.00	18.00

Colonial, green creamer, $25; sugar, $12.

ITEM	CRYSTAL	GREEN	PINK
Goblet, 8-1/2 oz, 5-3/4" h	15.00	25.00	40.00
Iced tea tumbler, 12 oz,	28.00	55.00	45.00
Juice tumbler, 5 oz, 3" h	17.50	27.50	22.00
Lemonade tumbler, 15 oz	47.50	75.00	65.00
Milk pitcher, 8 oz, 5" h	25.00	25.00	65.00
Mug, 12 oz, 5-1/2" h	—	825.00	500.00
Pitcher, 54 oz, 7" h, ice lip	30.00	45.00	48.00
Pitcher, 54 oz, 7" h, no lip	40.00	45.00	48.00
Pitcher, 68 oz, 7-3/4" h, ice lip	35.00	72.00	65.00
Pitcher, 68 oz, 7-3/4" h, no lip	45.00	60.00	65.00
Plate, 6" d, sherbet	4.50	11.00	6.00
Plate, 8-1/2" d, luncheon	6.00	8.00	24.00
Plate, 10" d, dinner	35.00	65.00	55.00

ITEM	CRYSTAL	GREEN	PINK
Plate, 10"d, grill	17.50	27.00	27.50
Plate, 12" d, oval	17.50	25.00	30.00
Platter, 12" l, oval	21.50	25.00	35.00
Salt and pepper shakers, pr	65.00	160.00	150.00
Saucer	4.50	6.75	6.50
Sherbet, 3" h	—	—	24.00
Sherbet, 3-3/8" h	10.00	14.00	14.50
Soup bowl, 7" d	30.00	85.00	85.00
Spoon holder or celery vase	65.00	115.00	125.00
Sugar, cov	60.00	48.00	50.00
Sugar, 5", open	10.00	12.00	15.00
Tumbler, 3 oz, 3-1/4" h, ftd	12.00	25.00	20.00
Tumbler, 5 oz, 4" h, ftd	20.00	42.00	40.00
Tumbler, 9 oz, 4" h	15.00	20.00	20.00
Tumbler, 10 oz, 5-1/4" h, ftd	30.00	46.50	50.00
Tumbler, 11 oz, 5-1/8" h	25.00	40.00	45.00
Vegetable bowl, 10" l, oval	18.00	25.00	45.00
Whiskey, 2-1/2" h, 1-1/2 oz.	10.00	20.00	15.00
Wine, 4-1/2" h, 2-1/2 oz	15.00	25.00	18.00

Colonial, pink divided grill plate, $27.50.

Colonial, crystal wine, $15; cocktail, $18.

Colonial, green 3-3/8" h sherbet, $14.

COLONIAL BLOCK

Manufactured by Hazel Atlas Glass Company, Clarksburg, West Virginia, and Zanesville, Ohio, early 1930s.

Pieces were made in black, cobalt blue (rare), crystal, green, pink, and white (1950s).

ITEM	BLACK	CRYSTAL	GREEN	PINK	WHITE
Bowl, 4" d	—	6.00	10.00	10.00	—
Bowl, 7" d	—	16.00	20.00	20.00	—
Butter dish, cov	—	35.00	45.00	45.00	—
Butter tub, cov	—	35.00	40.00	40.00	—
Candy jar, cov	—	30.00	40.00	40.00	—
Comport, 4" h, 4-3/4" w	—	12.00	—	—	—
Creamer	—	15.00	16.00	12.00	7.50
Goblet, 5-3/4" h	—	9.00	12.00	15.00	—
Pitcher, 20 oz, 5-3/4" h	—	40.00	50.00	50.00	—
Powder jar, cov	30.00	20.00	40.00	24.00	—
Sherbet	—	6.00	10.00	9.50	—
Sugar, cov	—	20.00	25.00	35.00	20.00
Sugar, open	—	6.00	15.00	10.00	10.00

Colonial Block, green covered butter dish, $45.

Colonial Block, green covered candy jar, $40.

COLONIAL FLUTED

ROPE

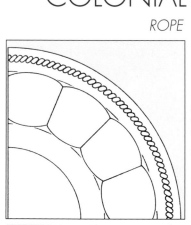

Manufactured by Federal Glass Company, Columbus, Ohio, from 1928 to 1933.

Pieces were made in crystal and green.

ITEM	CRYSTAL	GREEN
Berry bowl, 4" d	11.00	12.00
Berry bowl, 7-1/2" d	16.00	18.00
Cereal bowl, 6" d	15.00	18.00
Creamer, ftd	12.00	14.00
Cup	5.00	7.50
Plate, 6" d, sherbet	2.50	5.00
Plate, 8" d, luncheon	5.00	10.00
Salad bowl, 6-1/2" d, 2-1/2" deep	22.00	35.00
Saucer	2.50	4.00
Sherbet	6.00	8.50
Sugar, cov	21.00	25.00
Sugar, open	8.00	10.00

Colonial Fluted, green cup, $7.50.

Colonial Fluted, green 4" berry bowl, $12; 6" cereal bowl, $18.

COLONY
LINE #2412

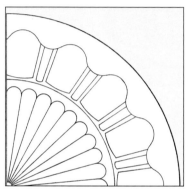

Manufactured by Fostoria Glass Company, Moundsville, West Virginia, from the 1930s until 1983. The pattern was designed by George Sakier.

Pieces were made in crystal. The pattern was reissued as "Maypole" in the 1980s in the following colors: amber, blue, green, red, yellow, and white.

ITEM	CRYSTAL
Almond bowl, ftd	15.00
Ashtray, 2-7/8" w, sq	8.75
Ashtray, 3" d, round	7.50
Ashtray, 3-1/2" w, sq	20.00
Ashtray, 4-1/2" d, round	15.00
Ashtray, 6" d, round	18.00
Bonbon, 5" d	25.00
Bonbon, 7"	15.00
Bowl, 4-1/2" d	15.00
Bowl, 5" d, handle	40.00
Bowl, 5-1/2" d, sq	30.00
Bowl, 8" d	35.00

Colony, crystal cup, $8.

Colony, crystal dinner plate, $22.50.

ITEM	CRYSTAL
Bowl, 10-1/2" d, high foot	95.00
Bowl, 10-1/2" d, low foot	45.00
Bowl, 11" l, flared	35.00
Bowl, 11" l, oval, ftd	70.00
Bud vase, 6" h	28.50
Butter dish, cov, quarter-pound	38.00
Cake plate, 10" d, handle	22.00
Candlesticks, pr, 3-1/2" h	35.00
Candlesticks, pr, 6-1/2" h, two-lite	60.00
Candlesticks, pr, 7" h	40.00
Candlesticks, pr, 7-1/2" h, prisms	150.00
Candlesticks, pr, 9" h	95.00
Candlesticks, pr, 9-3/4" h, prisms	172.00
Candlesticks, pr, 14-1/2" h, prisms	350.00
Candy dish, cov, 6-1/2"	45.00
Candy dish, cov, ftd, half-pound	75.00
Celery, 11-1/2"	32.00
Cheese and cracker	50.00
Cigarette box	48.00
Cocktail, 3-1/2 oz, 4"	5.00

ITEM	CRYSTAL
Comport, 4" h	18.00
Comport, cov, 6-1/2" d	38.00
Console bowl, 9" d or 13" d	65.00
Cornucopia, 9" h	70.00
Cream soup bowl, 5" d	48.00
Creamer	15.50
Creamer, individual size	11.00
Creamer and sugar tray, individual size	9.00
Cup	8.00
Finger bowl	45.00
Fruit bowl, 10" d	36.00
Fruit bowl, 14" d	155.00
Goblet, 5-1/4" h	18.00
Ice bucket	145.00
Iced tea tumbler, 12 oz	15.50
Juice tumbler, 5 oz. ftd	18.00
Lamp, electric	95.00
Lemon plate, 6-1/2" d, handle	12.50
Mayonnaise, three pcs	45.00
Milk pitcher, 16 oz	75.00
Oil bottle, orig stopper	40.00
Olive, 7" l, oblong	18.00
Oyster cocktail, 4 oz	14.00
Pickle	17.50
Pitcher, 48 oz, ice lip	150.00
Plate, 6" d, bread and butter	4.50
Plate, 7" d, salad	12.25
Plate, 8" d, luncheon	10.00
Plate, 9" d, dinner	22.50
Platter, 12" l	50.00
Punch bowl	695.00
Punch cup	12.00

Colony, crystal relish with two handles, $20.

ITEM	CRYSTAL
Relish, 10-1/2" d, three-part	35.00
Rose bowl	125.00
Salad bowl, 7-3/4" d	25.00
Salad bowl, 9-3/4" d	40.00
Salt and pepper shakers, pr, 2-1/2" h	45.00
Salt and pepper shakers, pr, 3-5/8" h	15.00
Salver, 12" d, ftd	65.00
Sandwich plate, center handle	45.00
Saucer	2.25
Sherbet, 3-5/8"	5.00
Sugar	15.50
Sugar, individual	11.50
Torte plate, 13" d	45.00
Torte plate, 15" d	60.00
Torte plate, 18" d	100.00
Tumbler, 5 oz, 4-1/2" h, ftd	30.00
Tumbler, 9 oz, 3-7/8" h	30.00
Tumbler, 12 oz, 5-3/4" h, ftd	24.00
Vase, 7" h	35.00
Vase, 7-1/2" h, flared	65.00
Vase, 12" h	150.00
Wine, 4-1/4" h	18.00

COLUMBIA

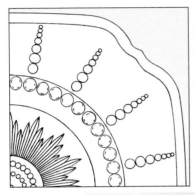

Manufactured by Federal Glass Company, Columbus, Ohio, from 1938 to 1942.

Pieces were made in crystal and pink. Several flashed (stained) colors have been found, and some decaled pieces are known.

Reproductions: † The 2-7/8-inch high juice tumbler has been reproduced. Look for the word "France" on the base to clearly identify the reproductions.

Columbia, crystal 11" d chop plate, $17; soup bowl, $25.

ITEM	CRYSTAL	FLASHED	PINK
Bowl, 10-1/2" d, ruffled edge	24.00	20.00	—
Butter dish, cov	20.00	25.00	—
Cereal bowl, 5" d	15.00	—	—
Chop plate, 11" d	17.00	12.00	—
Crescent-shaped salad	27.00	—	—
Cup	7.50	10.00	25.00
Juice tumbler, 4 oz, 2-3/4" h †	30.00	—	—
Plate, 6" d, bread and butter	10.00	4.00	14.00
Plate, 9-1/2" d, luncheon	9.00	12.00	20.00
Salad bowl, 8-1/2" d	10.00	—	—
Saucer	2.50	4050	10.00
Snack tray, cup	35.00	—	—
Soup bowl, 8" d, low	25.00	—	—
Tumbler, 9 oz.	42.50	—	—

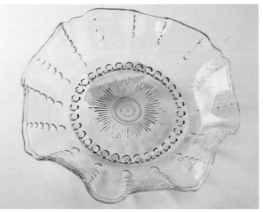

Columbia, crystal ruffled bowl, $24.

CONSTELLATION

PATTERN #300

Manufactured by Indiana Glass Company, Dunkirk, Indiana, circa 1940. Later reissued as Sunset Constellation by Tiara Home Products in the 1980s.

Indiana Glass Company made pieces in crystal and amber. Tiara Home Products made pieces in Amberina, emerald green, red, and yellow mist.

ITEM	AMBER	CRYSTAL	TIARA COLORS
Basket, 11"	—	30.00	25.00
Bowl, 11" d, two handles	—	25.00	12.00
Buffet plate, 18" d	—	40.00	—
Cake stand	—	45.00	—
Candlesticks, pr	—	45.00	15.00
Candy dish, cov	—	25.00	18.00
Celery tray	—	20.00	—
Console bowl, 11-1/2" d	—	25.00	20.00
Cookie jar, cov	—	28.00	24.00
Creamer	—	10.00	—

Constellation, crystal nut bowl, $12.

Constellation, amber water goblet, $15.

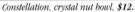

ITEM	AMBER	CRYSTAL	TIARA COLORS
Goblet, water	15.00	15.00	12.00
Mayonnaise bowl, ladle, underplate	—	28.00	—
Mug	—	15.00	—
Nappy, three toes	—	15.00	—
Nut bowl, 6" d, cupped	—	12.00	—
Pickle, oval	—	15.00	—
Pitcher, 7-1/2" d	65.00	45.00	60.00
Plate, dessert	—	5.00	—
Plate, lunch	—	8.00	—
Plate, salad	—	10.00	—
Platter, oval	—	20.00	—
Punch bowl	—	35.00	—
Relish, three-part	—	15.00	—
Salad bowl	—	22.00	—
Serving plate, 13-1/2" d	—	22.00	15.00
Sugar	—	10.00	—
Tumbler, 8 oz	—	15.00	—

CORONATION

BANDED FINE RIB, SAXON

Manufactured by Hocking Glass Company, Lancaster, Ohio, from 1936 to 1940.

Pieces were made in crystal, green, pink, and Royal Ruby.

ITEM	CRYSTAL	GREEN	PINK	ROYAL RUBY
Berry bowl, 4-1/4" d	—	50.00	7.50	12.00
Berry bowl, 8" d, handle	—	—	16.00	18.00
Berry bowl, 8" d	—	195.00		
Cup	5.00	—	6.00	7.50
Nappy bowl, 6-1/2" d	15.00	—	7.50	15.00
Pitcher, 68 oz, 7-3/4" h	—	—	500.00	—
Plate, 6" d, sherbet	2.00	—	14.50	—
Plate, 8-1/2" d, luncheon	5.00	60.00	12.00	8.50

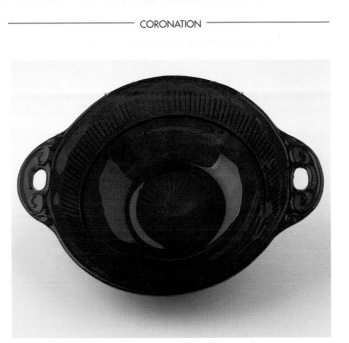

Coronation, royal ruby 8" handled berry bowl, $18.

ITEM	CRYSTAL	GREEN	PINK	ROYAL RUBY
Saucer	2.00	—	4.00	—
Sherbet	—	85.00	12.00	—
Tumbler, 10 oz, 5" h, ftd	—	195.00	25.00	—

CRACKED ICE

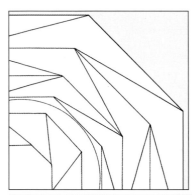

Manufactured by Indiana Glass, Dunkirk, Indiana, in the 1930s.

Pieces were made in pink and green. This pattern is often mistaken for Tea Room, so look for the additional diagonal line, giving it a more Art Deco style.

ITEM	GREEN	PINK
Creamer	30.00	35.00
Plate, 6-1/2" d	15.00	18.00
Sherbet	12.00	15.00
Sugar, cov	30.00	35.00
Tumbler	30.00	32.50

Cracked Ice, pink creamer, $35; covered sugar, $35.

CREMAX

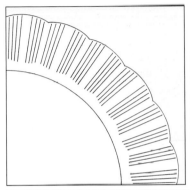

Manufactured by MacBeth-Evans Division of Corning Glass Works, late 1930s to early 1940s.

Pieces were made in Cremax, Cremax with fired-on colors, Delphite, and Robin's Egg Blue. One set is known as Bordette.

ITEM	BORDETTE	CREMAX	CREMAX, FIRED-ON	DELPHITE	ROBIN'S EGG BLUE
Cereal bowl, 5-3/4" d	5.00	6.00	9.00	10.00	10.00
Creamer	6.00	6.50	6.00	11.00	11.00
Cup	5.00	6.00	8.00	7.00	7.00
Demitasse cup	10.00	16.00	18.00	26.00	26.00
Demitasse saucer	6.00	7.00	8.00	12.00	20.00
Eggcup, 2-1/4" h	12.00	—	—	—	—
Plate, 6-1/4" d, bread and butter	4.00	4.50	5.50	7.00	7.00
Plate, 9-3/4" d, dinner	14.00	7.00	11.00	12.00	12.00
Sandwich plate, 11-1/2" d	9.50	10.00	15.00	17.00	17.00

ITEM	BORDETTE	CREMAX	CREMAX, FIRED-ON	DELPHITE	ROBIN'S EGG BLUE
Saucer	3.50	4.00	4.00	6.00	6.00
Sugar, open	6.00	6.50	6.00	11.00	11.00
Vegetable bowl, 9" d	10.00	11.00	10.00	20.00	20.00

Cremax, Bordette dinner plate with blue edge, $14.

CROCHETED CRYSTAL

Manufactured by Imperial Glass Company, Bellaire, Ohio, from 1943 to the early 1950s.

Pieces were made exclusively for Sears, Roebuck, and only in crystal.

ITEM	CRYSTAL
Basket, 6"	32.50
Basket, 9"	38.00
Basket, 12"	65.00
Buffet set, sauce bowl, ladle, 14" d plate	48.00
Cake stand, 12" d, ftd	42.00
Candlesticks, pr, 4-1/2" h, two lite	19.50
Candlesticks, pr, 6" w	20.00
Celery tray, 10" l, oval	25.00
Cheese and cracker, 12" d plate, ftd dish	42.00
Cocktail, 3-1/2 oz, 4-1/2" h	15.00
Console bowl, 12" d	25.00
Creamer, flat or footed	25.00

ITEM	CRYSTAL
Epergne, 11" h, ftd	140.00
Goblet, 9 oz, 7-1/8" h	15.00
Hors d'oeuvre dish, 10-1/2" d, four-part	30.00
Hurricane lamp, 11" h	48.00
Iced tea tumbler, 12 oz, 7" h, ftd	18.00
Juice tumbler, 6 oz, 6" h, ftd	12.00
Mayonnaise bowl, 5-1/4" d	15.00
Mayonnaise ladle	7.50
Mayonnaise plate, 7-1/2" d	8.00
Narcissus bowl, 7" d	42.00
Plate, 14" d	25.00
Plate, 17" d	40.00
Plate, 8" d, salad	9.50
Plate, 9-1/2" d, luncheon	12.50
Punch bowl, 14" d	70.00
Punch cup, closed handle	5.50
Punch cup, open handle	7.50
Relish, 11-1/2" d, three-part	24.50
Salad bowl, 10-1/2" d	35.00
Salad bowl liner, 13" d plate	25.00
Sherbet, 6 oz, 5" h	12.00
Sugar, flat or footed	15.00
Vase, 5" h, ftd	35.00
Vase, 8" h	35.00
Wine, 4-1/2 oz, 5-1/2" h	24.00

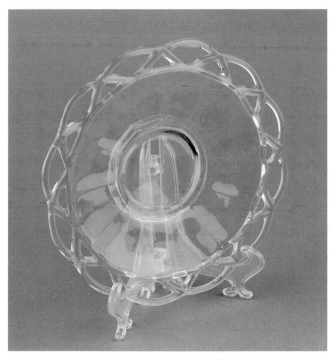

Crocheted Crystal, luncheon plate, $12.50.

CROW'S FOOT

LINE #412 AND LINE #890

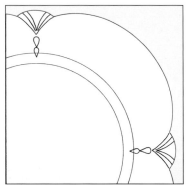

Manufactured by Paden City Glass Company, Paden City, West Virginia, in the 1930s. The square-shaped pieces are Line #412; the round line is Line #890.

Pieces were made in amber, amethyst, black, crystal, pink, Ritz blue, ruby red, white, and yellow.

ITEM	BLACK OR RITZ BLUE	COLORS	RUBY RED
Bowl, 4-7/8" w, sq	32.00	13.00	25.00
Bowl, 6" d	35.00	15.00	32.00
Bowl, 6-1/2" d, round, 2-1/2" h, 3-1/2" d base	50.00	24.00	45.00
Bowl, 8-1/2" d, sq, two handles	60.00	30.00	50.00
Bowl, 8-3/4" w, sq	55.00	25.00	45.00
Bowl, 10" d, ftd	75.00	35.00	70.00
Bowl, 10" w, sq, two handles	75.00	35.00	89.00
Bowl, 11" l, oval	45.00	20.00	40.00
Bowl, 11" w, sq	72.00	32.00	60.00
Bowl, 11" w, sq, rolled edge	75.00	35.00	70.00
Cake plate, sq, low pedestal foot	95.00	45.00	135.00

Crow's Foot, amber 8-1/2" square plate, $7.

ITEM	BLACK OR RITZ BLUE	COLORS	RUBY RED
Candlesticks, pr, 5-3/4" h	60.00	50.00	90.00
Candlesticks, pr, round base, tall	170.00	75.00	135.00
Candlesticks, pr, sq, mushroom	90.00	45.00	75.00
Candy, 6-1/8" w, 3-1/4" h, three legs, round	195.00	85.00	165.00
Candy, cov, 6-1/2" d, three parts	95.00	25.00	55.00
Cheese stand, 5" h	35.00	15.00	30.00
Comport, 3-1/4" h, 6-1/4" w	35.00	15.00	38.00
Comport, 4-3/4" h, 7-3/8" w	55.00	30.00	45.00
Comport, 6-5/8" h, 7" w	70.00	35.00	80.00
Console bowl, 11-1/2" d, three legs, round	100.00	50.00	150.00
Console bowl, 11-1/2" w, sq	95.00	40.00	80.00
Cracker plate, 11" d	50.00	25.00	45.00

ITEM	BLACK OR RITZ BLUE	COLORS	RUBY RED
Cream soup bowl, flat	28.00	12.00	22.00
Cream soup bowl, ftd	28.00	12.00	22.00
Creamer, flat	17.50	10.00	15.00
Creamer, footed	17.50	10.00	15.00
Cup, flat	18.50	8.00	15.00
Cup, ftd	18.50	6.00	15.00
Gravy boat, flat	100.00	45.00	85.00
Gravy boat, ftd	215.00	70.00	130.00
Mayonnaise, three legs	60.00	25.00	50.00
Nasturtium bowl, three legs	200.00	100.00	175.00
Plate, 5-3/4" d	4.00	2.00	3.00
Plate, 8" d, round	12.00	5.00	10.00
Plate, 8-1/2" w, sq	10.00	7.00	8.00
Plate, 9-1/4" d, round, dinner	40.00	20.00	35.00
Plate, 9-1/2" d, two handles	75.00	35.00	65.00
Plate, 10-3/8" d, round, two handles	65.00	30.00	55.00
Plate, 10-3/8" w, sq, two handles	65.00	30.00	55.00
Plate, 10-1/2" d, dinner	100.00	45.00	90.00
Platter, 12" l	50.00	17.50	30.00
Relish, 11" l, 3 part	100.00	48.00	85.00
Sandwich server, center handle, round	75.00	50.00	70.00
Sandwich server, center handle, sq	45.00	18.00	50.00
Saucer, 6" d, round	10.00	2.00	5.00
Saucer, 6" w, sq	10.00	2.00	5.00
Sugar, flat	17.50	10.00	15.00
Sugar, ftd	17.50	10.00	15.00
Tumbler, 4-1/4" h	80.00	35.00	75.00
Vase, 4-5/8" h	75.00	45.00	65.00
Vases, 10-1/4" h, cupped	110.00	50.00	90.00
Vases, 10-1/4" h, flared	85.00	35.00	70.00
Vases, 11-3/4" h, flared	185.00	125.00	240.00
Whipped cream bowl, three legs	70.00	30.00	60.00

CUBE
CUBIST

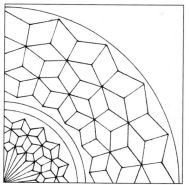

Manufactured by Jeannette Glass Company, Jeannette, Pennsylvania, from 1929 to 1933.

Pieces were made in amber, crystal, green, pink, ultramarine, and white. Production in white is limited in both the number of items made as well as collector interest.

ITEM	CRYSTAL	GREEN	PINK	ULTRAMARINE
Bowl, 4-1/2" d, deep	—	10.00	9.50	35.00
Bowl, 7-1/4" d		20.00	18.00	
Butter dish, cov		75.00	65.00	
Candy jar, cov, 6-1/2" h	—	25.00	30.00	—
Coaster, 3-1/4" d	—	9.50	10.00	
Creamer, 2-5/8" h	5.00	10.00	10.00	70.00
Creamer, 3-9/16" h	—	11.00	9.00	—
Cup	—	7.00	8.00	—
Dessert bowl, 4-1/2" d, pointed rim	7.00	8.50	12.50	—
Pitcher, 8-3/4" h, 45 oz	—	215.00	175.00	—
Plate, 6" d, sherbet	—	11.00	3.50	—

ITEM	CRYSTAL	GREEN	PINK	ULTRAMARINE
Plate, 8" d, luncheon	—	12.50	8.50	—
Powder jar, cov, three legs	—	30.00	30.00	—
Salad bowl, 6-1/2" d	6.00	20.00	15.00	—
Salt and pepper shakers, pr	—	35.00	36.00	—
Saucer	1.50	3.00	3.00	—
Sherbet, ftd	—	8.50	12.00	—
Sugar, cov, 2-3/8" h	4.00	22.00	6.00	—
Sugar, cov, 3" h	—	20.00	25.00	—
Sugar, open, 3"	5.00	8.00	6.00	—
Tray, 7-1/2" l	9.00	—	8.00	—
Tumbler, 9 oz, 4" h	—	70.00	65.00	—

Cube, green dessert bowl, $8.50; coaster, $9.50; sherbet, $8.50.

Cube, pink covered candy jar, $30.

Cube, green covered powder jar, $30.

Cube, pink luncheon plate, $8.50.

CUPID

Manufactured by Paden City Glass Company, Paden City, West Virginia, in the 1930s.

Pieces were made in amber, black, canary yellow, crystal, green, light blue, peacock blue, and pink. Prices for colors like amber, black, canary yellow, and light blue are still being established as more pieces of this pattern arrive on the secondary market. This expensive pattern is one to keep your eyes open for while searching at flea markets and garage sales.

ITEM	CRYSTAL	GREEN	PEACOCK BLUE	PINK
Bowl, 8-1/2" l, oval, ftd	—	300.00	—	300.00
Bowl, 9-1/4" d, center handle	—	275.00	—	275.00
Bowl, 10-1/2" d, rolled edge	—	250.00	—	250.00
Cake plate, 11-3/4" h	—	200.00	—	200.00
Cake stand, 2" h, ftd	—	235.00	—	235.00
Candlesticks, pr, 5" h	—	245.00	—	245.00
Candy, cov, 3 part	—	385.00	—	385.00
Candy, cov, 5-1/4" h	—	295.00	—	295.00
Champagne, 5-7/8" h	35.00	—	—	—
Cocktail, 5-1/8" h	25.00	—	—	—
Comport, 4-1/2" h, ftd	—	175.00	—	175.00
Comport, 6-1/4" h, ftd	—	185.00	225.00	290.00
Console bowl, 11" d	—	250.00	—	175.00

Cupid, pink 6-1/4" h low pedestal-foot comport, **$290.**

ITEM	CRYSTAL	GREEN	PEACOCK BLUE	PINK
Creamer, 4-1/2" h, ftd	45.00	150.00	—	150.00
Creamer, 5" h, ftd	—	150.00	—	150.00
Fruit bowl, 9-1/4" d, ftd	—	360.00	—	360.00
Fruit bowl, 10-1/4" d	—	245.00	—	275.00
Ice bucket, 6" h	—	325.00	—	325.00
Ice tub, 4-3/4" h	—	325.00	—	325.00
Mayonnaise, 6" d, spoon, 8" d plate	—	200.00	295.00	275.00
Plate, 10-1/2" d	—	150.00	175.00	150.00
Samovar	—	990.00	—	990.00
Sugar, 4-1/4" h, ftd	—	150.00	—	150.00
Sugar, 5" h, ftd	—	150.00	—	150.00
Tray, 10-3/4" d, center handle	—	200.00	—	200.00
Tray, 10-7/8" l, oval, ftd	—	250.00	—	250.00
Vase, 8-1/4" h, elliptical	—	650.00	—	650.00
Vase, 10" h	—	315.00	—	315.00
Wine, 5-1/8" h	12.50	—	—	—

DAISY
NO. 620

Manufactured by Indiana Glass Company, Dunkirk, Indiana, from late 1930s to 1980s.

Pieces were made in amber (1940s), crystal (1933-1940), dark green (1960s-1980s), fired-on red (late 1930s), and milk glass (1960s-1980s).

ITEM	AMBER OR FIRED-ON RED	CRYSTAL	DARK GREEN OR MILK WHITE
Berry bowl, 4-1/2" d	11.00	6.00	6.00
Berry bowl, 7-3/8" d deep	17.50	8.50	9.00
Berry bowl, 9-3/8" d, deep	35.00	14.00	14.00
Cake plate, 11-1/2" d	16.50	14.00	14.00
Cereal bowl, 6" d	25.00	10.00	10.00
Cream soup bowl, 4-1/2" d	12.50	7.50	9.50
Creamer, ftd	10.00	8.00	8.00
Cup	5.00	6.00	6.00
Plate, 6" d, sherbet	5.00	4.50	5.00
Plate, 7-3/8" d, salad	8.50	8.50	9.00
Plate, 8-3/8" d, luncheon	10.00	10.00	12.00
Plate, 9-3/8" d, dinner	12.00	12.00	15.00

ITEM	AMBER OR FIRED-ON RED	CRYSTAL	DARK GREEN OR MILK WHITE
Plate, 10-3/8" d, grill	15.00	15.00	18.00
Plate, 10-3/8" d, grill, indent for soup	15.00	8.00	10.00
Platter, 10-3/4" d	18.00	11.00	11.00
Relish dish, 8-3/8" d, 3 part	24.00	12.00	12.00
Sandwich plate, 11-1/2" d	17.50	14.00	14.00
Saucer	2.00	6.00	2.00

Daisy, green luncheon plate, $12.

ITEM	AMBER OR FIRED-ON RED	CRYSTAL	DARK GREEN OR MILK WHITE
Sherbet, ftd	6.00	5.00	5.00
Sugar, ftd	10.00	8.00	8.00
Tumbler, 9 oz, ftd	18.00	12.00	15.00
Tumbler, 12 oz, ftd	25.00	15.00	18.00
Vegetable bowl, 10" l, oval	18.00	12.00	12.00

Daisy, amber creamer, $10.

DELILAH

DELILAH BIRD, PEACOCK REVERSE, LINE #412

Manufactured by Paden City Glass Company, Paden City, West Virginia, in the 1930s.

Pieces were made in amber, black, cobalt blue, crystal, green, pink, red, and yellow.

ITEM	COLORS
Bowl, 4-7/8" w, sq	50.00
Bowl, 8-3/4" w, sq	115.00
Bowl, 8-3/4" w, sq, handles	125.00
Candlesticks, pr, 5-3/4" h	90.00
Candy dish, 6-1/2" w, sq	200.00
Comport, 3-1/4" h, 6-1/4" w	90.00
Comport, 4-1/4" h, 7-3/8" w	95.00
Console bowl, 11-3/4" d	400.00
Creamer, 2-3/4" h, flat	95.00
Cup	95.00
Plate, 5-3/4" d, sherbet	25.00
Plate, 8-1/2" d, luncheon	70.00

ITEM	COLORS
Plate, 10-3/8" d, two handles	155.00
Saucer	25.00
Server, center handle	85.00
Sherbet, two sizes	75.00
Tumbler, 10 oz, 4" h, flat	95.00
Vase, 6-3/4" h	125.00
Vase, 10" h	100.00

Above: Delilah Bird, amber candlesticks, $90. Left: Pink mayonnaise liner, $25.

DELLA ROBBIA

#1058

Manufactured by Westmoreland Glass Company, Grapeville, Pennsylvania, from the late 1920s to 1940s.

Pieces were made in crystal with applied luster colors and milk glass. Examples of milk glass prices are: hand-painted decorated candy jar, $45; creamer, $18; goblet, $35; tumbler, $22.50; and wine, $18.

ITEM	CRYSTAL
Basket, 9"	165.00
Basket, 12"	195.00
Bowl, 8" d, bell, handle	48.00
Bowl, 8"d, heart shape, handle	95.00
Bowl, 12" d, ftd	12.00
Bowl, 13" d, rolled edge	115.00
Bowl, 14" d, oval, flange	155.00
Bowl, 15" d, bell	175.00
Cake salver, 14" d, ftd	120.00
Candlesticks, pr, 4" h	65.00
Candlesticks, pr, 4" h, two-lite	160.00

ITEM	CRYSTAL
Candy jar, cov, scalloped edge	85.00
Champagne, 6 oz	25.00
Chocolate candy, round, flat	75.00
Cocktail, 3-1/4 oz	15.00
Comport, 12" d, ftd, bell	115.00
Comport, 13" d, flanged	125.00
Creamer, ftd	18.00
Cup, coffee	18.50
Finger bowl, 5" d	30.00
Ginger ale tumbler, 5 oz	25.00
Goblet, 8 oz, 6" h	28.00
Iced tea tumbler 11 oz, ftd	35.00
Iced tea tumbler 12 oz, 5-3/16" h, straight	40.00
Iced tea tumbler 12 oz, bell	32.00
Iced tea tumbler, 12 oz, bell, ftd	32.00
Mint comport, 6-1/2" d, 3-5/8" h, ftd	45.00
Nappy, 7-1/2" d	42.00
Nappy, 8" d, bell	45.00
Nappy, 4-1/2" d	30.00
Nappy, 6" d, bell	35.00
Nappy, 6-1/2"d, one handle	32.00
Nappy, 9" d	60.00
Pitcher, 32 oz	180.00
Plate, 6" d, finger bowl liner	12.00
Plate, 6-1/8" d, bread and butter	14.00
Plate, 7-1/4" d, salad	22.00
Plate, 9" d, luncheon	35.00
Plate, 10-1/2" d, dinner	95.00
Plate, 18" d	195.00
Platter, 14" l, oval	195.00
Punch bowl, 14" d	225.00
Punch bowl Liner, 18" d plate, upturned edge	200.00

ITEM	CRYSTAL
Punch cup	15.00
Salt and pepper shakers, pr	55.00
Saucer	10.00
Sherbet, 5 oz, low foot	22.00
Sherbet, 5 oz, 4-3/4" h, ftd	24.00
Sugar, ftd	27.50
Sweetmeat comport, 8" d	115.00
Torte plate, 14"d	125.00
Tumbler 8 oz, ftd	30.00
Tumbler, 8 oz, water	32.00
Wine, 3 oz	25.00

Della Robbia, crystal salad plate, $22.

Della Robbia, luster-decorated sweetmeat comport, $115.

DEWDROP

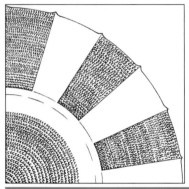

Manufactured by Jeannette Glass Company, Jeannette, Pennsylvania, from 1953 to 1956.

Pieces were made in crystal with a few forms also found iridized.

ITEM	CRYSTAL
Bowl, 4-3/4" d	9.00
Bowl, 8-1/2" d	22.00
Bowl, 10-3/8" d	24.00
Butter, cov	32.00
Candy dish, cov, 7" d	30.00
Casserole, cov	27.50
Creamer	8.50
Iced tea tumbler, 15 oz	17.50
Lazy Susan, 13" d tray	25.00
Pitcher, half-gallon, ftd	48.00
Plate, 11-1/2" d	20.00
Punch cup	4.00
Punch bowl set, bowl, 12 cups	75.00

ITEM	CRYSTAL
Snack cup	4.00
Snack plate, indent for cup	5.00
Relish, leaf-shape, handle	9.00
Sugar, cov	14.00
Tray, 10" d	22.00
Tumbler, 9 oz	35.00

Dewdrop, crystal tumbler, $35; iridescent pitcher, $60.

DIAMOND QUILTED

FLAT DIAMOND

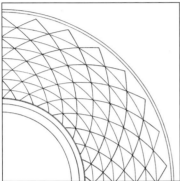

Manufactured by Imperial Glass Company, Bellaire, Ohio, from the late 1920 to the early 1930s.

Made in amber, black, blue, crystal, green, pink, and red. Amber and red prices are valued slightly higher than black.

ITEM	BLACK	BLUE	CRYSTAL
Bowl, 5-1/2" d, one handle	20.00	—	—
Bowl, 7" d, crimped edge	22.00	—	—
Bowl, 10" d	65.00	60.00	15.00
Cake salver, 10" d, tall	—	—	—
Candlesticks, pr	50.00	—	40.00
Candy jar, cov, ftd	—	—	25.00
Cereal bowl, 5" d	15.00	—	8.00
Champagne, 9 oz, 6" h	—	—	—
Comport, 6" h, 7-1/4" w	—	—	—
Comport, cov, 11-1/2" d	—	—	—
Console bowl, 10-1/2" d, rolled edge	65.00	60.00	15.00
Cordial, 1 oz	—	—	—
Cream soup bowl, 4-3/4" d	22.00	20.00	20.00

ITEM	BLACK	BLUE	CRYSTAL
Creamer	18.50	20.00	15.00
Cup	18.00	18.50	7.00
Ice bucket	90.00	90.00	—
Iced tea tumbler, 12 oz	—	—	—
Mayonnaise set, comport, plate, ladle	60.00	65.00	25.00
Pitcher, 64 oz	—	—	—
Plate, 6" d, sherbet	10.00	8.50	7.50
Plate, 7" d, salad	10.00	10.00	8.00
Plate, 8" d, luncheon	12.00	12.00	9.00
Punch bowl and stand	—	—	—
Sandwich plate, 14" d	—	—	—
Sandwich server, center handle	50.00	50.00	20.00
Saucer	5.00	5.00	2.00
Sherbet	16.00	16.00	14.00
Sugar	20.00	25.00	12.00
Tumbler, 6 oz, ftd	—	—	—
Tumbler, 9 oz	—	—	—
Tumbler, 9 oz, ftd	—	—	—
Tumbler, 12 oz, ftd	—	—	—
Vase, fan	80.00	75.00	—
Whiskey, 1-1/2" oz	—	—	—
Wine, 2 oz	—	—	—
Wine, 3 oz	—	—	—

ADDITIONAL COLORS

ITEM	GREEN	PINK
Bowl, 5-1/2" d, one handle	15.00	18.00
Bowl, 7" d, crimped edge	18.00	20.00
Bowl, 10" d	20.00	22.00
Cake salver, 10" d, tall	60.00	65.00
Candlesticks, pr	32.00	28.00
Candy jar, cov, ftd	65.00	65.00
Cereal bowl, 5" d	9.00	8.50

ITEM	GREEN	PINK
Champagne, 9 oz, 6" h	12.00	—
Compote, 6" h, 7-1/4" w	45.00	48.00
Compote, cov, 11-1/2" d	80.00	75.00
Console bowl, 10-1/2" d, rolled edge	20.00	24.00
Cordial, 1 oz	12.00	15.00
Cream soup bowl, 4-3/4" d	12.00	14.00
Creamer	12.00	12.00
Cup	10.00	10.00
Ice bucket	50.00	50.00
Iced tea tumbler, 12 oz	10.00	10.00
Mayonnaise set, comport, plate, ladle	37.50	40.00
Pitcher, 64 oz	50.00	55.00
Plate, 6" d, sherbet	4.00	7.50
Plate, 7" d, salad	8.50	8.50
Plate, 8" d, luncheon	6.50	8.50
Punch bowl and stand	450.00	450.00
Sandwich plate, 14" d	15.00	15.00
Sandwich server, center handle	25.00	25.00
Saucer	4.00	4.00
Sherbet	12.00	10.00
Sugar	15.00	13.50

Diamond Quilted, pink sugar, $13.50; creamer, $12.

ITEM	GREEN	PINK
Tumbler, 6 oz, ftd	9.00	10.00
Tumbler, 9 oz	14.00	16.00
Tumbler, 9 oz, ftd	14.00	16.00
Tumbler, 12 oz, ftd	15.00	15.00
Vase, fan	50.00	50.00
Whiskey, 1-1/2" oz	10.00	12.00
Wine, 2 oz	12.50	12.50
Wine, 3 oz	15.00	15.00

Diamond Quilted, green one-handled bowl, $15.

Diamond Quilted, green two-handled cream soup, $12.

DIANA

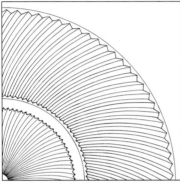

Manufactured by Federal Glass Company, Columbus, Ohio, 1937-1941.

Pieces were made in amber, crystal, and pink.

Reproductions: † A 13-1/8-inch diameter scalloped pink bowl has been made, which was not original to the pattern.

ITEM	AMBER	CRYSTAL	PINK
Ashtray, 3-1/2" d	—	4.00	5.00
Bowl, 12" d, scalloped edge	20.00	18.00	32.00
Candy jar, cov, round	40.00	18.50	45.00
Cereal bowl, 5" d	15.00	6.50	13.00
Coaster, 3-1/2" d	12.00	4.00	7.00
Console/fruit bowl, 11"d	10.00	20.00	44.00
Cream soup bowl, 5-1/2" d	12.00	14.00	24.00
Creamer, oval	9.00	4.00	12.50
Cup	10.00	5.00	20.00
Demitasse cup and saucer, 2 oz, 4-1/2" d saucer	—	9.00	50.00
Junior set, six cups and saucers, rack	—	125.00	300.00
Plate, 6" d, bread and butter	3.50	3.00	6.50
Plate, 9-1/2" d, dinner	9.00	7.00	18.50

ITEM	AMBER	CRYSTAL	PINK
Platter, 12" l, oval	15.00	12.00	28.00
Salad bowl, 9"d	18.00	15.00	30.00
Salt and pepper shakers, pr	100.00	30.00	75.00
Sandwich plate, 11-3/4" d	15.00	12.50	30.00
Sandwich plate, 11-3/4" d, advertising in center	—	15.00	—
Saucer	2.25	2.00	6.00
Sherbet	10.00	7.00	12.00
Sugar, open, oval	10.00	10.00	16.00
Tumbler, 9 oz, 4-1/8" h	27.50	18.00	45.00

Diana, pink 5" cereal bowl, $13; pink 9" salad bowl, $30.

Diana, crystal tumbler, $18.

DOGWOOD
APPLE BLOSSOM, WILD ROSE

Manufactured by MacBeth-Evans Company, Charleroi, Pennsylvania, from 1929 to 1932.

Pieces were made in Cremax, crystal, green, Monax, pink, and yellow. Yellow is rare; a cereal bowl is known and valued at $95. Crystal items are valued at 50 percent less than green.

ITEM	CREMAX OR MONAX	GREEN	PINK
Berry bowl, 8-1/2" d	40.00	100.00	55.00
Cake plate, 13" d, heavy solid foot	185.00	135.00	165.00
Cereal bowl, 5-1/2" d	12.00	35.00	30.00
Creamer, 2-1/2" h, thin	—	48.00	15.00
Creamer, 3-1/4" h, thick	—	—	15.00
Cup, thin	—	32.00	20.00
Cup, thick	36.00	40.00	22.50
Fruit bowl, 10-1/4" d	100.00	195.00	550.00
Pitcher, 8" h, 80 oz, decorated	—	450.00	225.00
Plate, 6" d, bread and butter	25.00	10.00	6.50
Plate, 8" d, luncheon	—	12.00	10.00
Plate, 9-1/4" d, dinner	—	—	25.00

ITEM	CREMAX OR MONAX	GREEN	PINK
Plate, 10-1/2" d, grill, AOP or border design	—	25.00	20.00
Salver, 12" d	165.00	—	35.00
Saucer	20.00	8.00	4.50
Sherbet, low, ftd	—	85.00	45.00
Sugar, 2-1/2" h, thin	—	50.00	20.00
Sugar, 3-1/4" h, thick, ftd	—	—	22.50
Tidbit, two-tier	—	—	90.00
Tumbler, 10 oz, 4" h, decorated	—	100.00	55.00
Tumbler, 11 oz, 4-3/4" h, decorated	—	95.00	45.00
Tumbler, 12 oz, 5" h, decorated	—	125.00	80.00
Tumbler, molded band	—	—	22.50

Dogwood, pink sugar, $22.50; creamer, $15; luncheon plate, $10.

DORIC

Manufactured by Jeannette Glass Company, Jeannette, Pennsylvania, from 1935 to 1938.

Pieces were made in Delphite, green, pink, and yellow. Yellow is rare.

ITEM	DELPHITE	GREEN	PINK
Berry bowl, 4-1/2" d	50.00	12.00	12.00
Berry bowl, 8-1/4" d	150.00	35.00	38.00
Bowl, 9" d, two handles	—	45.00	45.00
Butter dish, cov	—	90.00	75.00
Cake plate, 10" d, three legs	—	30.00	30.00
Candy dish, cov, 8" d	—	55.00	45.00
Candy dish, three parts	18.00	9.50	12.50
Cereal bowl, 5-1/2" d	—	65.00	70.00
Coaster, 3" d	—	28.00	20.00
Cream soup bowl, 5" d, two handles	—	325.00	—
Creamer, 4" h	—	17.00	14.00
Cup	—	10.00	10.00
Pitcher, 36 oz, 6" h, flat	1,200.00	55.00	45.00

ITEM	DELPHITE	GREEN	PINK
Pitcher, 48 oz, 7-1/2" h, ftd	—	1,000.00	750.00
Plate, 6" d, sherbet	—	7.50	7.50
Plate, 7" d, salad	—	22.00	18.00
Plate, 9" d, dinner	—	24.00	15.00
Plate, 9" d, grill	—	20.00	30.00
Platter, 12" l, oval	—	32.00	35.00
Relish tray, 4" x 4"	—	15.00	16.50
Relish tray, 4" x 8"	—	30.00	22.50
Salt and pepper shakers, pr	—	35.00	40.00
Saucer	—	7.00	4.00
Sherbet, ftd	12.00	20.00	15.00
Sugar, cov	—	35.00	32.00
Tray, 8" x 8", serving	—	40.00	40.00
Tray, 10" l, handle	—	25.00	24.00
Tumbler, 9 oz, 4-1/2" h, flat	—	75.00	50.00
Tumbler, 10 oz, 4" h, ftd	—	80.00	55.00
Tumbler, 12 oz, 5" h, ftd	—	125.00	85.00
Vegetable bowl, 9" l, oval	—	48.00	45.00

Doric, green cake plate, $30.

DORIC AND PANSY

Manufactured by Jeannette Glass Company, Jeannette, Pennsylvania, from 1937 to 1938.

Pieces were made in ultramarine with limited production in pink and crystal.

ITEM	CRYSTAL	PINK	ULTRAMARINE
Berry bowl, 4-1/2" d	12.00	12.00	24.00
Berry bowl, 8" d	—	24.00	75.00

Doric and Pansy, ultramarine child's sugar, $50; child's creamer, $45.

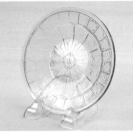

*Doric and
Pansy, pink
dinner
plate, $8.*

ITEM	CRYSTAL	PINK	ULTRAMARINE
Bowl, 9" d, handle	15.00	20.00	35.00
Butter dish, cov	—	—	475.00
Candy, cov, three parts	—	—	22.50
Cup	12.00	14.00	18.00
Creamer	72.00	90.00	145.00
Plate, 6" d, sherbet	8.00	12.00	12.50
Plate, 7" d, salad	—	—	40.00
Plate, 9" d, dinner	7.50	8.00	30.00
Salt shaker, orig top	—	—	325.00
Saucer	4.50	4.50	7.50
Sugar, open	80.00	85.00	145.00
Tray, 10" l, handles	45.00	—	25.00
Tumbler, 9 oz, 4-1/2" h	—	—	500.00

CHILDREN'S

ITEM	PINK	ULTRAMARINE
Creamer	35.00	45.00
Cup	30.00	35.00
Plate	12.00	14.50
Saucer	6.00	5.00
Sugar	35.00	50.00
14-pc set, orig box	400.00	425.00

EARLY AMERICAN PRESCUT

Manufactured by Anchor Hocking Glass Corp., Lancaster, Ohio, from 1960 to 1999.

Pieces were made in crystal with some limited production in colors.

ITEM	CRYSTAL
Ashtray, 4" d	5.00
Ashtray, 5" d	8.00
Ashtray, 7-3/4" d	12.00
Basket, 6" x 4-1/2"	20.00
Bowl, 4-1/4" d, plain rim	20.00
Bowl, 4-1/4" d, scalloped	7.50
Bowl, 5-1/4" d, scalloped	18.50
Bowl, 6-3/4" d, three legs	5.00
Bowl, 7-1/4" d, scalloped	20.00
Bowl, 8-3/4" d	10.00
Bowl, 9" d, oval	8.00
Bowl, 11-3/4" d, paneled	225.00
Bud vase, 5" h, ftd	475.00

ITEM	CRYSTAL
Butter, cov, 1/4 lb	8.50
Butter, cov, metal handle, knife	15.00
Cake plate	25.00
Candlesticks, pr, two-lite	32.50
Candy, cov, 5-1/4"	12.00
Candy, cov, 7-1/4"	14.50
Chip and dip, 10-1/4" bowl, metal holder	25.00

Early American Prescut, crystal cake plate, $25

ITEM	CRYSTAL
Coaster	6.00
Cocktail shaker, 30 oz	300.00
Console bowl, 9" d	15.00
Creamer	3.50
Creamer and sugar tray	3.00
Cruet, os	9.50
Dessert bowl, 5-3/8" d	3.00
Deviled egg plate, 11-3/4" d	35.00
Gondola dish, 9-1/2" l	7.50
Hostess tray, 6-1/2" x 12"	14.00
Iced tea tumbler, 15 oz, 6" h	20.00
Juice tumbler, 5 oz, 4' h	5.00
Lamp, oil	315.00
Lazy Susan, nine pcs	60.00
Pitcher, 18 oz	15.00
Pitcher, 40 oz, sq	30.00
Pitcher, 60 oz	20.00
Plate, 6-3/4" d, salad	55.00
Plate, 6-3/4" d, snack, ring for cup	40.00
Plate, 10" d, snack	15.00
Plate, 11" d	15.00
Punch cup	1.00
Punch set, 15 pcs	35.00
Relish, two parts, 10" l, tab handle	7.50
Relish, three parts, 8-1/2" l, oval	9.50
Relish, five parts, 13-1/2" d	30.00
Salad bowl, 10-3/4" d	15.00
Salt and pepper shakers, pr, individual size	72.00
Salt and pepper shakers, pr, metal tops	10.00
Salt and pepper shakers, pr, plastic tops	12.00
Serving plate, 11" d, four parts	90.00
Serving plate, 13-1/2" d	15.00

ITEM	CRYSTAL
Sherbet, 6 oz	90.00
Snack cup	3.00
Sugar, cov	4.50
Syrup pitcher, 12 oz	20.00
Tumbler, 10 oz, 4-1/2" h	6.50
Vase, 8-1/2" h	8.00
Vase, 10" h	15.00

Early American Prescut, crystal 10" h vase, $15; 8-1/2" h vase, $8.

ENGLISH HOBNAIL
LINE #555

Manufactured by Westmoreland Glass Company, Grapeville, Pennsylvania, from the 1920s to 1983.

Pieces were made in amber, cobalt blue, crystal, crystal with various color treatments, green, ice blue, pink, red, and turquoise blue. Values for cobalt blue, red, or turquoise blue pieces would be approximately 25 percent higher than ice blue values. Currently a turquoise basket is valued at $150. A red basket is valued at $90 and a red 8" diameter handled hexagonal footed bowl is $235. Crystal pieces with a color accent are slightly higher than crystal values.

Limited pieces were also made in milk white; a square-footed ivy ball is valued at $25, while a 4-inch diameter bowl with hand-painted decoration is $15.

Reproductions: † A creamer and sugar with a hexagonal foot, nut bowl, and pickle dish have been reproduced.

ITEM	AMBER	CRYSTAL	GREEN	ICE BLUE	PINK
Ashtray, 3" d	20.00	20.00	22.00	—	20.00
Ashtray, 4-1/2" d	9.00	9.00	15.00	24.00	15.00
Ashtray, 4-1/2" sq	9.50	9.50	15.00	—	15.00
Basket, 5" d, handle	20.00	20.00	—	—	—
Basket, 6" d, handle, tall	40.00	40.00	—	—	65.00
Bonbon, 6-1/2" h, handle	15.00	17.50	30.00	40.00	30.00

ITEM	AMBER	CRYSTAL	GREEN	ICE BLUE	PINK
Bowl, 7" d, six parts	17.50	17.50	—	—	—
Bowl, 7" d, oblong spoon	17.50	17.50			—
Bowl, 8" d, ftd	30.00	30.00	48.00	—	48.00
Bowl, 8" d, hexagonal foot, two handles	38.00	38.00	75.00	115.00	75.00
Bowl, 8", six pt	24.00	24.00	—	—	—
Bowl, 9-1/2" d, round, crimped	30.00	30.00	—	—	—
Bowl, 10" d, flared	35.00	35.00	40.00	—	40.00
Bowl, 10" l, oval, crimped	40.00	40.00	—	—	—
Bowl, 11" d, bell	35.00	35.00			
Bowl, 11" d, rolled edge	35.00	35.00	40.00	85.00	40.00
Bowl, 12" d, flared	32.00	32.00	40.00	—	95.00
Bowl, 12" l, oval crimped	32.00	32.00	—	—	—
Candelabra, two-lite	20.00	20.00	—	—	—
Candlesticks, pr, 3-1/2" h, round base	24.00	32.00	36.00	—	60.00
Candlesticks, pr, 5-1/2" h, sq base	30.00	32.00	—	—	—
Candlesticks, pr, 9" h, round base	50.00	40.00	72.00	85.00	125.00
Candy dish, three feet	45.00	38.00	50.00	—	50.00
Candy dish, cov, 1/2 lb, cone shape	45.00	22.00	55.00	—	90.00
Celery, 12" l, oval	24.00	45.00	36.00	—	36.00
Celery, 9" d	18.00	20.00	32.00	—	32.00
Champagne, two ball, round foot	8.00	7.00	20.00	—	20.00
Chandelier, 17" shade, 200 prisms	425.00	400.00	—	—	—
Cheese, cov, 6" d	40.00	42.00	—	—	—
Cheese, cov, 8-3/4" d	50.00	48.00	—	—	—
Cigarette box, cov, 4-1/2 x 2-1/2"	24.50	24.50	30.00	—	55.00
Cigarette jar, cov, round	16.00	18.00	25.00	—	65.00
Claret, 5 oz, round	15.00	17.50	—	—	—
Coaster, 3"	6.00	8.00	—	—	—
Cocktail, 3 oz, round	8.50	12.00	—	—	37.50
Cocktail, 3-1/2 oz, round, ball	15.00	17.50	—	—	—
Compote, 5" d, round, round foot	22.00	20.00	35.00	—	25.00

ITEM	AMBER	CRYSTAL	GREEN	ICE BLUE	PINK
Compote, 5" d, round, sq foot	24.00	24.00	—	—	—
Compote, 5-1/2" d, bell	12.00	15.00	—	—	—
Compote, 5-1/2" d, bell, sq foot	20.00	20.00	—	—	—
Console bowl, 12" d, flange	30.00	30.00	40.00	—	40.00
Cordial, 1 oz, round, ball	16.50	24.50	—	—	—
Cordial, 1 oz, round, foot	16.50	19.50	—	—	—
Cream soup bowl, 4-5/8" d	18.00	18.00	—	—	—
Cream soup liner, round, 6-1/2" d	7.50	7.50	—	—	—
Creamer, hexagonal foot †	20.00	20.00	25.00	—	48.00
Creamer, low, flat	10.00	10.00	—	—	—
Creamer, sq foot	24.00	24.00	45.00	—	45.00
Cruet, 12 oz	—	25.00	—	—	—
Cup	8.00	12.00	18.00	—	25.00
Decanter, 20 oz	55.00	55.00	—	—	—
Demitasse cup	17.50	17.50	55.00	—	55.00
Dish, 6" d, crimped	15.00	15.00	—	—	—
Eggcup	15.00	15.00	—	—	—
Finger bowl, 4-1/2" d	7.50	17.50	15.00	35.00	15.00
Finger bowl, 4-1/2" sq, foot	9.50	9.50	18.00	40.00	18.00
Finger bowl liner, 6" sq	6.50	6.50	20.00	—	20.00
Finger bowl liner, 6-1/2" d, round	12.00	12.00	10.00	—	10.00
Ginger ale tumbler, 5 oz, flat	10.00	10.00	18.00	—	20.00
Ginger ale tumbler, 5 oz, round foot	10.00	10.00	—	—	—
Ginger ale tumbler, 5 oz, sq foot	8.00	8.00	32.00	—	35.00
Goblet, 8 oz, 6-1/4" h, round foot, water	12.00	10.00	24.00	50.00	35.00
Goblet, 8 oz, 6" h, sq foot, water	10.00	10.00	—	—	50.00
Grapefruit bowl, 6-1/2" d	12.00	12.00	22.00	—	24.00
Hat, high	18.00	18.00	—	—	—
Hat, low	15.00	15.00	—	—	—
Honey compote, 6" d, round foot	18.00	18.00	35.00	—	35.00
Honey compote, 6" d, sq foot	18.00	18.00	—	—	—

*English Hobnail, green 6" mayonnaise, **$22**; 6-1/2" plate, **$10**.*

ITEM	AMBER	CRYSTAL	GREEN	ICE BLUE	PINK
Ice tub, 4" h	18.00	18.00	50.00	—	85.00
Ice tub, 5-1/2" h	36.00	36.00	65.00	—	100.00
Iced tea tumbler, 10 oz	14.00	14.00	30.00	—	30.00
Iced tea tumbler, 11 oz, round, ball	12.00	12.00	—	—	—
Iced tea tumbler, 11 oz, sq foot	13.50	13.50	—	—	—
Iced tea tumbler, 12-1/2 oz, round foot	14.00	14.00	—	—	—
Iced tea tumbler, 12 oz, flat	14.00	14.00	32.00	—	32.00
Icer, sq base, patterned insert	45.00	45.00	—	—	—
Ivy bowl, 6-1/2" d, sq foot, crimp top	35.00	35.00	—	—	—
Juice tumbler, 7 oz, round foot	27.50	27.50	—	—	—
Juice tumbler, 7 oz, sq foot	6.50	6.50	—	—	—
Lamp shade, 17" d	175.00	165.00	—	—	—
Lamp, 6-1/2" h, electric	45.00	45.00	50.00	—	50.00
Lamp, 9-1/2" d, electric	45.00	50.00	115.00	—	115.00
Lamp, candlestick	32.00	32.00	—	—	—
Marmalade, cov	40.00	40.00	45.00	—	70.00
Mayonnaise, 6"	12.00	12.00	22.00	—	22.00

ITEM	AMBER	CRYSTAL	GREEN	ICE BLUE	PINK
Mustard, cov, sq, foot	18.00	18.00	—	—	—
Nappy, 4-1/2" d, round	8.00	8.00	15.00	30.00	15.00
Nappy, 4-1/2" w, sq	8.50	8.50	—	—	—
Nappy, 5" d, round	10.00	10.00	15.00	35.00	15.00
Nappy, 5-1/2" d, bell	12.00	12.00	—	—	—
Nappy, 6" d, round	10.00	10.00	17.50	—	17.50
Nappy, 6" d, sq	10.00	10.00	17.50	—	17.50
Nappy, 6-1/2" d, round	12.50	12.50	20.00	—	20.00
Nappy, 6-1/2" d, sq	14.00	14.00	—	—	—
Nappy, 7" d, round	14.00	14.00	24.00		24.00
Nappy, 7-1/2" d, bell	15.00	15.00	—	—	—
Nappy, 8" d, cupped	22.00	22.00	30.00	—	30.00
Nappy, 8" d, round	22.00	22.00	35.00	—	35.00
Nappy, 9" d, bell	25.00	25.00	—	—	—
Nut, individual, ftd †	6.00	6.00	14.50	—	14.50
Oil bottle, 2 oz, handle	25.00	25.00	—	—	—
Oil bottle, 6 oz, handle	27.50	27.50	—	—	—
Old fashioned tumbler, 5 oz	15.00	15.00	—	—	—

English Hobnail, crystal nappy with handle, $22.

ITEM	AMBER	CRYSTAL	GREEN	ICE BLUE	PINK
Oyster cocktail, 5 oz, sq foot	12.00	12.00	17.50	—	17.50
Parfait, round foot	17.50	17.50	—	—	—
Pickle, 8" d, l	15.00	15.00	—	—	—
Pitcher, 23 oz, rounded	48.00	48.00	150.00	—	165.00
Pitcher, 32 oz, straight side	50.00	50.00	175.00	—	175.00
Pitcher, 38 oz, rounded	65.00	65.00	215.00	—	215.00
Pitcher, 60 oz, rounded	70.00	70.00	295.00	—	295.00
Pitcher, 64 oz, straight side	7500	75.00	310.00	—	310.00
Plate, 5-1/2" d, round	7.00	7.00	10.00	—	10.00
Plate, 6" w, sq	5.00	5.00	—	—	—
Plate, 6-1/2" d, round	6.25	6.25	10.00	—	10.00
Plate, 6-1/2" d, round, depressed center	6.00	6.00	—	—	—
Plate, 8" d, round	9.00	9.00	14.00	24.00	14.00
Plate, 8" d, round, ftd	13.00	13.00	—	—	—
Plate, 8-1/2" d, plain edge	9.00	9.00	—	—	—
Plate, 8-1/2" d, round	7.00	9.00	12.50	—	22.00
Plate, 8-3/4" w, sq	9.25	9.25	—	—	—
Plate, 10" d, round	15.00	15.00	45.00	—	65.00
Plate, 10" w, sq	15.00	15.00	—	—	—
Plate, 10-1/2" d, round, grill	18.00	15.00	—	—	—
Plate, 12" w, sq	20.00	20.00	—	—	—
Plate, 15" w, sq	28.00	28.00	—	—	—
Preserve, 8" d	15.00	15.00	—	—	—
Puff box, cov, 6" d, round	20.00	20.00	45.00	—	80.00
Punch bowl and stand	215.00	215.00	—	—	—
Punch cup	7.00	7.00	—	—	—
Relish, 8" d, three parts	18.00	18.00	—	—	—
Rose bowl, 4" d	17.50	17.50	48.00	—	50.00
Rose bowl, 6" d	20.00	20.00	—	—	—
Salt and pepper shakers, pr, round foot	27.50	27.50	150.00	—	165.00

ITEM	AMBER	CRYSTAL	GREEN	ICE BLUE	PINK
Salt and pepper shakers, pr, sq foot	30.00	42.00	—	—	—
Saucer, demitasse, round	10.00	10.00	15.00	—	17.50
Saucer, demitasse, sq	10.00	10.00	—	—	—
Saucer, round	2.00	2.00	6.00	—	6.00
Saucer, sq	2.00	2.00	—	—	—
Sherbet, high, round foot	7.00	8.00	18.00	—	37.50
Sherbet, high, sq foot	8.00	8.00	18.00	—	—
Sherbet, high, two ball, round foot	10.00	10.00	—	—	—
Sherbet, low, one ball, round foot	12.00	10.00	—	—	15.00
Sherbet, low, round foot	12.50	7.00	—	—	—
Sherbet, low, sq foot	6.50	6.00	15.00	—	17.50
Straw jar, 10" h	65.00	60.00	—	—	—
Sundae	9.00	9.00	—	—	—
Sugar, hexagonal, ftd †	9.00	9.00	25.00	—	22.00
Sugar, low, flat	8.00	8.00	45.00	—	—
Sugar, sq foot	9.00	9.00	48.00	—	55.00
Sweetmeat, 5-1/2" d, ball stem	30.00	30.00	—	—	—
Sweetmeat, 8" d, ball stem	40.00	40.00	60.00	—	65.00
Tidbit, two tiers	27.50	27.50	65.00	85.00	80.00
Toilet bottle, 5 oz	25.00	25.00	40.00	25.00	25.00
Torte plate, 14" d, round	35.00	30.00	48.00	—	48.00
Torte plate, 20-1/2" round	55.00	50.00	—	—	—
Tumbler, 8 oz, water	10.00	10.00	24.00	—	24.00
Tumbler, 9 oz, round, ball, water	10.00	10.00	—	—	—
Tumbler, 9 oz, round, ftd water	10.00	10.00	—	—	—
Tumbler, 9 oz, sq foot, water	10.00	10.00	—	—	—
Urn, cov, 11" h	35.00	35.00	350.00	—	350.00
Vase, 6-1/2" h, sq foot	24.00	24.00	—	—	—
Vase, 7-1/2" h, flip	27.50	27.50	70.00	—	70.00
Vase, 7-1/2" h, flip jar with cov	55.00	55.00	85.00	—	85.00
Vase, 8" h, sq foot	35.00	35.00	—	—	—
Vase, 8-1/2" h, flared top	40.00	40.00	120.00	—	235.00

ITEM	AMBER	CRYSTAL	GREEN	ICE BLUE	PINK
Whiskey, 1-1/2 oz	10.00	10.00	—	—	—
Whiskey, 3 oz	12.00	15.00	—	—	—
Wine, 2 oz, round foot	15.00	15.00	—	—	—
Wine, 2 oz, sq ft	24.00	24.00	35.00	—	65.00
Wine, 2-1/2 oz, ball, foot	20.00	20.00	—	—	—

English Hobnail, crystal tumbler, $10.

FAIRFAX
NO. 2375

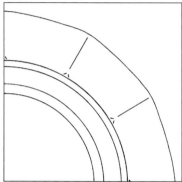

Manufactured by Fostoria Glass Company, Moundsville, Virginia, from 1927 to 1944. While many collect this pattern as Fairfax, the blanks were also used for some Fostoria etchings, such as June, Trojan, and Versailles. The values listed below are for the Fairfax pattern; expect to pay more for the etched patterns.

Pieces were made in amber, azure blue, black, blue, green, orchid, rose, topaz, and wisteria, with limited production in ruby.

ITEM	AMBER	AZURE BLUE, BLACK, BLUE	GREEN	ORCHID, ROSE, WISTERIA	TOPAZ
After dinner cup and saucer	15.00	30.00	18.00	30.00	18.00
Ashtray, 2-1/2" d	9.00	15.00	12.00	15.00	12.00
Ashtray, 4"	10.00	17.50	12.50	17.50	22.50
Ashtray, 5-1/2"	12.00	20.00	15.00	20.00	15.00
Baker, oval, 9" l	17.50	35.00	24.00	35.00	24.00
Baker, oval, 10-1/2" l	20.00	42.00	25.00	42.00	25.00
Bonbon	10.00	12.50	12.00	12.50	12.00
Bouillon, ftd	8.50	14.50	10.00	14.50	10.00
Bowl, 7" d, three-ftd	10.00	15.00	14.00	15.00	14.00
Bowl, 12" d	22.00	42.00	24.00	42.00	24.00

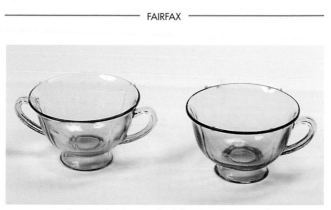

Fairfax, topaz bouillon soup bowl, $10; footed green cup, $9.

ITEM	AMBER	AZURE BLUE, BLACK, BLUE	GREEN	ORCHID, ROSE, WISTERIA	TOPAZ
Bread plate, 12" d	27.50	45.00	30.00	45.00	30.00
Butter dish, cov	80.00	130.00	100.00	140.00	100.00
Cake plate, 10" d	15.00	40.00	15.00	24.00	15.00
Canapé plate	12.00	20.00	15.00	20.00	15.00
Candlesticks, pr, 3" h	20.00	40.00	30.00	45.00	35.00
Candy, cov, three parts	40.00	65.00	50.00	65.00	50.00
Candy, cov, ftd	45.00	70.00	60.00	85.00	60.00
Celery Tray, 11-1/4" l	12.00	25.00	17.50	25.00	17.50
Centerpiece bowl, 12" d	20.00	40.00	25.00	40.00	35.00
Centerpiece bowl, 13" l, oval	24.00	45.00	35.00	45.00	35.00
Centerpiece bowl, 15" d	27.50	48.00	37.50	110.00	40.00
Cereal bowl, 6" d	12.00	24.00	14.50	24.00	18.00
Cheese and cracker set	20.00	45.00	25.00	45.00	25.00
Chop plate, 13" d	15.00	25.00	17.50	25.00	17.50

ITEM	AMBER	AZURE BLUE, BLACK, BLUE	GREEN	ORCHID, ROSE, WISTERIA	TOPAZ
Cigarette box	20.00	48.00	24.00	48.00	24.00
Claret, 4 oz, 6" h	25.00	40.00	35.00	40.00	35.00
Cocktail, 3 oz, 5-1/4" h	12.00	24.00	20.00	24.00	20.00
Comport, 5"	15.00	30.00	20.00	30.00	20.00
Comport, 7"	15.00	48.00	24.00	45.00	24.00
Cordial, 3/4 oz, 4" h	25.00	65.00	45.00	65.00	45.00
Cream soup bowl, ftd	10.00	20.00	15.00	20.00	15.00
Cream soup underplate	5.00	8.00	5.00	8.00	5.00
Creamer, flat	12.00		15.00	—	15.00
Creamer, ftd	10.00	15.00	12.00	15.00	12.00
Creamer, tea size	9.00	18.50	12.50	18.50	12.50
Cup, flat	4.50	—	6.50	—	6.50
Cup, ftd	7.50	15.00	9.00	10.00	9.00
Dessert bowl, large, handle	15.00	40.00	24.00	40.00	24.00
Flower holder, oval	25.00	85.00	40.00	85.00	40.00
Fruit bowl, 5" d	8.00	15.00	9.00	15.00	9.00
Goblet, 10 oz, 8-1/4" h	17.50	32.00	22.00	35.00	22.00
Grapefruit	17.50	35.00	25.00	35.00	25.00
Grapefruit liner	15.00	32.00	20.00	32.00	22.00
Ice bowl	12.00	20.00	20.00	23.00	20.00
Ice bowl liner	12.00	22.00	12.00	22.00	16.50
Ice bucket	32.00	50.00	65.00	50.00	35.00
Juice tumbler, 2-1/2 oz, ftd	12.00	10.00	18.50	32.00	18.50
Lemon bowl, two handles, ftd	6.50	12.50	7.50	12.50	7.50
Mayonnaise	10.00	15.00	10.00	15.00	10.00
Mayonnaise ladle	20.00	30.00	24.00	30.00	24.00
Mayonnaise underplate	5.00	8.00	4.00	8.00	5.00
Nappy, 8" d	18.00	40.00	24.00	40.00	24.00
Nut cup	15.00	20.00	20.00	20.00	20.00

Fairfax, green nut cup, $20; rare topaz two-part chilled juice tumbler, $12, and ice bowl with liner, $36.50.

ITEM	AMBER	AZURE BLUE, BLACK, BLUE	GREEN	ORCHID, ROSE, WISTERIA	TOPAZ
Oil bottle, ftd, os	85.00	150.00	110.00	150.00	110.00
Pickle, 8-1/2" l	10.00	25.00	15.00	25.00	15.00
Pitcher	115.00	200.00	145.00	175.00	200.00
Plate, 6" d, bread and butter	2.50	12.50	3.00	4.50	10.00
Plate, 7-1/2" d, salad	7.00	7.50	4.50	5.50	12.00
Plate, 8-3/4" d, salad	4.50	15.00	5.50	7.50	5.50
Plate, 9-1/2" d, luncheon	8.00	25.00	7.50	12.00	7.50
Plate, 10-1/4" d, dinner	18.00	30.00	30.00	40.00	30.00
Plate, 10-1/4" d, grill	17.50	40.00	27.50	40.00	27.50
Platter, 10-1/2" l	18.00	35.00	25.00	35.00	25.00
Platter, 12" l	20.00	40.00	32.00	40.00	32.00
Platter, 15" l	30.00	70.00	42.00	70.00	42.00

ITEM	AMBER	AZURE BLUE, BLACK, BLUE	GREEN	ORCHID, ROSE, WISTERIA	TOPAZ
Relish, 3-part, 8-1/2" l	12.00	22.00	14.00	22.00	14.00
Relish, 11-1/2" l	14.00	24.00	17.50	24.00	17.50
Salad dressing bowl	75.00	180.00	90.00	180.00	90.00
Salt and pepper shakers, pr, ftd	32.00	90.00	40.00	60.00	40.00
Salt and pepper shakers, pr, individual size	20.00	—	25.00	—	25.00
Sauce boat and underplate	30.00	65.00	38.00	115.00	40.00
Saucer	3.00	6.50	3.00	4.50	3.00
Sherbet, 6 oz, 6" h	10.00	14.00	12.50	20.00	22.50
Soup bowl, 7" d	18.00	40.00	24.00	40.00	24.00
Sugar bowl, flat	12.00	—	14.00	—	14.00
Sugar bowl, ftd	8.00	15.00	10.00	12.00	10.00
Sugar bowl, tea size	10.00	15.00	14.50	20.00	14.50
Sugar bowl lid	20.00	35.00	25.00	35.00	25.00
Sugar pail	25.00	60.00	40.00	60.00	40.00
Sweetmeat	12.00	17.50	15.00	17.50	15.00
Tray, 11" d, center handle	15.00	25.00	20.00	25.00	20.00
Tumbler, 5 oz, 4-1/2" h, ftd	10.00	17.50	12.00	17.50	12.00
Tumbler, 9 oz, 5-1/4" h, ftd	14.50	20.00	17.50	20.00	17.50
Tumbler, 12 oz, 6", ftd	17.50	27.50	25.00	27.50	25.00
Vase, 8" h	35.00	50.00	35.00	50.00	35.00
Whipped cream pail	25.00	55.00	40.00	55.00	40.00
Whipped cream underplate	9.00	12.00	10.00	12.00	10.00
Wine, 3 oz, 5-1/2" h	20.00	30.00	25.00	30.00	25.00

FLORAGOLD

LOUISA

Manufactured by Jeannette Glass Company, Jeannette, Pennsylvania, in the 1950s.

Pieces were made in iridescent. Some large comports were later made in ice blue, crystal, red-yellow, and shell pink.

ITEM	IRIDESCENT
Ashtray, 4" d	10.00
Bowl, 4-1/2" sq	4.50
Bowl, 5-1/4" d, ruffled	16.00
Bowl, 8-1/2" d, sq	22.00
Bowl, 8-1/2" d, ruffled	8.00
Butter dish, cov, 1/4 pound, oblong	30.00
Butter dish, cov, round, 5-1/2" w sq base	800.00
Butter dish, cov, round, 6-1/4" w sq base	40.00
Candlesticks, pr, double branch	70.00
Candy dish, one handle	7.50
Candy or cheese dish, cov, 6-3/4" d	90.00

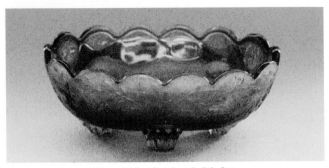

Floragold, four-footed candy dish, $12.

ITEM	IRIDESCENT
Candy, 5-3/4" l, four feet	12.00
Celery vase	420.00
Cereal bowl, 5-1/2" d, round	40.00
Coaster, 4" d	10.00
Comport, 5-1/4", plain top	795.00
Comport, 5-1/4", ruffled top	895.00
Creamer	15.00
Cup	10.00
Fruit bowl, 5-1/2" d, ruffled	8.50
Fruit bowl, 12" d, ruffled, large	15.00
Nappy, 5" d, one handle	12.00
Pitcher, 64 oz	45.00
Plate, 5-1/4" d, sherbet	12.00
Plate, 8-1/2" d, dinner	35.00
Platter, 11-1/4" d	30.00
Salad bowl, 9-1/2" d, deep	42.50
Salt and pepper shakers, pr, plastic tops	68.00

Floragold, iridescent dinner plate, $35; ruffled 5-1/4" d bowl, $16.

ITEM	IRIDESCENT
Saucer, 5-1/4" d	10.00
Sherbet, low, ftd	15.00
Sugar	15.00
Sugar lid	15.00
Tidbit, wooden post	35.00
Tray, 13-1/2" d	75.00
Tray, 13-1/2" d, with indent	25.00
Tumbler, 11 oz, ftd	10.00
Tumbler, 10 oz, ftd	15.00
Tumbler, 15 oz, ftd	110.00
Vase	425.00

FLORAL
POINSETTIA

Manufactured by Jeannette Glass Company, Jeannette, Pennsylvania, from 1931 to 1935.

Pieces were made in amber, crystal, Delphite, green, Jadite, pink, red, and yellow. Production in amber, crystal, red, and yellow was very limited. A crystal 6-7/8-inch vase is valued at $295.

Reproductions: † Reproduction salt and pepper shakers have been made in cobalt blue, dark green, green, pink, and red.

ITEM	DELPHITE	GREEN	JADITE	PINK
Berry bowl, 4" d	50.00	25.00	—	25.00
Butter dish, cov	—	85.00	—	115.00
Candlesticks, pr, 4" h	—	90.00	—	70.00
Candy jar, cov	80.00	45.00	—	45.00
Casserole, cov	—	45.00	—	40.00
Coaster, 3-1/4" d	—	15.00	—	12.00
Comport, 9"	—	875.00	—	795.00
Cream soup bowl, 5-1/2" d	—	700.00	—	700.00
Creamer, flat	—	24.00	—	18.00
Cup	—	15.00	—	10.00
Dresser tray, 9-1/4" l, oval	—	200.00	—	

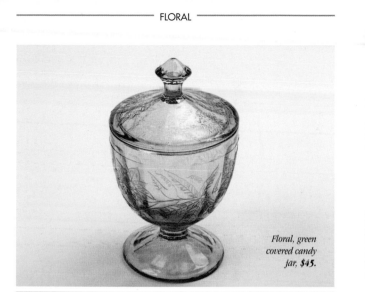

Floral, green covered candy jar, $45.

ITEM	DELPHITE	GREEN	JADITE	PINK
Flower frog	—	695.00	—	—
Ice tub, 3-1/2" h, oval	—	850.00	—	825.00
Juice tumbler, ftd	—	30.00	—	25.50
Juice tumbler, 5 oz, 4" h, flat	—	30.00	—	25.00
Lamp	—	325.00	—	260.00
Lemonade pitcher, 48 oz, 10-1/4" h	—	295.00	—	395.00
Lemonade tumbler, 9 oz, 5-1/4" h, ftd	—	64.00	—	60.00
Pitcher, 23 or 24 oz, 5-1/2" h	—	595.00	—	—
Pitcher, 32 oz, ftd, cone, 8" h	—	60.00	—	42.00
Plate, 6" d, sherbet	—	8.50	—	6.50
Plate, 8" d, salad	—	15.00	—	17.00

Floral, pink dinner plate, $22.50.

ITEM	DELPHITE	GREEN	JADITE	PINK
Plate, 9" d, dinner	145.00	27.50	—	22.50
Plate, 9" d, grill	—	185.00	—	—
Plate, 10-3/4" l, oval	—	20.00	—	17.50
Platter, 11" l	150.00	30.00	—	25.00
Refrigerator dish, cov, 5" sq	—	—	15.00	—
Relish, two-part oval	165.00	24.00	—	24.00
Rose bowl, three legs	—	500.00	—	—
Salad bowl, 7-1/2" d	—	40.00	—	38.00
Salad bowl, 7-1/2" d, ruffled	65.00	115.00	—	120.00
Salt and pepper shakers, pr, 4" h, ftd †	—	50.00	—	50.00
Salt and pepper shakers, pr, 6" flat	—	—	—	60.00
Saucer	—	12.50	—	12.50

Floral, green 9" oval vegetable bowl, $35.

ITEM	DELPHITE	GREEN	JADITE	PINK
Sherbet	90.00	24.00	—	20.00
Sugar, cov	—	28.00	—	28.00
Sugar, open	75.00	—	—	—
Tray, 6" sq, closed handles	—	195.00	—	—
Tumbler, 3 oz, 3-1/2" h, ftd	—	18.00	—	25.00
Tumbler, 7 oz, 4-1/2", ftd	175.00	25.00	—	20.00
Tumbler, 5-1/4" h, ftd	—	60.00	—	55.00
Vase, flared, three legs	—	485.00	—	—
Vase, 6-7/8" h	—	475.00	—	—
Vegetable bowl, 8" d, cov	—	50.00	—	65.00
Vegetable bowl, 8" d, open	80.00	—	—	40.00
Vegetable bowl, 9" l, oval	—	35.00	—	30.00

FLORAL AND DIAMOND BAND

Manufactured by U. S. Glass Company, Pittsburgh, Pennsylvania, in the late 1920s.

Pieces were made in pink and green with limited production in black, crystal, and iridescent.

ITEM	GREEN	PINK
Berry bowl, 4-1/2" d	12.00	15.00
Berry bowl, 8" d	20.00	18.00
Butter dish, cov	140.00	175.00
Compote, 5-1/2" h	18.00	17.50
Creamer, 4-3/4"	20.00	17.50
Iced tea tumbler, 5" h	45.00	50.00
Nappy, 5-3/4" d, handle	12.00	11.00
Pitcher, 42 oz, 8" h	100.00	90.00
Plate, 8" d, luncheon	40.00	40.00
Sherbet	7.00	9.50

ITEM	GREEN	PINK
Sugar, 5-1/4"	15.00	15.00
Tumbler, 4" h, water	25.00	25.00

*Floral and Diamond Band, green luncheon plate, **$40.***

FLORENTINE NO. 1
OLD FLORENTINE, POPPY NO. 1

Manufactured by Hazel Atlas Glass Company, Clarksburg, West Virginia, and Zanesville, Ohio, from 1932 until 1935.

Pieces were made in crystal, green, pink, and yellow, with limited production in cobalt blue.

Reproductions: † Salt and pepper shakers have been reproduced in cobalt blue, pink, and red.

ITEM	COBALT BLUE	CRYSTAL	GREEN	PINK	YELLOW
Ashtray, 5-1/2" d	—	24.00	24.00	30.00	28.00
Berry bowl, 5" d	24.00	12.00	12.00	15.00	15.00
Berry bowl, 8-1/2" d	—	24.00	25.00	28.00	28.00
Butter dish, cov	—	110.00	115.00	165.00	160.00
Cereal bowl, 6" d	—	32.00	32.00	35.00	35.00
Coaster/ashtray, 3-3/4" d	—	18.00	20.00	25.00	25.00
Comport, 3-1/2" h, ruffled	60.00	25.00	25.00	30.00	—
Cream soup bowl, 5" d, ruffled	50.00	12.00	14.00	20.00	—
Creamer	—	10.00	10.00	25.00	25.00

Florentine No. 1, green creamer, $10; covered sugar, $12.50.

ITEM	COBALT BLUE	CRYSTAL	GREEN	PINK	YELLOW
Creamer, ruffled	65.00	15.00	35.00	45.00	45.00
Cup	85.00	10.00	9.50	8.00	12.50
Iced tea tumbler, 12 oz, 5-1/4" h, ftd	—	28.00	28.00	30.00	24.00
Juice tumbler, 5 oz, 3-3/4" h, ftd	—	16.00	14.00	20.00	22.00
Lemonade tumbler, 9 oz, 5-1/4" h	—	—	—	100.00	—
Pitcher, 36 oz, 6-1/2", ftd	850.00	45.00	45.00	65.00	50.00
Pitcher, 48 oz, 7-1/2", flat, with or without ice llp	—	75.00	75.00	135.00	195.00
Plate, 6" d, sherbet	—	7.50	9.00	7.50	9.00
Plate, 8-1/2" d, salad	—	8.00	10.00	12.00	12.00
Plate, 10" d, dinner	—	16.00	16.00	22.00	24.00
Plate, 10" d, grill	—	12.00	12.50	20.00	22.00
Platter, 11-1/2" l, oval	—	19.00	10.00	22.00	28.00

Florentine No. 1, pink 8-1/2" berry bowl, $28.

ITEM	COBALT BLUE	CRYSTAL	GREEN	PINK	YELLOW
Salt and pepper shakers, pr, ftd †	—	30.00	42.00	65.00	65.00
Saucer	18.00	3.50	3.50	4.00	3.00
Sherbet, 3 oz, ftd	—	8.00	10.00	15.00	15.50
Sugar, cov	—	10.00	12.50	25.00	25.00
Sugar, ruffled	55.00	15.00	30.00	45.00	45.00
Tumbler, 4 oz, 3-1/4" h, ftd	—	15.00	16.00		
Tumbler, 9 oz, 4" h	—	50.00	18.00	25.00	—
Tumbler, 10 oz, 4-3/4" h, ftd	—	22.00	20.00	22.00	24.00
Vegetable bowl, cov, 9-1/2" l, oval	—	42.00	42.00	60.00	60.00

FLORENTINE NO. 2

POPPY NO. 2

Manufactured by Hazel Atlas Glass Company, Clarksburg, West Virginia, and Zanesville, Ohio, from 1932 to 1935.

Pieces were made in amber, cobalt blue, crystal, green, ice blue, pink, and yellow. Ice blue production is limited to a 7-1/2-inch pitcher valued at $525. Amber production is limited to 9-ounce and 12-ounce tumblers, both currently valued at $80; a cup and saucer valued at $75; and a sherbet valued at $45. Cobalt blue production is limited to a 3-1/2-inch comport valued at $60 and a 9-ounce tumbler valued at $80.

Reproductions: † 7-1/2-inch high cone-shaped pitcher and 4-inch high footed tumbler. Reproductions are found in amber, cobalt blue, crystal, deep green, and pink.

ITEM	CRYSTAL	GREEN	PINK	YELLOW
Ashtray, 3-1/2" d	18.50	18.50	—	25.00
Ashtray, 5-1/2" d	20.00	25.00	—	35.00
Berry bowl, 4-1/2" d	15.50	16.50	19.50	24.50
Berry bowl, 8" d	24.00	30.00	30.00	38.00
Bowl, 5-1/2" d	20.00	35.00	—	42.00
Bowl, 7-1/2" d, shallow	—	—	—	85.00
Bowl, 9" d, flat	27.50	27.50	—	—
Butter dish, cov	115.00	125.00	—	165.00

Florentine No. 2, green dinner plate, $12.

ITEM	CRYSTAL	GREEN	PINK	YELLOW
Candlesticks, pr, 2-3/4" h	45.00	48.00	—	70.00
Candy dish, cov	110.00	100.00	150.00	165.00
Cereal bowl, 6" d	28.00	28.00	—	40.00
Coaster, 3-1/4" d	—	—	—	25.00
Coaster, 3-3/4" d	18.50	18.50	—	25.00
Coaster, 5-1/2" d	20.00	25.00	—	35.00
Cocktail, 3-1/4" h, ftd	8.50	15.00	—	15.00
Comport, 3-1/2" d, ruffled	25.00	25.00	25.00	—
Condiment tray, round	—	—	—	65.00
Cream soup bowl, 4-3/4" d, two handles	16.50	16.00	18.50	22.00
Creamer	8.00	12.00	—	12.50
Cup	7.50	8.00	—	12.00

Florentine No. 2, green 7-1/2" footed cone pitcher, $40.

ITEM	CRYSTAL	GREEN	PINK	YELLOW
Custard cup	60.00	60.00	—	85.00
Gravy boat	—	—	—	65.00
Gravy boat underplate, 11-1/2" l	—	—	—	115.00
Iced tea tumbler, 12 oz, 5" h	35.00	32.00	—	45.00
Juice tumbler, 5 oz, 3-1/8" h, flat	14.50	14.50	14.50	22.00
Juice tumbler, 5 oz, 3-1/8" h, ftd	13.00	15.00	—	22.00
Parfait, 6" h	30.00	50.00	—	50.00
Pitcher, 24 oz, cone, ftd, 6-1/4" h	—	—	—	35.00
Pitcher, 28 oz, cone ftd, 7-1/2" h †	60.00	40.00	—	50.00
Pitcher, 48 oz, 7-1/2" h	60.00	70.00	120.00	295.00
Pitcher, 76 oz, 8-1/4" h	90.00	95.00	225.00	400.00
Plate, 6" d, sherbet	6.00	6.00	—	7.50

ITEM	CRYSTAL	GREEN	PINK	YELLOW
Plate, 6-1/2" d, indent	16.00	17.50	—	30.00
Plate, 8-1/2" d, salad	8.50	9.50	9.00	10.00
Plate, 10" d, dinner	12.50	12.00	—	17.50
Plate, 10-1/4" d, grill	15.00	15.00	—	17.50
Plate, 10-1/4" d, grill, cream soup ring	35.00	35.00	—	—
Platter, 11" oval	15.00	16.00	18.50	22.00
Relish, 10" d, divided, three parts	22.50	24.00	26.00	35.00

Florentine No. 2, yellow cup, **$12.**

ITEM	CRYSTAL	GREEN	PINK	YELLOW
Relish, 10" d, plain	22.50	24.00	26.00	32.00
Salt and pepper shakers, pr	24.00	48.00	—	45.00
Saucer	5.00	4.00	—	2.50
Sherbet, ftd	10.00	12.50	—	12.50
Sugar, cov	8.50	12.00	—	38.00
Tumbler, 5 oz, 3-1/4" h, ftd	18.00	15.00	15.00	—
Tumbler, 5 oz, 4" h, ftd †	15.00	15.00	18.00	20.00
Tumbler, 5 oz, 3-5/16" h, blown	18.50	18.50	—	—
Tumbler, 6 oz, 3-9/16" h, blown	16.00	18.50	—	—
Tumbler, 9 oz, 4" h	14.50	18.50	16.00	24.50
Tumbler, 9 oz, 4-1/2" h, ftd	25.00	25.00	—	15.00
Tumbler, 10 oz, 4-11/16, blown	19.00	19.00	—	—
Tumbler, 12 oz, 5" h, blown	20.00	20.00	—	20.00
Vase, 6" h	30.00	32.00	—	65.00
Vegetable bowl, cov, 9" l, oval	55.00	60.00	—	80.00

*Florentine No. 2, green sugar, **$12**; creamer, **$12**.*

FLOWER GARDEN WITH BUTTERFLIES

BUTTERFLIES AND ROSES

Manufactured by U. S. Glass Company, Pittsburgh, Pennsylvania, in the late 1920s.

Pieces were made in amber, black, blue, blue-green, canary yellow, crystal, green, and pink.

ITEM	AMBER OR CRYSTAL	BLACK	BLUE-GREEN, GREEN OR PINK	BLUE OR CANARY YELLOW
Ashtray	175.00	—	185.00	225.00
Bonbon, cov, 6-5/8" d	—	265.00	—	—
Bowl, 9" d, rolled edge	—	225.00	—	—
Candlesticks, pr, 4" h	50.00	—	60.00	100.00
Candlesticks, pr, 8" h	90.00	325.00	145.00	145.00
Candy, cov, 6" d, flat	135.00	—	165.00	—
Candy, cov, 7-1/2" cone shape	90.00	100.00	165.00	175.00

*Flower Garden with Butterflies, blue comport, 5-7/8" h, 11" w, **$95.***

ITEM	AMBER OR CRYSTAL	BLACK	BLUE-GREEN, GREEN OR PINK	BLUE OR CANARY YELLOW
Candy, cov, heart shape	—	—	1,250.00	1,500.00
Cologne bottle, 7-1/2" h	—	—	225.00	365.00
Comport, 2-7/8" h	—	250.00	40.00	45.00
Comport, 3" h	25.00	—	30.00	35.00
Comport, 4-1/4" h, 4-3/4" w	—	—	—	65.00
Comport, 4-3/4" h, 10-1/4" w	50.00	250.00	70.00	90.00

ITEM	AMBER OR CRYSTAL	BLACK	BLUE-GREEN, GREEN OR PINK	BLUE OR CANARY YELLOW
Comport, 5-7/8" h, 11" w	60.00	—	—	95.00
Comport, 7-1/4" h, 8-1/4" w	65.00	175.00	85.00	—
Creamer	—	—	75.00	—
Cup	—	—	70.00	—
Mayonnaise, ftd, 4-3/4" h, 6-1/4" w, 7" d plate, ladle	70.00	—	95.00	145.00
Orange bowl, 11" d, ftd	—	250.00	—	—
Plate, 7" d	20.00	—	25.00	30.00
Plate, 8" d	17.50	—	20.00	27.50
Plate, 10" d	—	—	45.00	50.00
Plate, 10" d, indent	35.00	150.00	45.00	50.00
Powder jar, 3-1/2", flat	—	—	75.00	—
Powder jar, 6-1/4" h, ftd	225.00	—	130.00	175.00
Powder jar, 7-1/2" h, ftd	85.00	—	135.00	195.00
Sandwich server, center handle	55.00	135.00	75.00	100.00
Saucer	—	—	30.00	—
Tray, 5-1/2 x 10", oval	50.00	—	75.00	9.00
Tray, 11-3/4 x 7-3/4", rect	50.00	—	75.00	90.00
Tumbler, 7-1/2 oz	175.00	—	—	—
Vase, 6-1/4" h	75.00	145.00	135.00	145.00
Vase, 8" h, Dahlia, cupped	—	275.00	—	—
Vase, 10" h, two handles	—	250.00	—	—
Vase, 10-1/2" h	—	—	150.00	225.00
Wall pocket, 9" l	—	365.00	—	—

FOREST GREEN

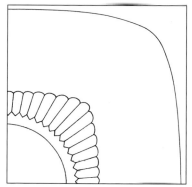

Manufactured by Anchor Hocking Glass Corp., Lancaster, Ohio, and Long Island City, New York, from 1950 to 1957.

Pieces were made only in forest green.

ITEM	FOREST GREEN
Ashtray, 3-1/2" sq	3.00
Ashtray, 4-5/8" sq	4.50
Ashtray, 5-3/4" hexagon	8.00
Ashtray, 5-3/4" sq	7.50
Batter bowl, spout	35.00
Berry bowl, large	15.00
Berry bowl, small	7.50
Bonbon, 6-1/4" w, tricorn	12.00
Bowl, 4-1/2" w, sq	7.00
Bowl, 5-1/4" deep	8.50
Bowl, 6" w, sq	18.00
Bowl, 6-1/2" d, scalloped	9.00

Forest Green, cup $7; saucer, $3.

ITEM	FOREST GREEN
Bowl, 6-3/8" d, three toes	15.00
Bowl, 7-3/8" w, sq	30.00
Bowl, 7-1/2" d, crimped	10.00
Candy dish, leaf shape	7.50
Cocktail, 3-1/2 oz	12.00
Cocktail, 4-1/2 oz	14.00
Creamer, flat	7.50
Cup, sq	7.00
Dessert bowl, 4-3/4" d	18.00
Goblet, 9 oz	12.00
Goblet, 9-1/2 oz	14.00

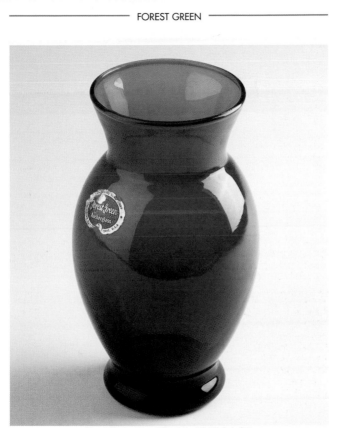

Forest Green, vase with original foil label, $12.

ITEM	FOREST GREEN
Iced tea tumbler, 13 oz	6.00
Iced tea tumbler, 14 oz, Boopie	8.00
Iced tea tumbler, 15 oz, tall	10.00
Iced tea tumbler, 32 oz, giant	18.00
Ivy ball, 4" h	5.00
Juice tumbler, 4 oz	5.00
Juice tumbler, 5-1/2 oz	12.50
Juice Roly Poly tumbler, 3-3/8" h	10.00
Ladle, all green glass	60.00
Mixing bowl, 6" d	9.50
Pitcher, 22 oz	24.00
Pitcher, 36 oz	25.00
Pitcher, 86 oz, round	42.00
Plate, 6-3/4" d, salad	7.50
Plate, 7" w, sq	6.75
Plate, 8-3/8" d, luncheon	9.00
Plate, 9-1/4" d, dinner	35.00
Platter, 11" l, rect	20.00
Popcorn bowl, 5-1/4" d	10.00
Punch bowl	25.00
Punch bowl and stand	60.00
Punch cup	2.25
Relish tray, 4-3/4" x 6-3/4" l, two handles	25.00
Roly Poly tumbler, 5-1/8" h	7.50
Salad bowl, 7-3/8" d	15.00
Sandwich plate, 13-3/4" d	45.00
Saucer, 5-3/8" w	3.00
Sherbet, 6 oz	9.00
Sherbet, 6 oz, Boopie	7.00
Sherbet, flat	7.50
Soup bowl, 6" d	18.00
Sugar, flat	30.00

Forest Green, tricorn bonbon, $12.

ITEM	FOREST GREEN
Tray, 6" x 10", two handles	30.00
Tumbler, 5 oz, 3-1/2" h	4.00
Tumbler, 7 oz	4.50
Tumbler, 5-1/4" h	4.00
Tumbler, 9-1/2 oz, tall	8.00
Tumbler, 9 oz, fancy	7.00
Tumbler, 9 oz, table	4.00
Tumbler, 10 oz, 4-1/2" h, ftd	7.50
Tumbler, 11 oz	7.00
Tumbler, 14 oz, 5" h	8.00
Tumbler, 15 oz, long boy	10.00
Vase, 6-3/8" h, Harding	10.00
Vase, 7" h, crimped	15.00
Vase, 9" h	12.00
Vegetable bowl, 8-1/2" l, oval	22.50

FORTUNE

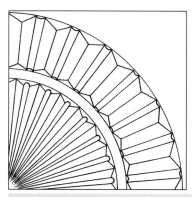

Manufactured by Hocking Glass Company, Lancaster, Ohio, from 1937 to 1938.

Pieces were made in crystal and pink.

*Fortune, pink 6" plate, **$20**; 4" berry bowl, **$11**; 4-1/2" bowl with one handle, **$10.***

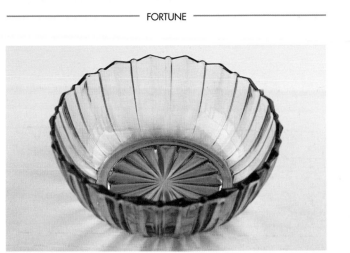

Fortune, pink 7-3/4" d berry bowl, $28.

ITEM	CRYSTAL	PINK
Berry bowl, 4" d	10.00	11.00
Berry bowl, 7-3/4" d	25.00	28.00
Bowl, 4-1/2" d, handle	12.00	10.00
Bowl, 5-1/4" d, rolled edge	20.00	20.00
Candy dish, cov, flat	28.00	45.00
Cup	12.00	15.00
Dessert bowl, 4-1/2" d	12.00	15.00
Julce tumbler, 5 oz, 3-1/2" h	12.00	15.00
Plate, 6" d, sherbet	8.00	20.00
Plate, 8" d, luncheon	25.00	25.00
Salad bowl, 7-3/4" d	25.00	25.00
Saucer	2.00	8.50
Tumbler, 9 oz, 4" h	15.00	15.50

FRUITS

Manufactured by Hazel Atlas Company and several other small glass companies from 1931 to 1935.

Pieces were made in crystal, green, iridized, and pink. Iridized production includes only a 4-inch tumbler valued at $10.

ITEM	CRYSTAL	GREEN	PINK
Berry bowl, 5" d	17.50	32.00	28.00
Berry bowl, 8" d	40.00	85.00	45.00
Console bowl, rolled edge, 7-1/4" d	—	—	275.00
Cup	5.00	15.00	10.00
Juice tumbler, 5 oz, 3-1/2" h	20.00	60.00	22.00
Pitcher, 7" h	50.00	95.00	—
Plate, 8" d, luncheon	12.00	15.00	12.00
Saucer	2.50	5.00	4.50
Sherbet	10.00	15.00	12.00
Tumbler, 4" h, multiple fruits	25.00	24.00	22.00
Tumbler, 4" h, single fruit	20.00	30.00	25.00
Tumbler, 12 oz, 5" h	70.00	200.00	95.00

Fruits, green luncheon plate, $15.

Fruits, green cup, $15; saucer, $5.

GEORGIAN

LOVEBIRDS

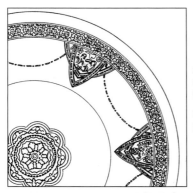

Manufactured by Federal Glass Company, Columbus, Ohio, from 1931 to 1936.

Pieces were made in green. A crystal hot plate is valued at $25.

ITEM	GREEN
Berry bowl, 4-1/2" d	15.00
Berry bowl, 7-1/2" d, large	65.00
Bowl, 6-1/2" d, deep	65.00
Butter dish, cov	95.00
Cereal bowl, 5-3/4" d	30.00
Cold cuts server, 18-1/2" d, wood, seven openings for 5" d coasters	750.00
Creamer, 3" d, ftd	12.00
Creamer, 4" d, ftd	17.50
Cup	10.00
Hot plate, 5" d, center design	48.00

Georgian, green sherbet, $16.

ITEM	GREEN
Plate, 6" d, sherbet	12.00
Plate, 8" d, luncheon	10.00
Plate, 9-1/4" d, center design only	25.00
Plate, 9-1/4" d, dinner	36.00
Platter, 11-1/2" l, closed handle	65.00
Saucer	4.50
Sherbet, ftd	16.00
Sugar cover, 3" d	12.00
Sugar cover, 4" d	18.00
Sugar, 3" d, ftd	15.00
Sugar, 4" d, ftd	15.00
Tumbler, 9 oz, 4" h, flat	85.00
Tumbler 12 oz, 5-1/4" h, flat	135.00
Vegetable bowl, 9" l, oval	65.00

Georgian, green 4-1/4" berry bowl, $15; 6" plate, $12.

HARP

Manufactured by Jeannette Glass Company, Jeannette, Pennsylvania, from 1954 to 1957.

Pieces were made in crystal and crystal with gold trim; limited pieces were made in ice blue, iridescent white, pink, and shell pink.

ITEM	CRYSTAL	ICE BLUE	SHELL PINK
Ashtray	10.00	—	—
Cake stand, 9" d	28.00	42.00	40.00
Coaster	3.00	—	—
Cup	20.00	—	—
Parfait	20.00	—	—
Plate, 7" d	20.00	25.00	—
Saucer	12.00	—	—
Snack set, cup, saucer, 7" plate	40.00	—	—
Tray, two handles, rectangular	35.00	35.00	65.00
Vase, 7-1/2" h	28.00	—	—

*Harp, crystal gold-edge plate, **$20**; cake stand, **$28**.*

HERITAGE

Manufactured by Federal Glass Company, Columbus, Ohio, from 1940 to 1955.

Pieces were made in blue, crystal, green, and pink.

Reproductions: † Bowls have been reproduced in amber, crystal, and green. Some are marked with an N or MC.

ITEM	BLUE	CRYSTAL	GREEN	PINK
Berry bowl, 5" d †	80.00	15.00	75.00	75.00
Berry bowl, 8-1/2" d †	195.00	40.00	175.00	150.00
Creamer, ftd	—	21.00	—	—
Cup	—	4.00	—	—
Fruit bowl, 10-1/2" d	—	18.00	—	—
Plate, 8" d, luncheon	—	8.00	—	—
Plate, 9-1/4" d, dinner	—	10.00	—	—
Sandwich plate, 12" d	—	15.00	—	—
Saucer	—	2.00	—	—
Sugar, open, ftd	—	22.50	—	—

Heritage, crystal cup, $4; saucer, $2.

Heritage, crystal dinner plate, $10.

HEX OPTIC
HONEYCOMB

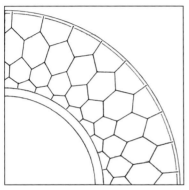

Manufactured by Jeannette Glass Company, Jeannette, Pennsylvania, from 1928 to 1932.

Pieces were made in green and pink. Ultramarine tumblers have been found. Iridescent tumblers and pitchers were made around 1960; it is assumed that Jeannette made them.

ITEM	GREEN	PINK
Berry bowl, 4-1/4" d, ruffled	12.50	8.50
Berry bowl, 7-1/2" d	25.00	12.00
Bucket reamer	65.00	60.00
Butter dish, cov, rect, one- lb size	90.00	90.00
Creamer, two style handles	8.00	16.00
Cup, two style handles	10.00	10.00
Goblet, 8 oz, 5-3/4" h	—	12.00
Ice bucket, metal handle	80.00	70.00
Mixing bowl, 7-1/4" d	15.00	15.00
Mixing bowl, 8-1/4" d	18.00	18.00
Mixing bowl, 9" d	20.00	20.00

ITEM	GREEN	PINK
Mixing bowl, 10" d	40.00	40.00
Pitcher, 32 oz, 5" h	38.00	35.00
Pitcher, 48 oz, 9" h, ftd	48.00	50.00
Pitcher, 96 oz, 8" h	225.00	230.00
Plate, 6" d, sherbet	3.00	3.00
Plate, 8" d, luncheon	6.00	8.00
Platter, 11" d, round	14.00	16.00
Refrigerator dish, 4 x 4"	20.00	18.00
Refrigerator stack set, four pcs	75.00	75.00
Salt and pepper shakers, pr	60.00	60.00

Hex Optic, green 4-3/4" cone-shaped footed tumbler, $8; 5" flat tumbler, $10.

ITEM	GREEN	PINK
Saucer	4.00	4.00
Sherbet, 5 oz, ftd	12.00	10.00
Sugar, two styles of handles	10.00	12.00
Sugar shaker	290.00	275.00
Tumbler, 12 oz, 5" h	10.00	10.00
Tumbler, 5-3/4" h, ftd	10.00	10.00
Tumbler, 7" h, ftd	12.00	12.00
Tumbler, 7 oz, 4-3/4" h, ftd	8.00	8.00
Tumbler, 9 oz, 3-3/4" h	10.00	10.00
Whiskey, 1 oz, 2" h	8.50	8.50

Hex Optic, green luncheon plate, $6; bucket reamer, $65.

HOBNAIL

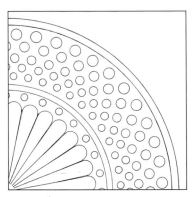

Manufactured by Hocking Glass Company, Lancaster, Ohio, from 1934 to 1936.

Pieces were made in crystal, crystal with red trim, and pink.

ITEM	CRYSTAL	CRYSTAL, RED TRIM	PINK
Cereal bowl, 5-1/2" d	4.25	4.25	—
Cordial, 5 oz, ftd	6.00	6.00	—
Creamer, ftd	4.00	4.00	—
Cup	5.00	5.00	6.00
Decanter and stopper, 32 oz	27.50	65.00	—
Goblet, 10 oz	7.50	7.50	—
Iced tea goblet, 13 oz	8.50	8.50	—
Iced tea tumbler, 15 oz	8.50	8.50	—
Juice tumbler, 5 oz	4.00	4.00	—
Milk pitcher, 18 oz	22.00	22.00	—
Pitcher, 67 oz	25.00	25.00	—
Plate, 6" d, sherbet	2.50	2.50	3.50

ITEM	CRYSTAL	CRYSTAL, RED TRIM	PINK
Plate, 8-1/2" d, luncheon	5.50	5.50	8.50
Salad bowl, 7" d	5.00	5.00	—
Saucer	2.00	2.00	3.00
Sherbet	4.00	4.00	6.00
Sugar, ftd	4.00	4.00	—
Tumbler, 9 oz, 4-3/4" h, flat	5.00	5.00	—
Whiskey, 1-1/2 oz	5.00	5.00	—
Wine, 3 oz, ftd	6.50	6.50	—

Hobnail, pink sherbet, $6.

HOLIDAY
BUTTON AND BOWS

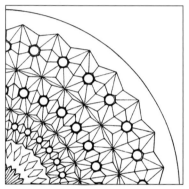

Manufactured by Jeannette Glass Company, Jeannette, Pennsylvania, from 1947 to the 1950s.

Pieces were made in crystal, iridescent, pink, and shell pink. Shell pink production was limited to the console bowl valued at $48.

ITEM	CRYSTAL	IRIDESCENT	PINK
Berry bowl, 5-1/8" d	—	—	12.00
Berry bowl, 8-1/2" d	—	—	55.00
Butter dish, cov	—	—	55.00
Cake plate, 10-1/2" d, three legs	—	—	180.00
Candlesticks, pr, 3" h	—	—	75.00
Chop plate, 13-3/4" d	—	—	140.00
Console bowl, 10-1/4" d	—	—	125.00
Creamer, ftd	—	—	12.00
Cup, plain	—	—	6.00
Cup, rayed bottom, 2" d base	—	—	12.00
Cup, rayed bottom, 2-3/8" d base	—	—	16.00

ITEM	CRYSTAL	IRIDESCENT	PINK
Juice tumbler, 5 oz, 4" h, ftd	—	25.00	35.00
Pitcher, 16 oz, 4-3/4" h	17.50	35.00	50.00
Pitcher, 52 oz, 6-3/4" h	—	—	45.00
Plate, 6" d, sherbet	—	—	2.50
Plate, 9" d, dinner	—	—	18.00
Platter, 11-3/8" l, oval	—	17.50	35.00
Sandwich tray, 10-1/2" d	—	20.00	22.00
Saucer, plain center	—	—	3.00
Saucer, rayed center, 2-1/8" d ring	—	—	4.50
Saucer, rayed center, 2-1/2" d ring	—	—	4.50
Sherbet	—	—	9.00
Soup bowl, 7-3/4" d	—	—	80.00
Sugar, cov	—	—	35.00
Sugar lid	—	—	20.00
Tumbler, 5 oz, 4" h, ftd	—	15.00	20.00
Tumbler, 5-1/4 oz, 4-1/4" h, ftd	8.00	—	45.00
Tumbler, 6" h, ftd	—	—	195.00
Tumbler, 9 oz, 4" h, ftd	—	—	55.00
Tumbler, 10 oz, 4" h, flat	—	—	28.00
Vegetable bowl, 9-1/2" l, oval	—	—	32.00

Holiday, pink 4" tumbler, $28; cup, $12.   *Holiday, pink 9" dinner plate, $18.*

HOMESPUN
FINE RIB

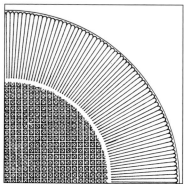

Manufactured by Jeannette Glass Company, Jeannette, Pennsylvania, from 1939 to 1949.

Pieces were made in crystal and pink.

ITEM	CRYSTAL	PINK
Ashtray	6.00	6.00
Berry bowl, 4-1/2" d, closed handles	12.00	17.50
Berry bowl, 8-1/4" d	20.00	20.00
Butter dish, cov	55.00	60.00
Cereal bowl, 5" d, closed handles	30.00	30.00
Coaster	6.00	6.00
Creamer, ftd	12.50	12.50
Cup	24.00	24.00
Iced tea tumbler, 13 oz, 5-1/4" h	32.00	32.00
Plate, 6" d, sherbet	6.50	6.50
Plate, 9-1/4" d, dinner	16.00	16.00

Homespun, pink sugar, $18.50; tumbler, $22.50.

Homespun, pink 9-1/4" dinner plate, $16.

ITEM	CRYSTAL	PINK
Platter, 13" d, closed handles	20.00	20.00
Saucer	8.50	8.50
Sherbet, low, flat	17.50	15.00
Sugar, ftd	12.50	18.50
Tumbler, 5 oz, 4" h, ftd	8.00	8.00
Tumbler, 6 oz, 3-7/8" h, straight	7.00	7.00
Tumbler, 9 oz, 4" h, flared top	17.50	24.50
Tumbler, 9 oz, 4-1/4" h, band at top	17.50	22.50
Tumbler, 15 oz, 6-1/4" h, ftd	38.00	38.00
Tumbler, 15 oz, 6-3/8" h, ftd	36.00	36.00

CHILDREN'S

ITEM	CRYSTAL	PINK
Cup	25.00	35.00
Plate	10.00	15.00
Saucer	9.00	8.00
Teapot	—	125.00

Homespun, pink 4" footed tumbler, $8.

HORSESHOE
NO. 612

Manufactured by Indiana Glass Company, Dunkirk, Indiana, from 1930 to 1933.

Pieces were made in crystal, green, pink, and yellow. There is limited collector interest in crystal and pink at the current time.

ITEM	GREEN	YELLOW
Berry bowl, 4-1/2" d	30.00	25.00
Berry bowl, 9-1/2" d	45.00	35.00
Butter dish, cov	750.00	—
Candy dish, metal holder	175.00	—
Cereal bowl, 6-1/2" d	25.00	40.00
Creamer, ftd	18.00	35.00
Cup	15.00	10.00
Pitcher, 64 oz, 8-1/2" h	295.00	350.00
Plate, 6" d, sherbet	9.00	9.00
Plate, 8-3/8" d, salad	10.00	10.00
Plate, 9-3/8" d, luncheon	15.00	20.00

ITEM	GREEN	YELLOW
Plate, 10-3/8" d, grill	90.00	135.00
Platter, 10-3/4" l, oval	25.00	45.00
Relish, three parts, ftd	45.00	55.00
Salad bowl, 7-1/2" d	24.00	24.00
Sandwich plate, 11-1/2" d	30.00	27.50
Saucer	6.00	6.50
Sherbet	15.00	16.50
Sugar, open	18.50	25.00
Tumbler, 9 oz, ftd	27.00	30.00
Tumbler, 12 oz, ftd	140.00	150.00
Tumbler, 12 oz, 4-3/4" h	150.00	—
Vegetable bowl, 8-1/2" d	30.00	30.00
Vegetable bowl, 10-1/2" d, oval	25.00	28.50

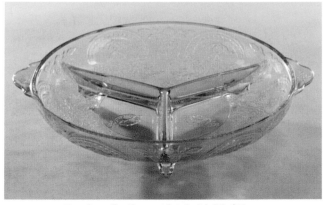

Horseshoe, yellow three-part footed relish dish, $55.

Horseshoe, yellow cup, $10.

IRIS

IRIS AND HERRINGBONE

Manufactured by Jeannette Glass Company, Jeannette, Pennsylvania, from 1928 to 1932 and in the 1950s and 1970s.

Pieces were made in crystal, iridescent, some green, and pink. Recent color combinations of yellow and red and blue and green and white have been made.

Reproductions: † Some collectors and dealers feel strongly that the newer re-issues of this pattern are actually reproductions. Forms that have the potential to fool buyers are the 4-1/2-inch berry bowl, covered candy jar, 10-inch diameter dinner plate, 6-1/2-inch high-footed tumbler, and vase. Careful examination of the object, plus careful consideration of the color, should help determine age.

A record price of $495 is noted for a rare amethyst demitasse cup and saucer.

ITEM	CRYSTAL	GREEN	IRIDESCENT	PINK
Berry bowl, 4-1/2" d, beaded edge †	50.00	—	14.00	—
Berry bowl, 8" d, beaded edge	135.00	—	40.00	—
Bowl, 5-1/2" d, scalloped	6.75	—	18.00	—
Bowl, 9-1/2" d, scalloped	16.50	—	15.00	—
Bread plate, 11-3/4" d	20.00	—	38.00	—
Butter dish, cov	60.00	—	65.00	—
Candlesticks, pr	45.00	—	55.00	—
Candy jar, cov †	195.00	—	—	—
Cereal bowl, 5" d	100.00			

Iris, iridescent 9" vase, $25.

ITEM	CRYSTAL	GREEN	IRIDESCENT	PINK
Coaster †	70.00	—	—	—
Cocktail, 4 oz, 4-1/4" h	28.00	—	—	—
Creamer, ftd	25.00	150.00	12.50	150.00
Cup	16.00	—	20.00	—
Demitasse cup and saucer	200.00	—	350.00	—
Fruit bowl, 11" d, straight edge	70.00	—	—	—
Fruit bowl, 11-1/2" d, ruffled	2.00	—	14.00	—
Fruit set	110.00	—	—	—
Goblet, 4 oz, 5-3/4" h	15.00	—	115.00	—
Goblet, 8 oz, 5-3/4" h	25.00	—	155.00	—
Iced tea tumbler, 6-1/2" h, ftd †	42.00	—	12.00	—
Lampshade, 11-1/2"	95.00	—	—	—
Nut set	145.00	—	—	—
Pitcher, 9-1/2" h, ftd	45.00	—	45.00	—
Plate, 5-1/2" d, sherbet	15.00	—	14.00	—
Plate, 7" d	95.00	—	—	—
Plate, 8" d, luncheon	110.00	—	115.00	—

Iris, crystal candlesticks, $45; iridescent sandwich plate, $35.

ITEM	CRYSTAL	GREEN	IRIDESCENT	PINK
Plate, 9" d, dinner †	35.00	—	40.00	—
Salad bowl, 9-1/2" d, ruffled	15.00	150.00	20.00	135.00
Sandwich plate, 11-3/4" d	50.00	—	35.00	—
Sauce, 5" d, ruffled	12.50	—	30.00	—
Saucer	12.00	—	11.00	—
Sherbet, 2-1/2" h, ftd	25.00	—	15.50	—
Sherbet, 4" h, ftd	25.00	—	15.50	—
Soup bowl, 7-1/2" d	185.00	—	75.00	—
Sugar, cov	40.00	150.00	16.00	150.00
Tumbler, 4" h, flat †	150.00	—	18.00	—
Tumbler, 6" h, ftd †	15.00	—	25.00	—
Tumbler, 6-1/2" h, ftd †	20.00	—	—	—
Tumbler, flat, water †	150.00	—	—	—
Vase, 9" h †	30.00	—	25.00	200.00
Wine, 4" h	18.00	—	32.50	—
Wine, 4-1/4" h, 3 oz	20.00	—	—	—
Wine, 5-1/2" h	24.50	—	—	—

Iris, crystal 5-3/4" footed stem goblet, $25; iridescent 6" cone-shaped tumbler, $25; pink 4" footed stem wine, value unknown.

JAMESTOWN

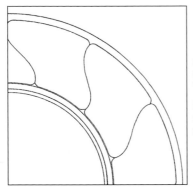

Manufactured by Fostoria Glass Company, Moundsville, West Virginia, from 1958 to 1982.

Items were made in amber, amethyst, blue, brown, crystal, green, pink, and red.

ITEM	AMBER OR BROWN	AMETHYST	BLUE OR RED	CRYSTAL OR GREEN	PINK
Butter, cov	25.00	48.00	60.00	48.00	60.00
Cake plate	25.00	45.00	60.00	45.00	60.00
Celery	20.00	35.00	40.00	35.00	40.00
Creamer, ftd	12.00	20.00	25.00	20.00	25.00
Dessert bowl, 4-1/2" d	8.50	14.00	17.50	13.50	15.00
Goblet, 9 oz or 10 oz	14.00	17.50	28.00	15.00	26.00
Iced tea tumbler, 11 or 12 oz	15.00	20.00	30.00	22.00	24.00
Jelly, cov	35.00	60.00	80.00	60.00	80.00
Juice tumbler, 5 oz	10.00	20.00	24.00	20.00	26.00
Muffin tray	30.00	45.00	55.00	45.00	55.00
Pickle	20.00	40.00	48.00	40.00	48.00

Jamestown, pink goblet, $26; blue goblet, $28.

ITEM	AMBER OR BROWN	AMETHYST	BLUE OR RED	CRYSTAL OR GREEN	PINK
Pitcher, 48 oz, ice lip	48.00	95.00	145.00	95.00	145.00
Plate, 8" d	9.50	17.50	25.00	17.50	25.00
Relish, two parts	15.00	35.00	40.00	35.00	40.00
Salad bowl, 10" d	24.00	40.00	50.00	40.00	50.00
Salt and pepper shakers, pr, chrome top	30.00	42.00	55.00	42.00	45.00
Salver, 10" d, 7" h	60.00	120.00	125.00	135.00	125.00
Sauce dish, cov	20.00	35.00	42.00	35.00	42.00
Serving bowl, two handles, 10" d	22.00	45.00	60.00	45.00	60.00
Sherbet, 6 oz or 7 oz	9.50	15.00	21.50	15.00	17.50

ITEM	AMBER OR BROWN	AMETHYST	BLUE OR RED	CRYSTAL OR GREEN	PINK
Sugar, ftd	12.00	17.50	25.00	17.50	25.00
Torte plate, 14" d	30.00	45.00	60.00	45.00	60.00
Tumbler, 9 oz	7.50	18.00	25.00	18.00	25.00
Tumbler, 12 oz	9.50	25.00	30.00	20.00	25.00
Wine, 4 oz	12.00	20.00	30.00	35.00	32.50

Jamestown, amber 8" plate, $9.50.

JUBILEE

Manufactured by Lancaster Glass Company, Lancaster, Ohio, in the early 1930s.

Pieces were made in pink and yellow.

ITEM	PINK	YELLOW
Bowl, 8" d, 5-1/8" h, three legs	275.00	225.00
Bowl, 11-1/2" d, three legs	265.00	250.00
Bowl, 11-1/2" d, three legs, curved in	—	250.00
Bowl, 13" d, three legs	250.00	245.00
Cake tray, 11" d, two handles	75.00	65.00
Candlesticks, pr	190.00	195.00
Candy jar, cov, three legs	325.00	325.00
Cheese and cracker set	265.00	255.00
Cordial, 1 oz, 4" h	—	245.00
Creamer	35.00	20.00
Cup	40.00	17.50
Fruit bowl, 9" d, handle	—	125.00
Fruit bowl, 11-1/2" h, flat	200.00	165.00

ITEM	PINK	YELLOW
Goblet, 3 oz, 4-7/8" h	—	150.00
Goblet, 11 oz, 7-1/2" h	—	150.00
Iced tea tumbler, 12-1/2 oz, 6 1/8" h	—	85.00
Juice tumbler, 6 oz, 5" h, ftd	—	100.00
Mayonnaise, plate, orig ladle	315.00	285.00
Mayonnaise underplate	125.00	110.00
Plate, 7" d, salad	25.00	12.00
Plate, 8-3/4" d, luncheon	30.00	14.50
Plate, 14" d, three legs	—	210.00
Sandwich plate, 13-1/2" d	95.00	85.00
Sandwich tray, 11" d, center handle	215.00	250.00
Saucer	15.00	8.00
Sherbet, 8 oz, 3" h	—	75.00
Sherbet/champagne, 7 oz, 5-1/2" h	—	75.00
Sugar	35.00	20.00
Tumbler, 10 oz, 6" h, ftd	75.00	40.00
Vase, 12" h	—	385.00

Jubilee, yellow saucer, $8; cup, $17.50.

Jubilee, yellow goblet, $150.

LACED EDGE

KATY BLUE, SUGAR CANE

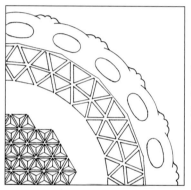

Manufactured by Imperial Glass Company, Bellaire, Ohio, in the early 1930s, known as Line 7455.

Pieces were made in blue and green with opalescent edges.

ITEM	BLUE	GREEN
Basket, 9" d	250.00	—
Bowl, 5" d	30.00	40.00
Bowl, 5-1/2" d	30.00	42.00
Bowl, 5-7/8" d	42.00	42.00
Bowl, 11" l, oval	295.00	285.00
Bowl, 11" l, oval, divided	165.00	165.00
Candlesticks, pr, double lite	80.00	150.00
Creamer	30.00	40.00
Cup	33.00	35.00
Fruit bowl, 4-1/2" d	32.00	30.00
Mayonnaise, three pieces	100.00	125.00

ITEM	BLUE	GREEN
Nappy, 6-1/2" d, belled	—	30.00
Plate, 6-1/2" d, bread and butter	24.00	24.00
Plate, 8" d, salad	35.00	25.00
Plate, 10" d, dinner	95.00	95.00
Plate, 12" d, luncheon	90.00	90.00
Platter, 13" l	185.00	165.00
Saucer	15.00	15.00
Soup bowl, 7" d	85.00	80.00
Sugar	30.00	40.00
Tidbit, two tiers, 8" and 10" plates	110.00	100.00
Tumbler, 9 oz	40.00	60.00
Vegetable bowl, 9" d	85.00	95.00

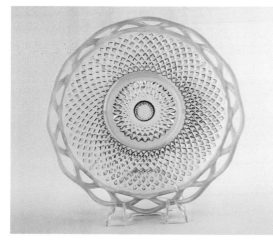

*Laced Edge,
blue 5-1/2"
bowl, $30.*

LAUREL

Manufactured by McKee Glass Company, Pittsburgh, Pennsylvania, in the 1930s. Pieces were made in French ivory, jade green, Poudre blue, and white opal. A 5-3/4" diameter plate featuring a bust of Jeannette McKee, 1888-1938, was made in the Laurel pattern in Delphite, back signed "McK," $195.

ITEM	FRENCH IVORY	JADE GREEN	POUDRE BLUE	WHITE OPAL
Berry bowl, 4-3/4" d	8.00	18.00	16.00	14.00
Berry bowl, 9" d	28.50	40.00	55.00	30.00
Bowl, 6" d, three legs	15.00	25.00	—	15.00
Bowl, 10-1/2" d, three legs	37.50	50.00	68.00	45.00
Bowl, 11" d	40.00	55.00	85.00	37.50
Candlesticks, pr, 4" h	40.00	55.00	—	45.00
Cereal bowl, 6" d	12.00	28.00	28.00	20.00
Cheese dish, cov	135.00	150.00	—	75.00
Creamer, short	12.00	25.00	—	18.00
Creamer, tall	15.00	28.00	40.00	24.00
Cup	9.50	15.00	20.00	12.00

Laurel, jade green dinner plate, $25.

ITEM	FRENCH IVORY	JADE GREEN	POUDRE BLUE	WHITE OPAL
Plate, 6" d, sherbet	5.00	15.00	10.00	8.00
Plate, 7-1/2" d, salad	10.00	20.00	17.50	12.00
Plate, 9-1/8" d, dinner	15.00	25.00	30.00	18.50
Plate, 9-1/8" d, grill, round	20.00	30.00	—	18.50
Plate, 9-1/8" d, grill, scalloped	15.00	25.00	—	18.50
Platter, 10-3/4" l, oval	30.00	48.00	45.00	30.00
Salt and pepper shakers, pr	60.00	85.00	—	65.00
Saucer	3.25	4.55	7.50	3.50
Sherbet	12.50	20.00	—	18.00
Sherbet/champagne, 5"	50.00	72.00	—	60.00
Soup bowl, 7-7/8" d	35.00	40.00	—	40.00
Sugar, short	12.00	25.00	—	18.00
Sugar, tall	15.00	35.00	40.00	24.00
Tumbler, 9 oz, 4-1/2" h, flat	45.00	60.00	—	60.00
Tumbler, 12 oz, 5" h, flat	60.00	—	—	—
Vegetable bowl, 9-3/4" l, oval	18.50	480.00	45.00	20.00

CHILDREN'S

ITEM	PLAIN	GREEN OR DECORATED	SCOTTY DOG GREEN	SCOTTY DOG IVORY
Creamer	35.00	100.00	200.00	115.00
Cup	25.00	50.00	100.00	50.00
Plate	15.00	18.00	75.00	40.00
Saucer	12.00	14.00	75.00	40.00
Sugar	40.00	75.00	200.00	115.00

LINCOLN INN

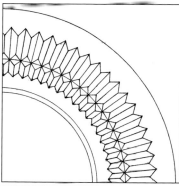

Manufactured by Fenton Art Glass Company, Williamstown, West Virginia, in the late 1920s.

Made in amber, amethyst, black, cobalt blue, crystal, green, green opalescent, light blue, opaque jade, pink, and red.

Production in black was limited to salt and pepper shakers valued at $325. Some rare pieces have been identified in several other colors.

ITEM	COBALT BLUE	CRYSTAL	OTHER COLORS	RED
Ashtray	17.50	12.00	12.00	17.50
Bonbon, oval, handle	17.50	12.00	14.00	18.00
Bonbon, sq, handle	15.00	12.00	14.00	15.00
Bowl, 6" d, crimped	14.50	7.50	10.00	14.50
Bowl, 9" d, shallow	—	9.00	—	—
Bowl, 9-1/4" d, ftd	42.00	18.00	20.00	45.00
Bowl, 10-1/2" d, ftd	50.00	75.00	30.00	50.00
Candy dish, ftd, oval	24.00	14.50	14.50	24.00
Cereal bowl, 6" d	12.50	7.50	9.50	12.50
Comport	25.00	14.00	15.00	25.00
Creamer	24.00	12.00	15.00	24.00
Cup	17.50	8.50	9.50	18.00

ITEM	COBALT BLUE	CRYSTAL	OTHER COLORS	RED
Finger bowl	20.00	14.00	14.50	20.00
Fruit bowl, 5" d	14.00	7.00	9.00	14.00
Goblet, 6" h	30.00	17.50	40.00	40.00
Iced tea tumbler, 12 oz, ftd	50.00	25.00	45.00	45.00
Juice tumbler, 4 oz, flat	32.50	9.00	14.00	27.50
Nut dish, ftd	20.00	14.50	16.00	20.00
Olive bowl, handle	15.00	8.50	65.00	15.00
Pitcher, 46 oz, 7-1/4" h	800.00	700.00	715.00	800.00
Plate, 6" d	19.50	12.00	12.50	19.50
Plate, 8" d	27.50	15.00	14.00	27.50
Plate, 9-1/4" d	30.00	15.00	16.50	30.00
Plate, 12" d	35.00	16.00	18.00	35.00
Salt and pepper shakers, pr	265.00	175.00	175.00	265.00
Sandwich server, center handle	175.00	110.00	110.00	175.00
Saucer	5.00	4.00	4.50	5.00
Sherbet, 4-1/2" h, cone shape	18.00	12.00	14.00	18.00
Sherbet, 4-3/4" h	20.00	14.00	32.50	20.00
Sugar	24.00	12.00	15.00	24.00
Tumbler, 5 oz, ftd	55.00	14.00	14.50	24.00
Tumbler, 9 oz, flat	—	14.00	15.00	15.00
Tumbler, 9 oz, ftd	28.00	32.00	35.00	30.00
Vase, 9-3/4" h	195.00	85.00	95.00	145.00
Vase, 12" h, ftd	225.00	115.00	125.00	175.00
Wine	38.00	20.00	65.00	40.00

Lincoln Inn, pink 8" plate, $14.

Lincoln Inn, cobalt blue goblet, $30.

LORAIN
BASKET, NO. 615

Manufactured by Indiana Glass Company, Dunkirk, Indiana, from 1929 to 1939.

Pieces were made in crystal, green, and yellow.

Reproductions: † A fantasy sherbet has been reported in both milk white and avocado green.

ITEM	CRYSTAL	GREEN	YELLOW
Berry bowl, 8" d	125.00	190.00	250.00
Cereal bowl, 6" d	45.00	50.00	65.00
Creamer, ftd	20.00	20.00	30.00
Cup and saucer	32.00	32.00	25.00
Plate, 5-1/2" d, sherbet	10.00	12.00	15.00
Plate, 7-3/4" d, salad	15.00	18.00	15.00
Plate, 8-3/4" d, luncheon	20.00	24.00	30.00
Plate, 10-1/4" d, dinner	30.00	40.00	90.00
Platter, 11-1/2" l	32.50	32.50	48.00
Relish, 8" d, four parts	32.00	32.00	40.00
Salad bowl, 7-3/4" d	40.00	40.00	75.00
Saucer	6.00	6.00	5.00

ITEM	CRYSTAL	GREEN	YELLOW
Sherbet, ftd †	32.00	20.00	24.00
Snack tray, crystal trim	32.00	37.50	—
Sugar, ftd	18.00	24.00	30.00
Tumbler, 9 oz, 4-3/4" h, ftd	32.00	30.00	28.00
Vegetable bowl, 9-3/4" l, oval	50.00	60.00	85.00

Lorain, yellow luncheon plate, $30; tumbler, $28.

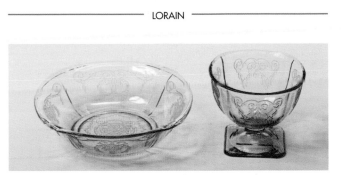

Lorain, yellow 6" cereal bowl, $65; green sherbet, $20.

Lorain, green cup and saucer, $32.

MADRID

Manufactured by Federal Glass Company, Lancaster, Ohio, from 1932 to 1939.

Pieces were made in amber, blue, crystal, green, iridescent, and pink. Iridized pieces are limited to a console set, consisting of a low bowl and pair of candlesticks, valued at $40.

Reproductions: † Reproductions include candlesticks, cups, saucers, and a vegetable bowl. Reproductions are found in amber, blue, crystal, and pink. Federal Glass Company reissued this pattern under the name "Recollection." Some of these pieces were dated 1976.

When Federal went bankrupt, the molds were sold to Indiana Glass, which removed the date and began production of crystal, then pink. Several pieces have been made recently that were not part of the original production and include a footed cake stand, goblet, two-section grill plate, preserves stand, squatty salt and pepper shakers, 11-ounce tumbler, and vase.

ITEM	AMBER	BLUE	CRYSTAL	GREEN	PINK
Ashtray, 6" sq	300.00	—	—	295.00	—
Berry bowl, small	8.50	—	6.50	—	—
Berry bowl, 9-3/8" d	25.00	—	25.00	—	25.00
Bowl, 7" d	17.50	—	12.00	17.50	—
Butter dish, cov	60.00	—	65.00	80.00	—
Cake plate, 11-1/4" d	24.00	—	20.00	—	27.50
Candlesticks, 2-1/4" h, pr †	20.00	—	14.50	—	24.00

ITEM	AMBER	BLUE	CRYSTAL	GREEN	PINK
Coaster, 5" d	40.00	—	40.00	35.00	—
Console bowl, 11" d	20.00	—	18.00	—	36.00
Cookie jar	40.00	—	45.00	—	40.00
Creamer	20.00	18.00	7.00	10.00	—
Cream soup bowl 4-3/4" d	25.00	—	15.50	—	—
Cup †	6.00	18.00	7.50	12.00	16.50
Gelatin mold, 2-1/2" h	15.00	—	10.00	—	—
Gravy boat	1,950.00	—	900.00	—	—
Gravy boat platter	900.00	—	900.00	—	—
Hot dish coaster, 3-1/2" d	95.00	—	40.00	45.00	—
Iced tea tumbler, round	25.00	—	24.50	22.00	—
Jam dish, 7" d	24.00	50.00	12.00	25.00	—
Juice pitcher	40.00	—	45.00	—	—
Juice tumbler, 5 oz, 3-7/8 h, ftd	32.50	40.00	35.00	30.00	—
Pitcher, jug-type	50.00	—	24.00	190.00	—
Pitcher, 60 oz, 8" h, sq	450.00	125.00	135.00	120.00	50.00
Pitcher, 80 oz, 8-1/2" h, ice lip	65.00	—	30.00	215.00	—
Plate, 6" d, sherbet	5.50	12.00	4.00	4.50	4.00
Plate, 7-1/2" d, salad	12.00	17.00	12.00	9.00	9.00
Plate, 8-7/8" d, luncheon	14.00	20.00	7.50	12.00	10.00
Plate, 10-1/2" d, dinner	50.00	60.00	24.00	45.00	—
Plate, 10-1/2" d, grill	15.00	—	10.00	18.50	—
Platter, 11-1/2" oval	20.00	32.00	20.00	18.00	18.00
Relish dish, 10-1/2" d	14.50	—	7.00	16.00	20.00
Salad bowl, 8" d	17.00	—	9.50	15.50	—
Salad bowl, 9-1/2" d	28.00	—	30.00	—	—
Salt and pepper shakers, 3-1/2" h	135.00	145.00	95.00	110.00	—
Sauce bowl, 5" d	8.50	—	7.50	8.50	11.00
Saucer †	2.00	8.00	4.00	7.00	5.00
Sherbet, cone	5.00	18.00	6.50	14.00	—
Sherbet, ftd	12.50	15.00	6.00	11.00	—
Soup bowl, 7" d †	15.50	20.00	8.00	19.50	—

ITEM	AMBER	BLUE	CRYSTAL	GREEN	PINK
Sugar, cov †	50.00	145.00	35.00	75.00	—
Sugar, open †	20.00	15.00	8.00	10.00	—
Tumbler, 9 oz, 4-1/2" h	25.00	35.00	17.50	25.00	20.00
Tumbler, 12 oz, 5-1/4" h, ftd or flat	30.00	—	32.00	42.00	—
Vegetable bowl, 10" l, oval †	28.00	35.00	24.00	24.00	30.00

Madrid, amber sugar, $20; creamer, $20.

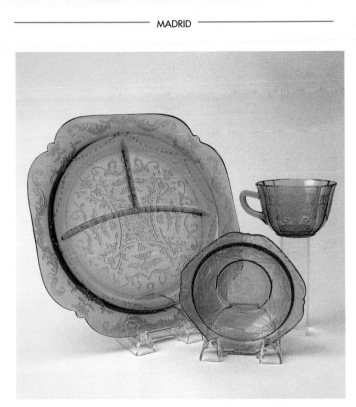

Madrid, amber grill plate, $15; berry bowl, $8.50; cup, $6.

MANHATTAN
HORIZONTAL RIBBED

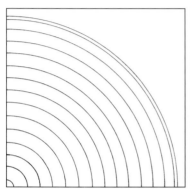

Manufactured by Anchor Hocking Glass Corp. from 1938 to 1943.

Pieces were made in crystal, green, iridized, pink, and ruby. Ruby pieces were limited to relish tray inserts, currently valued at $9 each. Green and iridized production was limited to footed tumblers, currently valued at $17.50.

Anchor Hocking introduced a similar pattern, Park Avenue, in 1987. Anchor Hocking was very careful to preserve the Manhattan pattern. Collectors should pay careful attention to measurements if they are uncertain of the pattern.

ITEM	CRYSTAL	PINK
Ashtray, 4" d, round	22.00	10.00
Ashtray, 4-1/2" w, sq	25.00	—
Berry bowl, 5-3/8" d, handles	22.50	24.00
Berry bowl, 7-1/2" d	28.00	—
Bowl, 4-1/2" d	7.00	—
Bowl, 8" d, closed handles	16.00	25.00
Bowl, 8" d, metal handle	25.00	—
Bowl, 9-1/2" d, handle	—	45.00
Candlesticks, pr, 4-1/2" h	25.00	—
Candy dish, three legs	—	16.00
Candy dish, cov	40.00	

ITEM	CRYSTAL	PINK
Cereal bowl, 5-1/4" d, no handles	95.00	—
Coaster, 3-1/2"	20.00	—
Cocktail	18.00	—
Comport, 5-3/4" h	40.00	55.00
Creamer, oval	9.00	20.00
Cup	18.00	140.00
Fruit bowl, 9-1/2" d, two open handles	40.00	50.00
Juice pitcher, 24 oz	20.00	—
Pitcher, 80 oz, tilted	55.00	85.00
Plate, 6" d, sherbet	7.00	50.00
Plate, 8-1/2" d, salad	24.00	—
Plate, 10-1/4" d, dinner	30.00	120.00

Manhattan, small crystal bowl (on pedestal), $7; pink creamer; $20, and sugar, $15; crystal salt and pepper shakers, $35; crystal tumbler, $18; crystal pitcher, $55; relish with metal stand, $85; pink footed candy dish, $16.

ITEM	CRYSTAL	PINK
Relish tray insert	8.50	9.50
Relish tray, 14" d, inserts	85.00	50.00
Relish tray, 14" d, four parts	65.00	—
Salad bowl, 9" d	20.00	—
Salt and pepper shakers, pr, 2" h, sq	35.00	70.00
Sandwich plate, 14" d	22.00	—
Sauce bowl, 4-1/2" d, handles	12.00	—
Saucer	7.00	50.00
Sherbet	10.00	15.00
Sugar, oval	14.50	15.00
Tumbler, 10 oz, 5-1/4" h, ftd	18.00	25.00
Vase, 8" h	20.00	—
Wine, 3-1/2" h	5.00	—

Manhattan, relish tray with ruby inserts and crystal base, $85; crystal comport, $40; crystal vase, $20; crystal fruit bowl with open handles, $40.

MAYFAIR

Manufactured by Federal Glass Company, Columbus, Ohio, in 1934.

Pieces were made in amber, crystal, and green.

ITEM	AMBER	CRYSTAL	GREEN
Cereal bowl, 6" d	18.50	15.00	22.00
Cream soup bowl, 5" d	20.00	12.00	20.00
Creamer, ftd	17.50	14.00	16.00
Cup	8.50	6.00	8.50
Plate, 6-3/4" d, salad	7.00	4.50	8.50
Plate, 9-1/2" d, dinner	18.00	12.00	14.50
Plate, 9-1/2" d, grill	18.50	15.00	17.50
Platter, 12" l, oval	27.50	22.00	30.00
Sauce bowl, 5" d	8.50	7.00	12.00
Saucer	4.50	3.50	4.50
Sugar, ftd	14.00	12.00	14.00
Tumbler, 9 oz, 4-1/2" h	32.50	18.50	32.00
Vegetable, 10" l, oval	32.00	32.00	32.00

*Mayfair Federal, amber dinner plate, **$18.***

MAYFAIR
OPEN ROSE

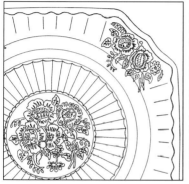

Manufactured by Hocking Glass Company, Lancaster, Ohio, from 1931 to 1937.

Pieces were made in crystal, green, ice blue, pink, and yellow.

Reproductions: † This pattern has been plagued with reproductions since 1977. Items reproduced include cookie jars, salt and pepper shakers, juice pitchers, and whiskey glasses. Reproductions are found in amethyst, blue, cobalt blue, green, pink, and red.

ITEM	CRYSTAL	GREEN	ICE BLUE
Bowl, 11-3/4" l, flat	—	35.00	75.00
Butter dish, cov	—	1,295.00	325.00
Cake plate, 10" d, ftd	—	115.00	75.00
Cake plate, 12" d, handles	—	40.00	95.00
Candy dish, cov	—	555.00	225.00
Celery dish, 9" l, divided	—	155.00	55.00
Celery dish, 10" l, divided	—	—	90.00
Celery dish, 10" l, not divided	—	115.00	80.00
Cereal bowl, 5-1/2" d	—	24.00	48.00
Cocktail, 3 oz, 4" h	—	875.00	—

ITEM	CRYSTAL	GREEN	ICE BLUE
Cookie jar, cov †	—	575.00	295.00
Cream soup bowl, 5" d	—	—	—
Creamer, ftd	—	—	50.00
Cup	—	150.00	40.00
Decanter, stopper, 32 oz	—	—	—
Fruit bowl, 12" d, scalloped	—	50.00	85.00
Goblet, 9 oz, 5-3/4" h	—	400.00	—
Goblet, 9 oz, 7-1/4" h, thin	—	—	225.00
Iced tea tumbler, 13-1/2 oz, 5-1/4" h	—	—	225.00
Iced tea tumbler, 15 oz, 6-1/2" h, ftd	—	250.00	285.00
Juice pitcher, 37oz, 6" h †	30.00	525.00	150.00

Mayfair Open Rose, green fruit bowl, $50.

ITEM	CRYSTAL	GREEN	ICE BLUE
Juice tumbler, 3 oz, 3-1/4" h, ftd	—	—	
Juice tumbler, 5 oz, 3-1/2"	—	—	225.00
Pitcher, 60 oz, 8" h	—	475.00	195.00
Pitcher, 80 oz, 8-1/2" h	—	700.00	225.00
Plate, 5-3/4" d	—	90.00	25.00
Plate, 6-1/2" d, off-center indent	—	115.00	42.00
Plate, 6-1/2" d, sherbet	—	—	24.00
Plate, 8-1/2" d, luncheon	—	85.00	45.00
Plate, 9-1/2" d, dinner	—	150.00	90.00
Plate, 9-1/2" d, grill	—	75.00	70.00
Plate, 11-1/2" d, grill, handles	—	—	—
Platter, 12" l, oval, open handles	17.50	175.00	60.00
Platter, 12-1/2" oval, 8" wide, closed handles	—	245.00	—
Relish, 8-3/8" d, four parts	—	160.00	65.00
Relish, 8-3/8" d, non-partitioned	—	275.00	—
Salt and pepper shakers, pr, flat †	20.00	800.00	295.00
Sandwich server, center handle	—	40.00	85.00
Saucer	—	70.00	30.00
Sherbet, 2-1/4" flat	—	—	125.00
Sherbet, 3" ftd	—	—	—
Sherbet, 4-3/4" ftd	—	150.00	75.00
Sugar, ftd	—	195.00	95.00
Sweet pea vase	—	285.00	145.00
Tumbler, 9 oz, 4-1/4" h	—	—	100.00
Tumbler, 10 oz, 5-1/4" h	—	—	125.00
Tumbler, 11 oz, 4-3/4" h	—	200.00	250.00
Vegetable bowl, 7" d, two handles	—	33.00	75.00
Vegetable bowl, 9-1/2" l, oval	—	110.00	60.00
Vegetable bowl, 10" d cov	—	—	120.00
Vegetable bowl, 10" d open	—	—	85.00
Whiskey, 1-1/2 oz, 2-1/4" h †	—	—	—
Wine, 3 oz, 4-1/2" h	—	450.00	—

Mayfair Open Rose, ice blue handled vegetable bowl, $75.

ITEM	PINK	PINK SATIN	YELLOW
Bowl, 11-3/4" l, flat	50.00	70.00	195.00
Butter dish, cov	65.00	95.00	1,295.00
Cake plate, 10" d, ftd	28.00	45.00	—
Cake plate, 12" d, handles	45.00	50.00	—
Candy dish, cov	65.00	85.00	465.00
Celery dish, 9" l, divided	—	—	150.00
Celery dish, 10" l, divided	295.00	—	—
Celery dish, 10" l, not divided	45.00	50.00	115.00
Cereal bowl, 5-1/2" d	25.00	35.00	75.00
Cocktail, 3 oz, 4" h	65.00	—	—
Cookie jar, cov †	65.00	37.00	860.00
Cream soup bowl, 5" d	50.00	68.00	—
Creamer, ftd	30.00	30.00	—
Cup	18.00	29.50	150.00
Decanter, stopper, 32 oz	175.00	—	—
Fruit bowl, 12" d, scalloped	50.00	75.00	215.00
Goblet, 9 oz, 5-3/4" h	70.00	—	—
Goblet, 9 oz, 7-1/4" h, thin	250.00	—	—
Iced tea tumbler, 13-1/2 oz, 5-1/4" h	55.00	—	—
Iced tea tumbler, 15 oz, 6-1/2" h, ftd	65.00	65.00	—
Juice pitcher, 37oz, 6" h †	55.00	65.00	525.00
Juice tumbler, 3 oz, 3-1/4" h, ftd	80.00	—	—
Juice tumbler, 5 oz, 3-1/2"	60.00	—	—
Pitcher, 60 oz, 8" h	75.00	100.00	425.00
Pitcher, 80 oz, 8-1/2" h	115.00	125.00	715.00
Plate, 5-3/4" d	12.00	15.00	90.00
Plate, 6-1/2" d, off-center indent	30.00	35.00	—
Plate, 6-1/2" d, sherbet	14.50	—	—
Plate, 8-1/2" d, luncheon	30.00	35.00	80.00
Plate, 9-1/2" d, dinner	45.00	60.00	150.00
Plate, 9-1/2" d, grill	50.00	35.00	80.00
Plate, 11-1/2" d, grill, handles	—	—	100.00

*Mayfair Open Rose, pink tumbler, 11 oz, **$225**;*
*pink satin-finish covered cookie jar, **$37**.*

ITEM	PINK	PINK SATIN	YELLOW
Platter, 12" l, oval, open handles	30.00	35.00	115.00
Platter, 12-1/2" oval, 8" wide, closed handles	—	—	245.00
Relish, 8-3/8" d, four parts	30.00	37.50	160.00
Relish, 8-3/8" d, non-partitioned	200.00	—	275.00
Salt and pepper shakers, pr, flat †	65.00	70.00	700.00
Sandwich server, center handle	45.00	50.00	120.00
Saucer	30.00	30.00	70.00
Sherbet, 2-1/4" flat	185.00	—	—
Sherbet, 3" ftd	15.00	—	—
Sherbet, 4-3/4" ftd	75.00	75.00	150.00
Sugar, ftd	25.00	40.00	185.00
Sweet pea vase	200.00	165.00	—
Tumbler, 9 oz, 4-1/4" h	35.00	—	—
Tumbler, 10 oz, 5-1/4" h	45.00	—	185.00
Tumbler, 11 oz, 4-3/4" h	225.00	225.00	215.00
Vegetable bowl, 7" d, two handles	65.00	70.00	195.00
Vegetable bowl, 9-1/2" l, oval	30.00	30.00	125.00
Vegetable bowl, 10" d cov	120.00	120.00	900.00
Vegetable bowl, 10" d open	15.00	19.00	200.00
Whiskey, 1-1/2 oz, 2-1/4" h †	58.00	—	—
Wine, 3 oz, 4-1/2" h	120.00	—	—

MELBA
LINE #707

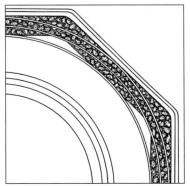

Manufactured by L. E. Smith Glass Company, Mount Pleasant, Pennsylvania, in the early 1930s.

Pieces were made in amethyst, black, green, and pink.

ITEMS	AMETHYST	BLACK	GREEN	PINK
Baker, oval	20.00	22.00	18.00	18.00
Bowl, 10-1/2" d, ruffled	18.00	20.00	15.00	15.00
Candleholder	15.00	17.00	12.00	12.00
Creamer	15.00	18.00	12.00	12.00
Cup	6.50	8.50	5.00	5.00
Dessert bowl	4.50	5.00	3.50	3.50
Plate, 6" d, bread and butter	5.00	7.50	4.00	4.00
Plate, 7" d, salad	7.00	9.50	6.00	6.00
Plate, 9" d, luncheon	9.00	12.00	8.00	8.00
Platter	15.00	18.00	12.00	12.00
Salad bowl	18.00	20.00	15.00	15.00

ITEMS	AMETHYST	BLACK	GREEN	PINK
Saucer	3.50	4.50	3.00	3.00
Serving plate, 9" d, handles	15.00	18.00	12.00	12.00
Sugar	15.00	18.00	12.00	12.00
Vegetable bowl, 9-1/2" l	18.00	20.00	15.00	15.00

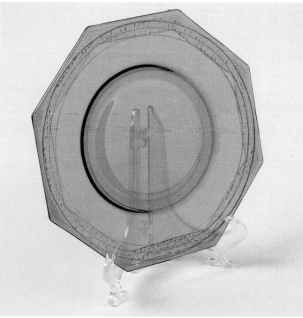

Melba, amethyst luncheon plate, $9.

MISS AMERICA
DIAMOND PATTERN

Manufactured by Hocking Glass Company, Lancaster, Ohio, from 1935 to 1938.

Pieces were made in crystal, green, ice blue, jade-ite, pink, and royal ruby.

Reproductions: † Reproductions include the butter dish (including a new importer), creamer, 8-inch pitcher, salt and pepper shakers, sugar, and tumbler. Reproductions are found in amberina, blue, cobalt blue, crystal, green, pink, and red.

ITEM	CRYSTAL	GREEN	ICE BLUE	PINK	ROYAL RUBY
Berry bowl, 4-1/2" d	—	30.00	—	—	—
Bowl, 8" d, curved at top	48.00	—	—	95.00	—
Bowl, 8" d, straight sides	—	—	—	85.00	—
Bowl, 11" d, shallow	—	—	—	—	850.00
Butter dish, cov †	200.00	—	—	550.00	—
Cake plate, 12" d, ftd	27.50	—	—	45.00	—
Candy jar, cov, 11-1/2"	65.00	—	—	200.00	—
Celery dish, 10-1/2" l, oval	20.00	—	160.00	42.00	—
Cereal bowl, 6-1/4" d	10.00	18.00	—	30.00	—
Coaster, 5-3/4" d	15.50	—	—	45.00	—
Comport, 5" d	18.00	—	—	30.00	—

Miss America, pink goblet, $40; comport, $30; 10 oz tumbler with original label, $40.

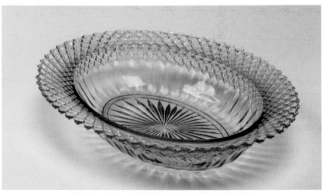

Miss America, pink 10" oval vegetable bowl, $55.

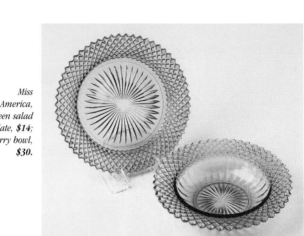

Miss America, green salad plate, $14; berry bowl, $30.

ITEM	CRYSTAL	GREEN	ICE BLUE	PINK	ROYAL RUBY
Creamer, ftd †	10.00	—	—	24.00	215.00
Cup	9.50	12.00	16.00	30.00	200.00
Fruit bowl, 8-3/4" d	39.50	—	—	60.00	450.00
Goblet, 10 oz, 5-1/2" h	22.50	—	—	40.00	200.00
Iced tea tumbler, 14 oz, 5-3/4" h	25.00	—	—	85.00	—
Juice goblet, 5 oz, 4-3/4" h	27.50	—	—	125.00	250.00
Juice tumbler, 5 oz, 4" h	26.50	—	140.00	50.00	180.00
Pitcher, 65 oz, 8" h †	45.00	—	—	175.00	—
Pitcher, 65 oz, 8-1/2" h, ice lip	75.00	—	—	135.00	50.00
Plate, 5-3/4" d, sherbet	7.50	9.00	55.00	18.00	—
Plate, 6-3/4" d	—	12.00	—	—	—
Plate, 8-1/2" d, salad	9.00	14.00	—	25.00	150.00
Plate, 10-1/4" d, dinner	16.50	—	150.00	45.00	—

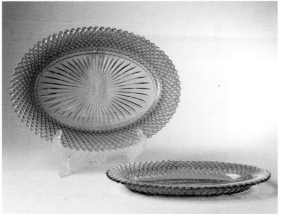

*Miss America, pink 12-1/2" l oval platter, **$55**; 10-1/2" l oval celery dish, **$42**.*

ITEM	CRYSTAL	GREEN	ICE BLUE	PINK	ROYAL RUBY
Plate, 10-1/4" d, grill	15.00	—	—	37.50	—
Platter, 12-1/4" l, oval	18.00	—	—	55.00	—
Relish, 8-3/4" l, four parts	20.00	—	—	40.00	—
Relish, 11-3/4" d, divided	35.00	—	—	40.00	—
Salt and pepper shakers, pr †	35.00	300.00	—	65.00	—
Saucer	4.00	—	—	8.00	60.00
Sherbet	10.00	—	60.00	20.00	175.00
Sugar	10.00	—	—	25.00	225.00
Tumbler, 10 oz, 4-1/2" h, flat †	18.00	45.00	—	40.00	—
Tumbler, 14 oz, 5-3/4" h	28.00	—	—	—	—
Vegetable bowl, 10" l, oval	20.00	—	—	55.00	—
Whiskey	24.00	—	—	—	—
Wine, 3 oz, 3-3/4" h	25.00	—	—	85.00	250.00

MODERNTONE

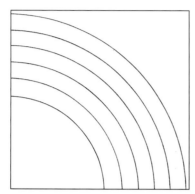

Manufactured by Hazel Atlas Glass Company, Clarksburg, West Virginia, and Zanesville, Ohio, from 1934 to 1942; also in the late 1940s to early 1950s.

Pieces were made in amethyst, cobalt blue, crystal, pink, and Platonite fired-on colors. Later period production saw plain white as well as white with blue or red stripes and a Willow-type design in blue or red on white. Collector interest in crystal is limited and prices remain low, less than 50 percent of Platonite.

ITEM	AMETHYST	COBALT BLUE	PLATONITE, DARKER SHADES
Ashtray, 7-3/4" d, match holder center	—	200.00	—
Berry bowl, 5" d, rim	25.00	30.00	—
Berry bowl, 5" d, without rim	—	—	12.50
Berry bowl, 8-3/4" d	42.00	55.00	—
Bowl, 8" d, no rim	—	—	40.00
Bowl, 8" d, rim	—	—	—
Butter dish, metal cov	—	98.00	—
Cereal bowl, 5" d, deep, no white	—	—	17.50

Moderntone, cobalt blue sugar, $12; creamer, $15.

ITEM	PLATONITE, PASTEL SHADES	WHITE OR WHITE WITH DEC	WILLOW—TYPE DEC
Ashtray, 7-3/4" d, match holder center	—	—	—
Berry bowl, 5" d, rim	7.00	5.00	15.00
Berry bowl, 5" d, without rim	25.00	—	—
Berry bowl, 8-3/4" d	—	7.50	28.00
Bowl, 8" d, no rim	50.00	—	—
Bowl, 8" d, rim	15.00	6.00	28.00
Butter dish, metal cov	—	—	—
Cereal bowl, 5" d, deep, no white	10.00	—	—

ITEM	AMETHYST	COBALT BLUE	PLATONITE, DARKER SHADES
Cereal bowl, 5" d, deep, with white	—	—	—
Cereal bowl, 6-1/2" d	70.00	70.00	—
Cheese dish, 7" d, metal cov	—	400.00	—
Cream soup bowl, 4-3/4" d	20.00	22.00	—
Cream soup bowl, 5" d, ruffled	30.00	65.00	—
Creamer	18.00	15.00	12.00
Cup	12.00	10.00	9.00
Custard cup	18.00	20.00	—
Mug, 4" h, 8 oz	—	—	—
Mustard, metal lid	—	25.00	—
Plate, 5-7/8" d, sherbet	8.00	9.50	—
Plate, 6-3/4" d, salad	12.50	12.00	12.00
Plate, 7-3/4" d, luncheon	10.00	14.00	—
Plate, 8-7/8" d, dinner	14.50	18.00	15.00
Platter, 11" l, oval	40.00	55.00	—
Platter, 12" l, oval	48.00	165.00	32.00
Salt and pepper shakers, pr	45.00	48.00	—
Sandwich plate, 10-1/2" d	35.00	75.00	—
Saucer	4.50	5.00	7.50
Sherbet	13.00	15.00	12.00
Soup bowl, 7-1/2" d	95.00	225.00	—
Sugar	18.00	12.00	12.00
Tumbler, 5 oz	40.00	75.00	—
Tumbler, 9 oz	30.00	40.00	45.00
Tumbler, 12 oz	85.00	95.00	—
Tumbler, cone, ftd	—	—	—
Whiskey, 1-1/2 oz	—	45.00	—

ITEM	PLATONITE, PASTEL SHADES	WHITE OR WHITE WITH DEC	WILLOW—TYPE DEC
Cereal bowl, 5" d, deep, with white	9.00	4.50	—
Cereal bowl, 6-1/2" d	—	—	—
Cheese dish, 7" d, metal cov	—	—	—
Cream soup bowl, 4-3/4" d	12.00	7.00	24.00
Cream soup bowl, 5" d, ruffled	—	—	—
Creamer	5.50	4.50	20.00
Cup	6.50	2.50	22.00
Custard cup	—	—	—
Mug, 4" h, 8 oz	—	8.50	—
Mustard, metal lid	—	—	—
Plate, 5-7/8" d, sherbet	—	—	—
Plate, 6-3/4" d, salad	9.00	6.00	10.00
Plate, 7-3/4" d, luncheon	—	—	—
Plate, 8-7/8" d, dinner	12.00	4.00	20.00
Platter, 11" l, oval	—	14.00	30.00
Platter, 12" l, oval	15.00	10.00	35.00
Salt and pepper shakers, pr	24.00	18.00	—
Sandwich plate, 10-1/2" d	20.00	12.50	—
Saucer	2.50	2.50	4.50
Sherbet	8.00	4.50	14.00
Soup bowl, 7-1/2" d	—	—	—
Sugar	8.00	7.50	20.00
Tumbler, 5 oz	—	—	—
Tumbler, 9 oz	12.00	—	—
Tumbler, 12 oz	—	—	—
Tumbler, cone, ftd	—	4.00	—
Whiskey, 1-1/2 oz	18.50	—	—

CHILDREN'S

Hazel Atlas also manufactured children's sets in the early 1950s, known as Little Hostess Party dishes. The original box adds to the value. Colorful combinations were found.

ITEM	GRAY/RUST/GOLD	GREEN/GRAY/CHARTREUSE	LEMON/BEIGE/PINK/AQUA
Creamer, 1-3/4"	17.50	16.00	15.00
Cup, 3/4"	15.00	12.00	20.00
Plate, 5-1/4" d	15.00	12.50	12.00
Saucer, 3-7/8" d	10.00	8.00	12.50
Sugar, 1-3/4"	12.00	15.00	20.00
Teapot, 3-1/2" d	125.00	115.00	95.00

ITEM	PASTEL PINK/GREEN/BLUE/YELLOW	PINK/BLACK/WHITE
Creamer, 1-3/4"	15.00	20.00
Cup, 3/4"	12.00	30.00
Plate, 5-1/4" d	12.00	15.00
Saucer, 3-7/8" d	8.00	15.00
Sugar, 1-3/4"	15.00	20.00
Teapot, 3-1/2" d	—	95.00

Children's Moderntone, darker shades of Platonite saucers: rust, $10; green, $8; and lemon yellow, $12.50.

*Moderntone, cobalt blue dinner plate, **$18**; salad plate, **$12**; sherbet (on pedestal), **$15**; cup, **$10**, and saucer, **$5**; cream soup bowl, **$22**.*

MONTICELLO
WAFFLE #698

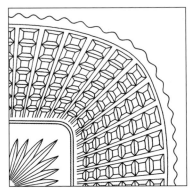

Manufactured by Imperial Glass Company, circa 1920 to the 1950s.

Pieces were made in crystal, Rubigold (Imperial's trademarked name for marigold carnival glass), teal, and white milk glass. Some other colors are known in very limited production runs, such as a basket in Rose Marie. Collector interest is highest for crystal.

ITEMS	CRYSTAL
Basket, 10" h	25.00
Bonbon, 5-1/2" d, handle	15.00
Bowl, 6" d	10.00
Bowl, 6-1/2" d or 7-1/2" d, belled	15.00
Bowl, 8-1/2" d or 10" d, belled	18.00
Bowl, 9" d	18.00
Bowl, 10" d	20.00
Butter tub, 5-1/2" d	35.00
Cake plate, 12" d	35.00
Celery tray, 9" l	20.00
Cheese dish, cov	75.00

Monticello, clear compote, stemmed, $15.

ITEMS	CRYSTAL
Coaster, 3-1/4" d	7.50
Cocktail	15.00
Compote, 5-1/4" d	12.50
Compote, 5-3/4" d, belled rim	15.00
Cream soup bowl, 5-1/2" d	12.50
Creamer	18.00
Cup	10.00
Finger bowl, 4-1/2" d	10.00
Fruit bowl, 4-1/2" d or 5" d	10.00
Goblet	15.00
Iced tea tumbler, 12 oz	15.00

ITEMS	CRYSTAL
Lily bowl, 5" d	20.00
Lily bowl, 6" d	25.00
Lily bowl, 7" d	30.00
Lily bowl, 8" d, cupped	35.00
Mayonnaise, 3 pcs	32.50
Nappy, 7" d	15.00
Pickle dish, 6" l, oval	12.00
Pitcher, 52 oz, ice lip	60.00
Plate, 6" d, bread and butter	5.00
Plate, 8" d, salad	8.00
Plate, 9" d, dinner	18.00
Plates, 10-1/2" w, sq	25.00
Punch bowl	65.00
Punch cup	8.50
Relish, 8-1/4" l, divided	18.00
Salad bowl, 7-1/2" sq	30.00
Salt and pepper shakers, pr, glass tops	24.00
Saucer	4.50
Serving plate, 16" d, cupped	50.00
Sherbet	13.00
Sugar	18.00
Tidbit, two tiers	45.00
Tumbler, 9 oz	12.00
Vase, 6" h	25.00
Vase, 10-1/2" h	35.00
Vegetable bowl, 8" d	25.00

MOONDROPS

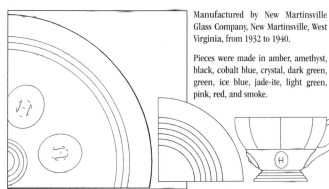

Manufactured by New Martinsville Glass Company, New Martinsville, West Virginia, from 1932 to 1940.

Pieces were made in amber, amethyst, black, cobalt blue, crystal, dark green, green, ice blue, jade-ite, light green, pink, red, and smoke.

ITEM	COBALT BLUE	CRYSTAL	OTHER COLORS	RED
Ashtray	30.00	—	18.00	30.00
Berry bowl, 5-1/4" d	20.00	—	12.00	20.00
Bowl, 8-1/2" d, ftd, concave top	40.00	—	25.00	40.00
Bowl, 9-1/2" d, three legs, ruffled	60.00	—	—	60.00
Bowl, 9-3/4" l, oval, handles	50.00	—	30.00	50.00
Butter dish, cov	150.00	150.00	275.00	295.00
Candlesticks, pr, 2" h, ruffled	40.00	—	25.00	40.00
Candlesticks, pr, 4" h, sherbet style	30.00	—	45.00	30.00
Candlesticks, pr, 5" h, ruffled	32.00	—	22.00	32.00
Candlesticks, pr, 5" h, wings	90.00	—	60.00	100.00
Candlesticks, pr, 5-1/4" h, triple light	100.00	65.00	65.00	100.00
Candlesticks, pr, 8-1/2" h, metal stem	40.00	—	32.00	40.00

Moondrops, pink saucer, $4; cup, $12.

ITEM	COBALT BLUE	CRYSTAL	OTHER COLORS	RED
Candy dish, 8" d, ruffled	40.00	—	20.00	40.00
Casserole, cov, 9-3/4" d	185.00	—	100.00	185.00
Celery bowl, 11" l, boat-shape	30.00	—	24.00	30.00
Cocktail shaker, metal top	60.00	—	35.00	60.00
Comport, 4" d	25.00	—	15.00	25.00
Comport, 11-1/2" d	60.00	—	30.00	60.00
Console bowl, 12" d, round, three ftd			40.00	
Console bowl, 13" d, wings	—	—	80.00	120.00
Cordial, 3/4 oz, 2-7/8" h	55.00	—	25.00	24.00
Cream soup bowl 4-1/4" d	90.00	—	35.00	90.00
Creamer, 2-3/4" h	15.00	—	10.00	20.00
Creamer, 3-3/4" h	12.00	—	12.00	16.00
Cup	16.00	10.00	12.00	18.00
Decanter, 7-3/4" h	70.00	—	40.00	70.00

Moondrops, red sugar, $20; creamer, $16.

ITEM	COBALT BLUE	CRYSTAL	OTHER COLORS	RED
Decanter, 8-1/2" h	72.00	—	45.00	72.00
Decanter, 10-1/4" h, rocket-shape	425.00	—	375.00	425.00
Decanter, 11-1/4" h	100.00	—	50.00	110.00
Goblet, 5 oz, 4-3/4" h	25.00	—	15.00	22.00
Goblet, 8 oz, 5-3/4" h	35.00	—	20.00	33.00
Goblet, 9 oz, 6-1/4" h, metal stem	15.00	—	17.50	15.00
Gravy boat	120.00	—	90.00	125.00
Juice tumbler, 3 oz, 3-1/4" h, ftd	15.00	—	10.00	15.00
Mayonnaise, 5-1/4" h	32.50	—	30.00	32.50
Mug, 12 oz, 5-1/8" h	40.00	—	24.00	42.00
Perfume bottle, rocket-shape	200.00	—	150.00	210.00
Pickle, 7-1/2" d	25.00	—	15.00	25.00
Pitcher, 22 oz, 6-7/8" h	175.00	—	90.00	175.00
Pitcher, 32 oz, 8-1/8" h	195.00	—	110.00	195.00
Pitcher, 50 oz, 8" h, lip	200.00	—	115.00	200.00
Pitcher, 53 oz, 8-1/8" h	195.00	—	120.00	195.00
Plate, 5-7/8" d	12.00	—	7.50	12.00
Plate, 6" d, round, off-center indent	12.50	—	10.00	12.50
Plate, 6-1/8" d, sherbet	8.00	—	6.00	8.00

ITEM	COBALT BLUE	CRYSTAL	OTHER COLORS	RED
Plate, 7-1/8" d, salad	12.00	—	10.00	12.00
Plate, 8-1/2" d, luncheon	17.50	—	12.00	15.00
Plate, 9-1/2" d, dinner	25.00	—	15.00	25.00
Platter, 12" l, oval	35.00	—	20.00	35.00
Powder jar, three ftd	175.00	—	100.00	185.00
Relish, 8-1/2" d, three ftd, divided	30.00	—	20.00	30.00
Sandwich plate, 14" d	40.00	—	20.00	40.00
Sandwich plate, 14" d, w handles	44.00	—	24.00	45.00
Saucer	6.00	2.00	4.00	6.50
Sherbet, 2-5/8" h	15.00	10.00	11.00	20.00
Sherbet, 3-1/2" h	25.00	—	15.00	25.00
Shot glass, 2 oz, 2-3/4" h	17.50	—	12.00	12.50
Shot glass, 2 oz, 2-3/4" h, handle	16.50	—	15.00	35.00
Soup bowl, 6-3/4" d	80.00	—	—	80.00
Sugar, 2-3/4" h	10.00	—	10.00	20.00
Tray, 7-1/2" l	15.00	—	20.00	16.00
Tumbler, 5 oz, 3-5/8" h	15.00	—	10.00	15.00
Tumbler, 7 oz, 4-3/8" h	17.50	—	10.00	18.00
Tumbler, 8 oz, 4-3/8" h	17.50	—	12.00	22.00
Tumbler, 9 oz, 4-7/8" h, handle	30.00	—	15.00	28.00
Tumbler, 9 oz, 4-7/8" h	20.00	—	15.00	19.00
Tumbler, 12 oz, 5-1/8" h	30.00	—	15.00	33.00
Vase, 7-1/4" h, flat, ruffled	60.00	—	60.00	60.00
Vase, 8-1/2" h, bud, rocket-shape	245.00	—	185.00	245.00
Vase, 9-1/4" h, rocket-shape	240.00	—	125.00	240.00
Vegetable bowl, 9-3/4" l, oval	48.00	—	24.00	48.00
Wine, 3 oz, 5-1/2" h, metal stem	17.50	—	10.00	20.00
Wine, 4-3/4" h, rocket-shape	27.50	—	30.00	85.00
Wine, 4 oz, 4" h	24.00	—	12.00	25.00
Wine, 4 oz, 5-1/2" h, metal stem	20.00	—	12.00	20.00

MOONSTONE

Manufactured by Anchor Hocking Glass Corp., Lancaster, Ohio, from 1941 to 1946.

Pieces were made in crystal with opalescent hobnails and ocean green with opalescent hobnails.

ITEM	CRYSTAL	OCEAN GREEN
Berry bowl, 5-1/2" d	25.00	—
Bonbon, heart shape, handle	18.00	13.50
Bowl, 6-1/2" d, crimped, handle	20.00	—
Bowl, 7-1/4" d, flat	15.00	—
Bowl, 9-1/2" d, crimped	30.00	—
Bud vase, 5-1/2" h	15.00	—
Candleholder, pr	20.00	—
Candy jar, cov, 6" h	30.00	—
Cigarette box, cov	25.00	—
Creamer	10.00	9.50
Cup	10.00	10.00
Dessert bowl, 5-1/2" d, crimped	22.50	—

ITEM	CRYSTAL	OCEAN GREEN
Goblet, 10 oz	28.00	24.00
Plate, 6-1/4" d, sherbet	5.00	9.00
Plate, 8-3/8" d, luncheon	12.50	17.50
Puff box, cov, 4-3/4" d, round	25.00	—
Relish, 7-1/4" d, divided	12.00	—
Relish, cloverleaf	20.00	—
Sandwich plate, 10-3/4" d	35.00	—
Saucer	6.00	6.00
Sherbet, ftd	10.00	7.00
Sugar, ftd	10.00	12.50
Vase, 6-1/2" h, ruffled	24.00	—

*Moonstone, crystal 4-3/4" puff box, covered, **$25**; cigarette box, covered, **$25**.*

*Moonstone, crystal 5-1/2" bud vase, **$15**; candleholders, pr, **$20**.*

MOROCCAN
AMETHYST

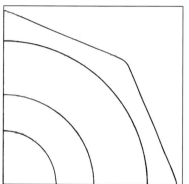

Manufactured by Hazel Ware, a division of Continental Can, in the 1960s.

Pieces were made in amethyst.

ITEM	AMETHYST
Ashtray, 3-1/4" d, round	5.75
Ashtray, 3-1/4" w, triangular	5.75
Ashtray, 6-7/8" w, triangular	12.50
Ashtray, 8" w, square	14.00
Bowl, 5-3/4" w, deep, square	12.00
Bowl, 6" d, round	18.00
Bowl, 7-3/4" l, oval	18.50
Bowl, 7-3/4" l, rectangular	18.00
Bowl, 7-3/4" l, rectangular, metal handle	24.50
Bowl, 10-3/4" d	30.00

ITEM	AMETHYST
Candy, cov, short	35.00
Candy, cov, tall	32.00
Chip and dip, 10-3/4" and 5-3/4" bowls in metal frame	40.00
Cocktail shaker, chrome lid	50.00
Cocktail, stirrer, 16 oz, 6-1/4" h, lip	35.00
Cup	7.50
Fruit bowl, 4-3/4" d, octagonal	8.50
Goblet, 9 oz, 5-1/2" h	12.50
Ice bucket, 6" h	35.00
Iced tea tumbler, 16 oz, 6-1/2" h	18.50
Juice goblet, 5-1/2 oz, 4-3/8" h	12.50
Juice tumbler, 4 oz, 2-1/2" h	8.00
Old fashioned tumbler, 8 oz, 3-1/4" h	15.00
Plate, 5-3/4" d, sherbet	4.50
Plate, 7-1/4" d, salad	4.75
Plate, 9-3/4" d, dinner	6.00
Punch bowl	85.00
Punch cup	6.00
Relish, 7-3/4" l	18.00
Salad fork and spoon	12.00
Sandwich plate, 12" d, metal handle	15.00
Saucer	1.00
Sherbet, 7-1/2 oz, 4-1/4" h	8.00
Snack plate, 10" l, fan shaped, cup rest	7.00
Snack set, square plate, cup	12.00
Tidbit, three tiers	75.00
Tumbler, 9 oz	12.50
Tumbler, 11 oz, 4-1/4" h, crinkled bottom	12.00
Tumbler, 11 oz, 4-5/8" h	12.00
Vase, 8-1/2" h, ruffled	25.00
Wine, 4-1/2 oz, 4" h	7.50

Moroccan, amethyst cocktail stirrer, $35.

Moroccan, amethyst cup, $7.50; saucer, $1.

MT. PLEASANT
DOUBLE SHIELD

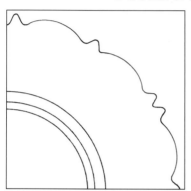

Manufactured by L. E. Smith, Mt. Pleasant, Pennsylvania, from the 1920s to 1934.

Pieces were made in amethyst, black, cobalt blue, crystal, green, pink, and white.

ITEM	AMETHYST	BLACK	COBALT BLUE	GREEN	PINK
Bonbon, 7" d, rolled edge	24.00	24.50	24.00	16.00	16.00
Bowl, 6" d, three legs	—	22.00	—	—	—
Bowl, 6" w, sq, two handles	27.50	18.00	24.00	15.00	15.00
Bowl, 7" d, three ftd, rolled out edge	18.50	24.50	18.50	17.50	17.50
Bowl, 8" d, scalloped, two handles	37.50	35.00	37.50	20.00	20.00
Bowl, 8" d, sq, two handles	38.00	40.00	38.00	20.00	20.00
Bowl, 9" d, scalloped, 1-3/4" deep, ftd	28.00	32.00	30.00	—	—
Bowl, 10" d, two handles, turned-up edge	30.00	34.00	32.00	—	—

Mt. Pleasant, black scalloped fruit bowl, $40.

ITEM	AMETHYST	BLACK	COBALT BLUE	GREEN	PINK
Cake plate, 10-1/2" d, 1-1/4" h, ftd	45.00	47.00	40.00	—	—
Cake plate, 10-1/2" d, two handles	26.00	40.00	28.00	17.50	17.50
Candlesticks, pr, single lite	28.00	42.50	30.00	24.00	28.00
Candlesticks, pr, two lite	48.00	48.00	50.00	30.00	32.00
Creamer	21.00	15.00	22.50	20.00	24.00
Cup	15.00	12.00	12.00	12.50	12.50
Fruit bowl, 4-7/8" sq	16.00	20.00	30.00	12.00	12.50
Fruit bowl, 9-1/4" sq	30.00	50.00	35.00	20.00	20.00
Fruit bowl, 10" d, scalloped	40.00	40.00	40.00	—	—
Leaf, 8" l	12.50	17.50	22.00	—	—
Leaf, 11-1/4" l	25.00	30.00	28.00	—	—

ITEM	AMETHYST	BLACK	COBALT BLUE	GREEN	PINK
Mayonnaise, 5-1/2" h, three ftd	25.00	25.00	25.00	17.50	17.50
Mint, 6" d, center handle	25.00	26.50	25.00	16.00	16.00
Plate, 7" h, two handles, scalloped	15.00	16.00	16.50	12.50	12.50
Plate, 8" d, scalloped	16.00	15.00	16.00	12.50	12.50
Plate, 8" d, scalloped, three ftd	17.50	27.00	17.50	12.50	12.50
Plate, 8" w, sq	17.50	25.00	17.50	12.50	12.50
Plate, 8-1/4" w, sq, indent for cup	17.50	19.00	17.50	—	—
Plate, 9" d, grill	20.00	20.00	20.00	—	—
Plate, 12" d, two handles	20.00	35.00	35.00	20.00	20.00
Rose bowl, 4" d	25.00	30.00	27.50	20.00	20.00
Salt and pepper shakers, pr	50.00	50.00	45.00	25.00	25.00
Sandwich server, center handle	35.00	37.50	40.00	—	—
Saucer	5.00	5.00	3.00	3.50	3.50
Sherbet	15.00	16.50	20.00	12.50	12.50
Sugar	9.00	20.00	15.00	20.00	20.00
Tumbler, ftd	25.00	27.50	25.00	—	—
Vase, 7-1/4" h	30.00	35.00	40.00	—	35.00

Mt. Pleasant, black creamer, $15; sugar (on pedestal), $20; scalloped bowl with two handles, $35; cup, $12.

NATIONAL

Manufactured by Jeannette Glass Company, Jeannette, Pennsylvania, from the late 1940s to the mid 1950s.

Pieces were made in crystal, pink, and shell pink. Collector interest is primarily with crystal. Prices for pink and shell pink are not yet firmly established but usually command slightly higher prices than crystal.

ITEM	CRYSTAL
Ashtray	4.50
Berry bowl, 4-1/2" d	4.00
Berry bowl, 8-1/2" d	8.00
Bowl, 12" d	w15.00
Candleholders, pr	25.00
Candy dish, cov, ftd	20.00
Cigarette box	15.00
Creamer	6.50
Creamer and sugar tray	6.00
Cup	4.00
Jar, cov	15.00
Lazy Susan	40.00

ITEM	CRYSTAL
Milk pitcher, 20 oz	25.00
Plate, 8" d	6.50
Punch bowl stand	10.00
Punch bowl, 12" d	25.00
Punch cup	3.50
Relish, three parts	15.00
Salt and pepper shakers, pr	10.00
Saucer	1.00
Serving plate, 15" d	17.50
Tray, two handles	17.50
Tumbler, ftd	8.50
Vase, 9"	20.00
Water pitcher, 64 oz	30.00

National, crystal candleholders, $25.

National, crystal tray with two handles, $17.50.

NEW CENTURY

Manufactured by Hazel Atlas Company, Clarksburg, West Virginia, and Zanesville, Ohio, from 1930 to 1935.

Pieces were made in crystal and green with limited production in amethyst, cobalt blue, and pink.

ITEM	AMETHYST	COBALT BLUE	CRYSTAL	GREEN	PINK
Ashtray/coaster, 5-3/8" d	—	—	15.00	30.00	—
Berry bowl, 4-1/2" d	—	—	35.00	35.00	—
Berry bowl, 8" d	—	—	30.00	30.00	—
Butter dish, cov	—	—	75.00	75.00	—
Casserole, cov, 9" d	—	—	115.00	115.00	—
Cocktail, 3-1/4 oz	—	—	42.00	42.00	—
Cream soup bowl 4-3/4" d	—	—	25.00	25.00	—
Creamer	—	—	12.00	14.00	—
Cup	20.00	20.00	10.00	12.00	20.00
Decanter, stopper	—	—	90.00	90.00	—
Pitcher, with or without ice lip, 60 oz	55.00	55.00	45.00	48.00	35.00

ITEM	AMETHYST	COBALT BLUE	CRYSTAL	GREEN	PINK
Pitcher, with or without ice lip, 80 oz	55.00	55.00	35.00	48.00	50.00
Plate, 6" d, sherbet	—	—	5.50	6.50	—
Plate, 7-1/8" d, breakfast	—	—	12.00	12.00	—
Plate, 8-1/2" d, salad	—	—	12.00	12.00	—
Plate, 10" d, dinner	—	—	24.00	24.00	—
Plate, 10" d, grill	—	—	15.00	18.00	—
Platter, 11" l, oval	—	—	30.00	30.00	—
Salt and pepper shakers, pr	—	—	45.00	45.00	—
Saucer	7.50	7.50	5.00	6.50	8.00
Sherbet, 3" h	—	—	9.00	12.00	—
Sugar, cov	—	—	40.00	35.00	—
Tumbler, 5 oz, 3-1/2" h	12.00	16.50	15.00	18.00	18.00

New Century, green salt and pepper shakers, $45.

ITEM	AMETHYST	COBALT BLUE	CRYSTAL	GREEN	PINK
Tumbler, 5 oz, 4" h, ftd	—	—	30.00	32.50	—
Tumbler, 8 oz, 3-1/2" h	—	—	25.00	27.50	—
Tumbler, 9 oz, 4-1/4" h	15.00	24.00	18.00	20.00	15.00
Tumbler, 9 oz, 4-7/8" h, ftd	—	—	25.00	25.00	—
Tumbler, 10 oz, 5" h	30.00	20.00	30.00	27.50	20.00
Tumbler, 12 oz, 5-1/4" h	35.00	30.00	32.50	35.00	20.00
Whiskey, 2-1/2" h, 1-1/2 oz	—	—	18.00	20.00	—
Wine, 2-1/2 oz	—	—	35.00	40.00	—

New Century, green dinner plate, **$24.**

NEWPORT

HAIRPIN

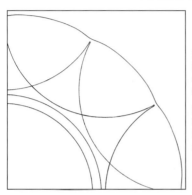

Manufactured by Hazel Atlas Glass Company, Clarksburg, West Virginia, and Zanesville, Ohio, from 1936 to the early 1950s.

Pieces were made in amethyst, cobalt blue, pink (from 1936 to 1940), Platonite white, and fired-on colors (from the 1940s to early 1950s).

ITEM	AMETHYST	COBALT BLUE	FIRED-ON COLOR	PINK	PLATONITE
Berry bowl, 4-3/4" d	20.00	25.00	9.00	12.50	5.00
Berry bowl, 8-1/4" d	50.00	50.00	16.00	25.00	10.00
Cereal bowl, 5-1/4" d	35.00	45.00	—	20.00	—
Cream soup bowl 4-3/4" d	15.00	20.00	10.00	17.50	8.50
Creamer	20.00	22.00	8.50	10.00	3.00
Cup	12.00	15.00	9.00	6.00	4.50

ITEM	AMETHYST	COBALT BLUE	FIRED-ON COLOR	PINK	PLATONITE
Plate, 6" d, sherbet	7.50	10.00	5.00	3.50	2.00
Plate, 8-1/2" d, luncheon	15.00	22.00	8.00	8.00	4.50
Plate, 8-13/16" d, dinner	32.00	35.00	15.00	15.00	12.00
Platter, 11-3/4" l, oval	35.00	48.00	18.00	20.00	12.00

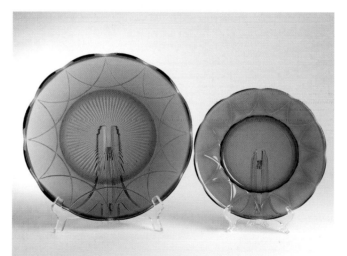

Newport, cobalt blue 11-1/2" d cupped edge round sandwich plate, $50; 8-1/2" d luncheon plate, $22.

Newport, cobalt blue 5-1/4" cereal bowl, $45; sherbet, $15.

ITEM	AMETHYST	COBALT BLUE	FIRED-ON COLOR	PINK	PLATONITE
Salt and pepper shakers, pr	70.00	65.00	32.00	30.00	30.00
Sandwich plate, 11-1/2" d	48.00	50.00	15.00	24.00	10.00
Saucer	5.25	6.00	3.00	2.50	2.00
Sherbet	15.00	15.00	10.00	8.00	4.00
Sugar	18.00	22.00	9.50	10.00	5.00
Tumbler, 9 oz, 4-1/2" h	40.00	48.00	15.00	20.00	—

NORMANDIE
BOUQUET AND LATTICE

Manufactured by Federal Glass Company, Columbus, Ohio, from 1933 to 1940.

Pieces were made in amber, crystal, iridescent, and pink.

ITEM	AMBER	CRYSTAL	IRIDESCENT	PINK
Berry bowl, 5" d	9.50	6.00	4.50	12.00
Berry bowl, 8-1/2" d	35.00	24.00	26.00	80.00
Cereal bowl, 6-1/2" d	12.00	20.00	8.00	35.00
Creamer, ftd	10.00	10.00	8.00	20.00
Cup	6.00	4.00	5.00	10.00
Iced tea tumbler, 12 oz, 5" h	40.00	—	—	—
Juice tumbler, 5 oz, 4" h	38.00	—	—	—
Pitcher, 80 oz, 8" h	80.00	—	—	245.00
Plate, 6" d, sherbet	4.50	2.00	3.50	5.00
Plate, 7-3/4" d, salad	10.00	5.00	55.00	18.00
Plate, 9-1/4" d, luncheon	12.50	6.00	16.50	100.00

ITEM	AMBER	CRYSTAL	IRIDESCENT	PINK
Plate, 11" d, dinner	32.00	15.00	25.00	18.00
Plate, 11" d, grill	15.00	8.00	12.00	25.00
Platter, 11-3/4" l	35.00	10.00	12.00	80.00
Salt and pepper shakers, pr	40.00	20.00	—	4.00
Saucer	4.00	1.50	3.50	10.00
Sherbet	7.50	6.50	9.00	10.00
Sugar	8.00	6.00	7.00	20.00
Tumbler, 9 oz, 4-1/4" h	25.00	10.00	—	70.00
Vegetable bowl, 10" l, oval	27.50	12.00	25.00	45.00

Normandie, iridescent cup, $5.

Normandie, iridescent dinner plate, $25.

OLD CAFÉ

Manufactured by Hocking Glass Company, Lancaster, Ohio, from 1936 to 1940.

Pieces were made in crystal, pink, and royal ruby.

ITEM	CRYSTAL	PINK	ROYAL RUBY
Berry bowl, 3-3/4" d	9.50	14.00	9.00
Bowl, 6-1/2" d	15.00	18.00	—
Bowl, 9" d, closed handles	10.00	10.00	15.00
Candy dish, 8" d, low	12.00	15.00	12.00
Candy jar, 5-1/2" d, crystal with ruby cover	25.00	32.00	25.00
Cereal bowl, 5-1/2" d	30.00	30.00	30.00
Cup	12.00	10.00	15.00
Juice tumbler, 3" h	18.00	18.00	22.00
Lamp	100.00	100.00	150.00
Olive dish, 6" l, oblong	7.50	14.50	—
Pitcher, 36 oz, 6" h	125.00	145.00	—
Pitcher, 80 oz	150.00	165.00	—

Old Café, royal ruby bowl with handles and original label, $15.

ITEM	CRYSTAL	PINK	ROYAL RUBY
Plate, 6" d, sherbet	5.00	5.00	—
Plate, 10" d, dinner	60.00	45.00	—
Relish, 5-1/2" d, metal handle	18.00	—	—
Saucer	5.00	5.00	—
Sherbet, low, ftd	15.00	16.00	12.00
Tumbler, 4" h, 9 oz	18.00	22.00	18.00
Vase, 7-1/4" h	40.00	45.00	50.00

Old Café, pink candy jar with ruby cover, $32.

OLD COLONY
LACE EDGE, OPEN LACE

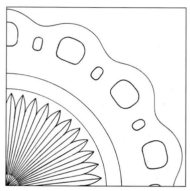

Manufactured by Hocking Glass Company, Lancaster, Ohio, from 1935 to 1938.

Pieces were made in crystal and pink. Crystal Old Colony pieces are valued at about 50 percent of pink, as are frosted or satin finish prices. Many other companies made a look-alike to Old Colony, so care must be exercised.

ITEM	PINK
Bonbon, cov	65.00
Bowl, 9-1/2" d, plain	30.00
Bowl, 9-1/2" d, ribbed	38.00
Butter dish, cov	55.00
Candlesticks, pr	350.00
Candy jar, cov, ribbed	65.00
Cereal bowl, 6-3/8" d	24.00
Comport, 7" d, cov	60.00
Comport, 9" d	950.00
Console bowl, 10-1/2" d, three legs	325.00
Cookie jar, cov	75.00

*Old Colony, pink 12-3/4" l platter, five parts, **$45.***

ITEM	PINK
Creamer	30.00
Cup	24.00
Flower bowl, crystal frog	30.00
Plate, 7-1/4" d, salad	24.50
Plate, 8-1/4" d, luncheon	28.00
Plate, 10-1/2" d, dinner	35.00
Plate, 10-1/2" d, grill	20.00
Plate, 13" d, four parts, solid lace	65.00
Plate, 13" d, solid lace	65.00
Platter, 12-3/4" l	45.00
Platter, 12-3/4" l, five parts	45.00

ITEM	PINK
Relish dish, 7-1/2" d, three parts, deep	60.00
Relish plate, 10-1/2" d, three parts	20.00
Salad bowl, 7-3/4" d, ribbed	60.00
Saucer	15.00
Sherbet, ftd	90.00
Sugar	25.00
Tumbler, 5 oz, 3-1/2" h, flat	120.00
Tumbler, 9 oz, 4-1/2" h, flat	22.00
Tumbler, 10-1/2 oz, 5" h, ftd	75.00
Vase, 7" h	650.00

Old Colony, pink 9-1/2" d bowl, ribbed, $38.

OLD ENGLISH
THREADING

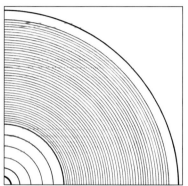

Manufactured by Indiana Glass Company, Dunkirk, Indiana, in the late 1920s.

Pieces were made in amber, crystal, green, and pink.

ITEM	AMBER	CRYSTAL	GREEN	PINK
Bowl, 4" d, flat	20.00	18.00	22.00	20.00
Bowl, 9-1/2" d, flat	35.00	25.00	35.00	35.00
Candlesticks, pr, 4" h	35.00	25.00	35.00	35.00
Candy dish, cov, flat	50.00	40.00	50.00	50.00
Candy jar, cov	55.00	45.00	55.00	55.00
Cheese compote, 3-1/2" h	17.50	12.00	17.50	17.50
Cheese plate, indent	20.00	10.00	20.00	20.00
Compote, 3-1/2" h, 6-3/8" w, two handles	24.00	12.00	24.00	24.00
Compote, 3-1/2" h, 7" w	24.00	12.00	24.00	24.00
Creamer	18.00	10.00	18.00	18.00
Egg cup	—	10.00	—	—

ITEM	AMBER	CRYSTAL	GREEN	PINK
Fruit bowl, 9" d, ftd	30.00	20.00	30.00	30.00
Fruit stand, 11" h, ftd	40.00	18.00	40.00	40.00
Goblet, 8 oz, 5-3/4" h	30.00	15.00	30.00	30.00
Pitcher	70.00	35.00	90.00	70.00
Pitcher, cov	125.00	55.00	125.00	125.00
Sandwich server, center handle	60.00	—	60.00	60.00
Sherbet	20.00	10.00	20.00	20.00
Sugar, cov	38.00	14.00	38.00	38.00
Tumbler, 4-1/2" h, ftd	18.00	12.00	28.00	24.00
Tumbler, 5-1/2" h, ftd	40.00	20.00	40.00	40.00
Vase, 5-3/8" h, 7" w, fan-shape	48.00	24.00	48.00	48.00
Vase, 8" h, 4-1/2" w, ftd	45.00	20.00	45.00	45.00
Vase, 8-1/4" h, 4-1/4" w, ftd	45.00	20.00	45.00	45.00
Vase, 12" h, ftd	72.00	35.00	72.00	72.00

Old English, green compote, $24.

Old English, green with silver edge 6-3/8" d cover for candy jar, keyhole finial, $30.

ORANGE BLOSSOM

Manufactured by Indiana Glass Company, Dunkirk, Indiana, in 1957. This pattern was originally made in a custard color in the 1930s. That pattern is known as Indiana Custard.

Made in milk white. Some plates have a decaled Currier and Ives—type scene in the center.

ITEM	MILK WHITE
Creamer, ftd	5.00
Cup	9.50
Dessert bowl, 5-1/2″ d	5.00
Plate, 5-3/8″ d, sherbet	3.50
Plate, 8-7/8″ d, lunch	8.50
Saucer	2.00
Sugar, ftd	5.00

Orange Blossom, milk white creamer, $5.

Orange Blossom, milk white open sugar, $5.

OVIDE

Manufactured by Hazel Atlas Glass Company, Clarksburg, West Virginia, and Zanesville, Ohio, from 1930-1935 and in the 1950s.

Pieces were made in black, green, and white Platonite with fired-on colors in the 1950s.

Ovide, green eggcup, $12; sherbet, $5.50.

ITEM	BLACK	GREEN	PLATONITE
Berry bowl, 4-3/4" d	—	7.50	10.00
Berry bowl, 8" d	—	—	22.00
Candy dish, cov	45.00	24.00	35.00
Cereal bowl, 5-1/2" d	8.00	—	9.00
Creamer	7.50	6.50	9.00
Cup	6.50	4.50	9.00
Eggcup	—	12.00	22.00
Fruit cocktail, ftd	5.00	4.50	—
Plate, 6" d, sherbet	—	2.50	5.00
Plate, 8" d, luncheon	—	4.50	12.00
Plate, 9" d, dinner	—	—	12.00
Platter, 11" d	—	—	24.00
Salt and pepper shakers, pr	28.00	28.00	25.00
Saucer	3.50	4.50	6.00
Sherbet	6.50	5.50	6.00
Sugar, open	9.00	7.00	20.00
Tumbler	18.00	—	12.00

Ovide, pink and gray Platonite luncheon plate, $12.

OYSTER & PEARL

Manufactured by Anchor Hocking Glass Corp. from 1938 to 1940.

Pieces were made in crystal, pink, royal ruby, and white with fired-on green or pink.

ITEM	CRYSTAL	PINK	ROYAL RUBY	WHITE, FIRED-ON GREEN	WHITE, FIRED-ON PINK
Bowl, 5-1/2" d, handle	8.00	15.00	38.00	10.00	—
Bowl, 5-1/4" w, handle, heart-shape	12.00	20.00	—	15.00	—
Bowl, 6-1/2" d, handle	12.00	12.00	28.00	—	—
Candleholders, pr, 3-1/2" h	35.00	45.00	60.00	25.00	25.00
Fruit bowl, 10-1/2" d, deep	20.00	38.00	60.00	30.00	28.00
Relish dish, 10-1/4" l, divided	10.00	27.00	—	—	—
Sandwich plate, 13-1/2" d	20.00	40.00	50.00	—	

Oyster and Pearl, ruby sandwich plate, $50.

Oyster and Pearl, royal ruby candlestick, $30; pink candlestick, $22.50.

PANELED GRAPE
PATTERN #188

Manufactured by Westmoreland Glass Company from 1950 to the 1970s.

Pieces were made in milk white glass. Some pieces were decorated. A limited production in mint green occurred in 1979. Decorated pieces are usually valued the same as the white pieces, providing the painted decoration is in very good condition. The resale market on green is very limited at the present time.

ITEM	MILK WHITE
Appetizer set, three pcs	60.00
Banana bowl, 12" d, ftd	175.00
Basket, 5-1/2", ruffled	50.00
Basket, 6-1/2", oval	24.50
Basket, 8"	110.00
Bowl, 4" d, crimped	22.00
Bowl, 6" d, crimped, stemmed	30.00
Bowl, 6" d, ruffled, stemmed	30.00
Bowl, 6-1/2" d, oval	30.00
Bowl, 8" d, cupped	40.00
Bowl, 9" d, ftd, skirted base	50.00
Bowl, 9-1/2" d, bell shape	45.00

ITEM	MILK WHITE
Bowl, 9-1/2" d, bell shape, ftd	90.00
Bowl, 10-1/2" d	70.00
Bowl, 11" l, oval, ftd	125.00
Bowl, 12" d, flat	120.00
Bowl, 12" d, ftd	125.00
Bowl, cov, 9" d, ftd	75.00
Bowl, cov, 9" w, sq	85.00
Bud vase, 10" h	30.00
Butter, cov, 1/4 pound	25.00
Cake plate, 10-1/2" d	65.00
Cake plate, 11" d, ftd, skirt	65.00
Candelabra, pr, three-lite	195.00
Candleholder, 4", octagonal	15.00
Candleholder, 5" h, handle	40.00
Candleholder, 9" h, two-lite	30.00
Candy jar, cov, 6-1/4"	40.00
Canister, cov, 7" h	175.00
Canister, cov, 9-1/2" h	185.00
Canister, cov, 11" h	195.00
Celery vase, 6-1/2" h	40.00
Cheese, cov, 7" d	60.00
Chocolate box, cov, 6-1/2" l	55.00
Chop plate, 14" d	125.00
Cigarette lighter, goblet or toothpick shape	25.00
Cologne, gold trim	50.00
Compote, cov, 7" d, ftd	35.00
Compote, cov, 9" d, ftd, crimped	48.00
Compote, open, 4-1/2" d, crimped	30.00
Condiment set, five pcs	130.00
Cordial, 2 oz	20.00
Creamer, individual	12.00
Creamer, table	15.00

ITEM	MILK WHITE
Creamer, tall	30.00
Cruet, stopper	20.00
Cup, flared	15.00
Decanter	120.00
Dresser set, four pcs	215.00
Egg plate, 10" d, center handle	75.00
Egg plate, 12" d	70.00
Epergne, 8-1/2" h	60.00
Epergne, 9" d bowl, two pcs	175.00
Flower pot	45.00
Fruit cocktail, 3-1/2" or 4-1/2"	18.00
Goblet, 8 oz	25.00
Iced tea tumbler, 12 oz	28.00
Ivy ball	65.00
Jardinière, 5", cupped or straight, ftd	25.00
Jardinière, 6-1/2" h, cupped or straight, ftd	35.00
Jelly, cov, 4-1/2" d	25.00
Juice tumbler, 5 oz	24.00
Ladle	10.00
Marmalade	55.00
Mayonnaise, 4" d, ftd	35.00
Napkin ring	12.00
Nappy, 4-1/2" d	20.00
Nappy, 5" d, bell shape	22.00
Nappy, 5" d, round, handle	24.00
Nappy, 7" d	26.00
Nappy, 8-1/2" d	28.00
Nappy, 9" d	30.00
Nappy, 10" d	35.00
Oil or vinegar bottle, stopper	40.00
Old fashioned tumbler, 6 oz	28.00
Parfait, 6" h	25.00

Paneled Grape, milk white dinner plate, $40.

ITEM	MILK WHITE
Pickle dish, oval	20.00
Pitcher, 16 oz	20.00
Pitcher, 32 oz	45.00
Planter, 3" x 8-1/2"	35.00
Planter, 4-1/2" x 4-1/2"	38.00
Planter, 5" x 9"	38.00
Plate, 6" d, bread and butter	8.00
Plate, 7" d, salad	25.00
Plate, 8-1/2" d, luncheon	25.00
Plate, 10-1/2" d, dinner	40.00
Puff box, cov	35.00
Punch bowl, 13" d, bell or flared	300.00

ITEM	MILK WHITE
Punch cup	15.00
Punch ladle	85.00
Relish, three parts, 9" l	40.00
Rose bowl, 4" d	20.00
Rose bowl, 4-1/2" d, cupped, ftd	35.00
Salt and pepper shakers, pr, ftd, three sizes	35.00
Sauce boat	40.00
Sauce boat underplate	20.00
Saucer	8.50
Serving plate, 18" d	165.00
Sherbet, 3-3/4" h	15.00
Sherbet, 4-3/4" h	17.50
Soap dish	100.00
Spooner, 6" h	40.00
Sugar, cov, individual	15.00
Sugar, cov, large	25.00
Sugar, cov, table	20.00
Sugar, open, 4-1/4"	15.00
Tidbit tray, metal handle, 8-1/2" d	30.00
Tidbit tray, metal handle, 10-1/2" d	65.00
Toothpick holder	25.00
Tray, 9" l, oval	55.00
Tray, 13-1/2" l, oval	90.00
Tumbler, 8 oz	20.00
Vase, 6" h, bell shape	20.00
Vase, 8-1/2" h or 9" h, bell shape	30.00
Vase, 9-1/2" h, straight sides	30.00
Vase, 11-1/2" h, bell or straight sides	35.00
Vase, 14" h, 16" h, 18" h, swung	30.00
Wall pocket, 6"	85.00
Wall pocket, 8"	95.00
Wine, 3 oz	20.00

PARK AVENUE

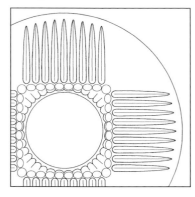

Manufactured by Federal Glass Company, Columbus, Ohio, from 1941 to the early 1970s.

Made in amber, crystal, and crystal with gold trim. Values for crystal and crystal with gold trim are the same.

ITEM	AMBER	CRYSTAL
Ashtray, 3-1/2" sq	—	5.00
Ashtray, 4-1/2" sq	—	6.50
Candleholder, pr, 5" d	—	9.00
Dessert bowl, 5" d	6.50	3.00
Iced tea tumbler, 12 oz	12.00	6.50
Juice tumbler, 4-1/2 oz	5.00	5.00
Tumbler, 9 oz	8.00	6.00
Tumbler, 10 oz	9.00	6.00
Vegetable bowl, 8-1/2" d	18.00	10.00
Whiskey tumbler, 1-1/4 oz	—	4.50

Park Avenue, crystal juice tumbler with gold band, $5.

PARROT

SYLVAN

Manufactured by Federal Glass Company, Columbus, Ohio, from 1931 to 1932.

Pieces were made in amber and green, with limited production in blue and crystal.

ITEM	AMBER	GREEN
Berry bowl, 5" d	42.00	30.00
Berry bowl, 8" d	75.00	80.00
Butter dish, cov	1,250.00	475.00
Creamer, ftd	65.00	65.00
Cup	35.00	25.00
Hot plate, 5" d, pointed	875.00	900.00
Hot plate, round	—	950.00
Jam dish, 7" d	35.00	—
Pitcher, 80 oz, 8-1/2" h	—	2,500.00
Plate, 5-3/4" d, sherbet	24.00	35.00
Plate, 7-1/2" d, salad	—	35.00

ITEM	AMBER	GREEN
Plate, 9" d, dinner	50.00	50.00
Plate, 10-1/2" d, grill, round	35.00	—
Plate, 10-1/2" d, grill, square	—	30.00
Platter, 11-1/4" l, oblong	65.00	60.00
Salt and pepper shakers, pr	—	270.00
Saucer	18.00	18.00
Sherbet, ftd, cone	25.00	27.50
Soup bowl, 7" d	35.00	45.00
Sugar, cov	450.00	265.00
Tumbler, 10 oz, 4-1/4" h	100.00	130.00
Tumbler, 10 oz, 5-1/2" h, ftd, Madrid mold	145.00	—
Tumbler, 12 oz, 5-1/2" h	115.00	160.00
Tumbler, 5-3/4" h, ftd, heavy	100.00	120.00
Vegetable bowl, 10" l, oval	75.00	65.00

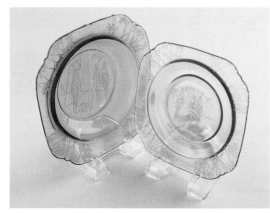

Parrot, amber jam dish, $35; green sherbet plate, $35.

PATRICIAN

SPOKE

Manufactured by Federal Glass Company, Columbus, Ohio, from 1933 to 1937.

Pieces were made in amber (also called Golden Glo), crystal, green, and pink.

ITEM	AMBER	CRYSTAL	GREEN	PINK
Berry bowl, 5" d	12.50	10.00	12.50	18.50
Berry bowl, 8-1/2" d	35.00	15.00	35.00	45.00
Butter dish, cov	115.00	100.00	145.00	225.00
Cereal bowl, 6" d	32.00	27.50	27.50	25.00
Cookie jar, cov	70.00	80.00	485.00	—
Cream soup bowl, 4-3/4" d	18.00	28.00	18.00	18.00
Creamer, ftd	12.50	9.00	12.00	12.50
Cup	8.00	12.00	9.00	12.50
Jam dish	30.00	25.00	35.00	30.00
Mayonnaise, three toes	—	—	—	165.00
Pitcher, 75 oz, 8" h, molded handle	110.00	95.00	125.00	115.00
Pitcher, 75 oz, 8-1/4" h, applied handle	150.00	140.00	150.00	145.00

Patrician, amber salt and pepper shakers, **$45.**

Patrician, amber 5" bowl, $12.50; 8-1/2" bowl, $35.

ITEM	AMBER	CRYSTAL	GREEN	PINK
Plate, 6" d, sherbet	10.00	8.50	10.00	10.00
Plate, 7-1/2" d, salad	12.50	15.00	20.00	15.00
Plate, 9" d, luncheon	15.00	12.50	12.00	12.50
Plate, 10-1/2" d, grill	15.00	13.50	20.00	20.00
Plate, 10-1/2 d, dinner	10.00	12.75	32.00	36.00
Platter, 11-1/2" l, oval	38.00	30.00	30.00	28.00
Salt and pepper shakers, pr	45.00	65.00	75.00	85.00
Saucer	4.00	9.25	9.50	9.50
Sherbet	12.00	10.00	12.00	16.00
Sugar	14.00	9.00	12.50	12.50
Sugar lid	55.00	50.00	75.00	60.00
Tumbler, 5 oz, 4" h	40.00	28.50	30.00	32.00
Tumbler, 8 oz, 5-1/4" h, ftd	40.00	42.00	50.00	—
Tumbler, 9 oz, 4-1/4" h	25.00	28.50	25.00	38.00
Tumbler, 12 oz	45.00	—	—	—
Tumbler, 14 oz, 5-1/2" h	45.00	40.00	50.00	48.00
Vegetable bowl, 10" l, oval	35.00	30.00	35.00	30.00

*Patrician, amber pitcher, molded handle, 8" h, 75 oz, **$110**.*

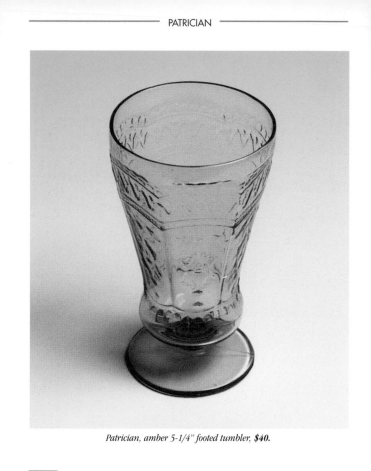

Patrician, amber 5-1/4" footed tumbler, $40.

PATRICK

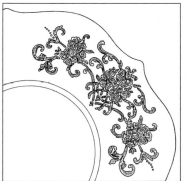

Manufactured by Lancaster Glass Company, Lancaster, Ohio, in the early 1930s.

Pieces were made in pink and yellow.

ITEM	PINK	YELLOW
Candlesticks, pr	200.00	160.00
Candy dish, three ftd	175.00	175.00
Cheese and cracker set	150.00	130.00
Cocktail, 4" h	85.00	85.00
Console bowl, 11" d	150.00	150.00
Creamer	75.00	40.00
Cup	70.00	40.00
Fruit bowl, 9" d, handle	175.00	130.00
Goblet, 10 oz, 6" h	85.00	75.00
Juice goblet, 6 oz, 4-3/4" h	85.00	75.00
Mayonnaise, three pieces	200.00	140.00
Plate, 7" d, sherbet	20.00	15.00
Plate, 7-1/2" d, salad	25.00	20.00

ITEM	PINK	YELLOW
Plate, 8" d, luncheon	45.00	30.00
Saucer	20.00	12.00
Sherbet, 4-3/4" d	72.00	60.00
Sugar	75.00	40.00
Tray, 11" d, center handle	165.00	120.00
Tray, 11" d, two handles	80.00	65.00

Patrick, yellow tray with caned center and two handles, $65.

PEACOCK & WILD ROSE
LINE #1300

Manufactured by Paden City Glass Company, Padenww City, West Virginia, in the 1930s.

Pieces were made in amber, black, cobalt blue, crystal, green, light blue, pink and red. A black 6-1/4-inch vase is valued at $100; a black 10-inch vase is valued at $165.

ITEM	AMBER, COBALT BLUE, CRYSTAL LIGHT BLUE, RED	GREEN	PINK
Bowl, 8-1/2" d, flat	110.00	175.00	185.00
Bowl, 8-3/4" d, ftd	115.00	125.00	135.00
Bowl, 9-1/2" d, center handle	175.00	185.00	195.00
Bowl, 9-1/2" d, ftd	85.00	95.00	95.00
Bowl, 10-1/2" d, center handle	85.00	115.00	195.00
Bowl, 10-1/2" d, ftd	95.00	165.00	195.00
Cake plate, low foot	195.00	195.00	100.00
Candlesticks, pr, 5" h	145.00	165.00	165.00
Candy dish, cov, 7"	250.00	250.00	250.00

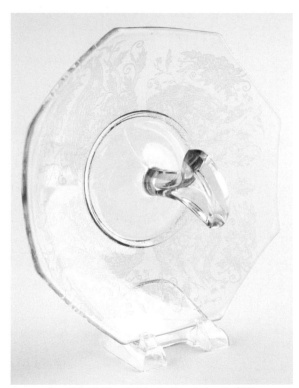

Peacock & Wild Rose, pink bowl with center handle, $195.

ITEM	AMBER, COBALT BLUE, CRYSTAL LIGHT BLUE, RED	GREEN	PINK
Cheese and cracker set	195.00	225.00	225.00
Comport, 3-1/4" h, 6-1/4" w	75.00	100.00	115.00
Console bowl, 11" d	165.00	175.00	175.00
Console bowl, 14" d	80.00	120.00	120.00
Fruit bowl, 8-1/2" l, oval, ftd	165.00	175.00	185.00
Fruit bowl, 10-1/2" d	175.00	185.00	185.00
Ice bucket	175.00	175.00	200.00
Ice Tub, 4-3/4"	185.00	195.00	195.00
Mayonnaise	115.00	120.00	125.00
Pitcher, 5" h	250.00	250.00	265.00
Relish, three parts	75.00	90.00	90.00
Sandwich tray, 10"	125.00	125.00	150.00
Tumbler, 3" h	55.00	60.00	65.00
Tumbler, 4" h	65.00	70.00	75.00
Tumbler 5-1/4" h	75.00	75.00	75.00
Vase, 8-1/4" h, elliptical	200.00	350.00	375.00
Vase, 10" h	250.00	145.00	225.00
Vase, 12" h	250.00	200.00	200.00

PEANUT BUTTER

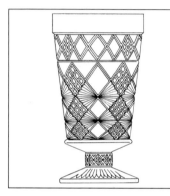

Unknown maker, 1950s.

Pieces were made in crystal and milk glass. Some pieces were originally filled with Big Top Peanut Butter.

ITEM	CRYSTAL	MILK GLASS
Cup	6.50	—
Juice tumbler, 5-1/4" h	10.00	12.00
Plate, 8" d	7.50	—
Saucer	3.50	—
Sherbet, ftd	5.00	5.00
Tumbler, 5-3/4" h	8.50	7.50

Peanut Butter, crystal tumbler, $8.50.

PETALWARE

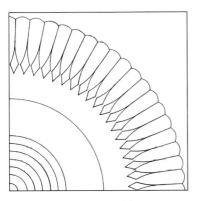

Manufactured by Macbeth-Evans Glass Company, Charleroi, Pennsylvania, from 1930 to 1940.

Made in cobalt blue, Cremax, crystal, fired-on red, blue, green, and yellow, Monax, and pink. Florette is the name given to a floral decorated with a pointed petal. There are other patterns, such as red flowers with a red rim, fruit, and other floral patterns.

Crystal values are approximately 50 percent less than those listed for Cremax. Cobalt blue production was limited, and the mustard is currently valued at $15 when complete with its metal lid. Monax Regency is priced the same as Monax Florette.

ITEM	CREMAX	CREMAX, GOLD TRIM	FIRED-ON COLORS	MONAX, FLORETTE	MONAX, PLAIN	PINK
Berry bowl, 9" d	30.00	32.00	—	35.50	18.00	20.00
Cereal bowl, 5-1/4" d	15.00	17.50	8.50	15.50	9.00	12.00
Cream soup bowl, 4-1/2" d	12.50	12.00	12.00	15.00	11.25	17.00
Creamer, ftd	12.50	18.00	8.50	11.50	7.50	10.00
Cup	8.00	10.00	9.50	9.50	4.50	10.00
Lampshade, 9" d	17.00	—	125.00	14.00	18.00	—

ITEM	CREMAX	CREMAX, GOLD TRIM	FIRED-ON COLORS	MONAX, FLORETTE	MONAX, PLAIN	PINK
Plate, 6" d, sherbet	4.50	50.00	6.00	6.00	2.50	4.50
Plate, 8" d, salad	8.00	10.00	9.50	9.00	5.00	14.00
Plate, 9" d, dinner	12.50	14.00	8.50	16.50	24.00	15.00
Platter, 13" l, oval	25.00	20.00	20.00	25.00	20.00	24.50
Salver, 11" d	14.00	17.00	14.00	27.50	28.00	20.00
Salver, 12" d	—	—	—	—	24.00	22.50
Saucer	3.50	4.00	4.00	4.50	2.50	5.00
Sherbet, 4" h, low ftd	—	—	—	—	20.00	—
Sherbet, 4-1/2" h, low ftd	15.00	12.00	8.00	12.00	10.00	8.50
Soup bowl, 7" d	65.00	60.00	70.00	65.00	90.00	—
Sugar, ftd	7.50	18.00	12.00	12.00	7.00	10.00
Tumbler, 12 oz, 4-5/8" h	—	—	—	—	—	25.00

Petalware, pink 5-1/4" cereal bowl, $12.

Petalware, Monax dinner plate, $24.

PHILBE

Manufactured by Anchor-Hocking Glass Corp., under its Fire King trademark from 1937 to 1938.

Pieces were made in blue, crystal, green, and pink. The only known example of Ruby Red Philbe is in the Anchor Hocking Glass Museum, San Antonio, Texas.

ITEM	BLUE	CRYSTAL	GREEN	PINK
Candy Jar, cov, 4" d, low	900.00	350.00	850.00	775.00
Cereal bowl, 5-1/2" d	70.00	25.00	45.00	45.00
Cookie Jar, cov	1,850.00	650.00	995.00	995.00
Creamer, 3-1/4", ftd	145.00	50.00	135.00	135.00
Cup	160.00	85.00	115.00	115.00
Goblet, 9 oz, 7-1/4" h	225.00	80.00	175.00	175.00
Iced tea tumbler, 15 oz, 6-1/2" h, ftd	195.00	45.00	75.00	75.00
Juice tumbler, 3-1/2" h, ftd	175.00	45.00	150.00	150.00
Pitcher, 36 oz, 6" h	900.00	300.00	625.00	625.00
Pitcher, 56 oz, 8-1/2" h	1.450.00	625.00	1,200.00	1,200.00
Plate, 6" d, sherbet	75.00	35.00	60.00	60.00

Fire King Philbe, green creamer, **$135.**

ITEM	BLUE	CRYSTAL	GREEN	PINK
Plate, 8" d, luncheon	50.00	22.00	40.00	40.00
Plate, 10-1/2" d, grill	75.00	25.00	65.00	65.00
Platter, 12" l, closed handles	200.00	65.00	175.00	175.00
Refrigerator dish, 4" x 5"	45.00	—	—	—
Refrigerator dish, 5" x 9"	50.00	—	—	—
Salad bowl, 7-1/4" d	85.00	30.00	50.00	50.00
Salver, 10-1/2" d	80.00	25.00	55.00	55.00
Salver, 11-5/8" d	95.00	25.00	65.00	65.00
Sandwich plate, 10" d	150.00	60.00	95.00	95.00
Saucer, 6" d	75.00	35.00	60.00	60.00
Sugar, 3-1/4", ftd	145.00	50.00	135.00	135.00
Tumbler, 9 oz, 4" h, flat	125.00	40.00	100.00	100.00
Tumbler, 10 oz, 5-1/4" h	95.00	35.00	75.00	75.00
Vegetable bowl, 10" l, oval	165.00	75.00	115.00	115.00

PINEAPPLE & FLORAL

NO. 618

Manufactured by Indiana Glass Company, Dunkirk, Indiana, from 1932 to 1937.

Pieces were made in amber, avocado (late 1960s), cobalt blue (1980s), crystal, fired-on green, fired-on red, and pink (1980s).

Reproductions: † A salad bowl and diamond-shaped comport have been reproduced in several different colors, including crystal, pink, and avocado green.

ITEM	AMBER	CRYSTAL	RED
Ashtray, 4-1/2" d	20.00	17.50	20.00
Berry bowl, 4-3/4" d	24.00	20.00	22.00
Cereal bowl, 6" d	24.00	30.00	22.00
Comport, diamond-shape	10.00	5.00	10.00
Creamer, diamond-shape	10.00	7.50	10.00
Cream soup	16.50	18.00	16.50
Cup	10.00	12.00	10.00
Plate, 6" d, sherbet	8.00	6.50	8.00
Plate, 8-3/8" d, salad	12.00	10.00	12.00
Plate, 9-3/8" d, dinner	17.50	18.00	17.50
Plate, 9-3/4" d, indentation	—	20.00	—

ITEM	AMBER	CRYSTAL	RED
Plate, 11" d, closed handles	24.00	20.00	24.00
Plate, 11-1/2" d, indentation	—	25.00	—
Platter, 11" l, closed handles	20.00	18.00	20.00
Relish, 11-1/2" d, divided	28.00	24.00	28.00
Salad bowl, 7" d †	10.00	5.00	10.00
Sandwich plate, 11-1/2" d	24.00	20.00	24.00
Saucer	7.50	6.00	7.50
Sherbet, ftd	28.00	24.00	28.00
Sugar, diamond-shape	10.00	7.50	10.00
Tumbler, 8 oz, 4-1/4" h	40.00	40.00	40.00
Tumbler, 12 oz, 5" h	48.00	47.50	48.00
Vase, cone shape	45.00	42.50	45.00
Vegetable bowl, 10" l, oval	22.00	30.00	32.00

Pineapple & Floral, amber cream soup bowl, $16.50.

Pineapple & Floral, crystal footed sherbet, $24.

Pineapple & Floral, crystal sugar, $7.50; creamer, $7.50.

PIONEER

Manufactured by Federal Glass Company, Columbus, Ohio, starting in the 1940s.

Pieces were originally made in pink; crystal was added later. The crystal 11-inch fluted bowl and 12-inch dinner plate were made until 1973.

ITEM	CRYSTAL	PINK
Bowl, 7" d, low, fruits center	8.00	10.00
Bowl, 7-3/4" d, ruffled, fruits center	10.00	12.00
Bowl, 10-1/2" d, fruits center	12.00	14.00
Bowl, 10-1/2" d, plain center	10.00	12.00
Bowl, 11" d, ruffled, fruits center	15.00	18.00
Bowl, 11" d, ruffled, plain center	12.00	15.00
Nappy, 5-3/8" d, fruits center	8.00	10.00
Nappy, 5-3/8" d, plain center	6.00	8.00
Plate, 8" d, luncheon, fruits center	6.00	8.00
Plate, 8" d, luncheon, plain center	6.00	8.00
Plate, 12" d, fruits center	10.00	12.00
Plate, 12" d, plain center	10.00	12.00

Pioneer, crystal luncheon plate, fruit center, $6.

Pioneer, pink luncheon plate, fruit center, $8.

PRETZEL

NO. 622

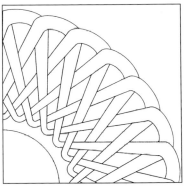

Manufactured by Indiana Glass Company, Dunkirk, Indiana, from late 1930s to 1960s.

Pieces were made in avocado, crystal, and teal. Some crystal pieces have a fruit decoration. There have been recent amber, blue, and opaque white issues. A teal cup and saucer is valued at $165.

ITEM	CRYSTAL, PLAIN	CRYSTAL, FRUITS
Berry bowl, 9-3/8" d	18.00	—
Bowl, 8" d	7.00	—
Celery tray, 10-1/4" l	9.50	—
Creamer	6.00	—
Cup	6.50	—
Fruit cup, 4-1/2" d	7.50	—
Iced tea tumbler, 12 oz, 5-1/2" h	70.00	—
Juice tumbler	35.00	—
Olive, 7" l, leaf-shape	5.00	—
Pickle, 8-1/2" d, two handles	3.00	—

ITEM	CRYSTAL, PLAIN	CRYSTAL, FRUITS
Pitcher, 39 oz	250.00	—
Plate, 6" d	4.00	8.00
Plate, 6" d, tab handle	7.00	—
Plate, 7" sq, wings	9.00	—
Plate, 7-1/4" w, sq, indent	8.00	—
Plate, 7-1/4" w, sq, indent, three parts	10.00	—
Plate, 8-3/8" d, salad	7.50	8.00
Plate, 9-3/8" d, dinner	10.00	18.00
Plate, 10" d, dinner	12.00	15.00
Relish, 7", three parts	10.00	—

Pretzel, crystal 4-1/2" d fruit cup, $7.50; 7-1/2" d soup bowl, $12.

ITEM	CRYSTAL, PLAIN	CRYSTAL, FRUITS
Sandwich plate, 11-1/2" d	12.50	12.00
Saucer	1.50	—
Soup bowl, 7-1/2" d	12.00	10.00
Sugar	8.00	—
Tumbler, 5 oz, 3-1/2" h	50.00	—
Tumbler, 9 oz, 4-1/2" h	70.00	—

Pretzel, crystal sugar, $8; creamer, $6.

PRIMO
PANELED ASTER

Manufactured by U.S. Glass Company, Pittsburgh, Pennsylvania, in the early 1930s.

Pieces were made in green and yellow.

ITEM	GREEN	YELLOW
Bowl, 4-1/2" d	20.00	25.00
Bowl, 7-3/4" d	38.00	40.00
Cake plate, 10" d, three ftd	40.00	45.00
Coaster/ashtray	8.75	8.75
Creamer	12.00	15.00
Cup	14.50	14.50
Hostess tray, 5-3/4" d, handles	42.00	45.00
Plate, 7-1/2" d	10.25	12.00
Plate, 10" d, dinner	27.50	30.00
Plate, 10" d, grill	18.00	20.00
Saucer	3.25	3.25

ITEM	GREEN	YELLOW
Sherbet	14.25	14.50
Sugar	12.00	12.00
Tumbler, 9 oz, 5-3/4" h, ftd	22.00	45.00

Primo, yellow cup, $14.50.

PRIMROSE

Manufactured by Anchor Hocking Glass Corp. under its Fire King trademark from 1960 to 1962.

Pieces were made in white with a red, pink, and black floral decoration.

ITEM	DECORATED
Baking pan, 6-1/2" x 10-1/2"	14.00
Baking pan, 8" x 12-1/2"	30.00
Baking pan, cov, 5" x 9"	18.00
Cake pan, 8" d, round	12.50
Cake pan, 8" w, square	12.50
Casserole, cov, one pint	9.50
Casserole, cov, 1/2 quart, oval	12.50
Casserole, cov, one quart	14.00
Casserole, cov, 1-1/2 quart	16.00
Casserole, cov, two quart	18.00
Creamer	9.00
Cup, 8 oz	4.00
Custard cup	3.50

ITEM	DECORATED
Dessert bowl, 4-5/8" d	3.00
Juice tumbler, 5 oz	35.00
Loaf pan, 5" x 9"	15.00
Plate, 7-3/8" d, salad	5.00
Plate, 9-1/8" d, dinner	12.00
Platter, 9" x 12"	16.00
Saucer, 5-3/4" d	1.50
Set, boxed, 19 pcs	150.00
Snack cup, 5 oz	3.00
Snack tray, 11" x 6"	7.00
Soup bowl, 6-5/8" d	8.50
Sugar, cov	10.00
Tumbler, 11 oz	25.00
Vegetable bowl, 8-1/4" d	12.00

Fire King Primrose, dinner plate with pink and red floral decoration, $12.

PRINCESS

Manufactured by Hocking Glass Company, Lancaster, Ohio, from 1931 to 1935.

Pieces were made in apricot yellow, blue, green, pink, and topaz yellow.

Reproductions: † The candy dish and salt and pepper shakers have been reproduced in blue, green, and pink.

ITEM	APRICOT YELLOW	BLUE	GREEN	PINK	TOPAZ YELLOW
Ashtray, 4-1/2" d	110.00	—	65.00	90.00	110.00
Berry bowl, 4-1/2" d	55.00	—	40.00	30.00	55.00
Butter dish, cov	700.00	—	75.00	115.00	700.00
Cake plate, 10" d, ftd	—	—	32.50	100.00	—
Candy dish, cov †	—	—	55.00	85.00	—
Cereal bowl, 5" d	—	—	35.00	45.00	—
Coaster	100.00	—	65.00	65.00	100.00
Cookie jar, cov	—	875.00	65.00	75.00	—
Creamer, oval	25.00	—	18.00	17.50	22.50
Cup	10.00	120.00	10.00	12.50	10.00
Hat-shaped bowl, 9-1/2" d	125.00	—	48.00	75.00	125.00

Princess, green octagonal salad bowl, $40; cookie jar, $65.

ITEM	APRICOT YELLOW	BLUE	GREEN	PINK	TOPAZ YELLOW
Iced tea tumbler, 13 oz, 5-1/2" h	45.00	—	125.00	115.00	40.00
Juice tumbler, 5 oz, 3" h	28.00	—	25.00	28.00	28.00
Pitcher, 24 oz, 7-3/8" h, ftd	—	—	550.00	475.00	—
Pitcher, 37 oz, 6" h	750.00	—	70.00	75.00	750.00
Pitcher, 60 oz, 8" h	95.00	—	75.00	70.00	95.00
Plate, 5-1/2" d, sherbet	6.75	65.00	9.00	12.00	6.75
Plate, 8" d, salad	18.00	—	18.00	15.00	10.00
Plate, 9-1/2" d, dinner	25.00	—	24.50	35.00	25.00
Plate, 9-1/2" d, grill	10.00	175.00	15.00	16.00	10.00
Plate, 10-1/2" d, grill, closed handles	10.00	—	15.00	15.00	10.00

ITEM	APRICOT YELLOW	BLUE	GREEN	PINK	TOPAZ YELLOW
Platter, 12" l, closed handles	60.00	—	30.00	25.00	60.00
Relish, 7-1/2" l, divided, four parts	100.00	—	35.00	30.00	100.00
Relish, 7-1/2" l, plain	225.00	—	195.00	195.00	225.00
Salad bowl, 9" d, octagonal	125.00	—	40.00	48.00	165.00
Salt and pepper shakers, pr, 4-1/2" h †	75.00	—	60.00	65.00	85.00
Sandwich plate, 10-1/4" d, two closed handles	175.00	—	30.00	35.00	175.00
Saucer, 6" sq	3.00	65.00	10.00	10.00	5.00

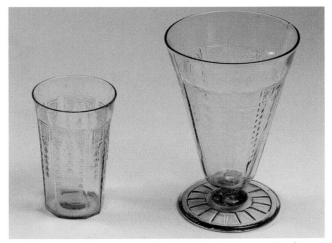

*Princess, topaz yellow 3" juice tumbler, **$28**; pink 5-1/4" footed tumbler, **$32**.*

ITEM	APRICOT YELLOW	BLUE	GREEN	PINK	TOPAZ YELLOW
Sherbet, ftd	40.00	—	15.00	25.00	40.00
Spice shakers, pr, 5-1/2" h	—	—	20.00	—	—
Sugar, cov	30.00	—	38.00	65.00	30.00
Tumbler, 9 oz, 4" h	25.00	—	25.00	25.00	25.00
Tumbler, 9 oz, 4-3/4" h, sq, ftd	—	—	65.00	25.00	—
Tumbler, 10 oz, 5-1/4" h, ftd	28.00	—	35.00	32.00	28.00
Tumbler, 12-1/2 oz, 6-1/2" h, ftd	25.00	—	180.00	95.00	25.00
Vase, 8" h	—	—	55.00	60.00	—
Vegetable bowl, 10" l, oval	60.00	—	32.00	35.00	65.00

Princess, pink cup, $12.50.

PYRAMID
NO. 610

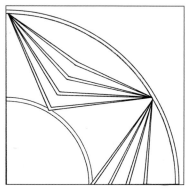

Manufactured by Indiana Glass Company, Dunkirk, Indiana, from 1926 to 1932.

Pieces were made in crystal, green, pink, white, and yellow. Tiara produced black and blue pieces from 1974 to 1975. Production was limited in blue and white. Prices for black have not been firmly established in the secondary market at this time.

ITEM	CRYSTAL	GREEN	PINK	YELLOW
Berry bowl, 4-3/4" d	20.00	35.00	35.00	55.00
Berry bowl, 8-1/2" d	30.00	65.00	55.00	75.00
Bowl, 9-1/2" l, oval	30.00	45.00	40.00	65.00
Creamer	20.00	35.00	35.00	40.00
Ice tub	95.00	145.00	155.00	225.00
Pickle dish, 9-1/2" l, 5-3/4" w	30.00	35.00	35.00	65.00
Pitcher	395.00	265.00	400.00	550.00
Relish, four parts, handles	25.00	65.00	60.00	70.00

ITEM	CRYSTAL	GREEN	PINK	YELLOW
Sugar	20.00	35.00	35.00	45.00
Tray for creamer and sugar	25.00	30.00	30.00	35.00
Tumbler, 8 oz, ftd	55.00	50.00	55.00	75.00
Tumbler, 11 oz, ftd	70.00	75.00	50.00	95.00

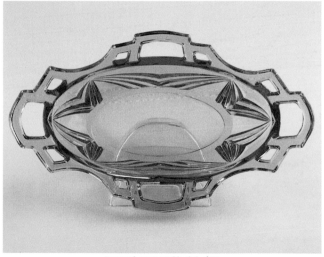

Pyramid, green pickle dish, $35.

QUEEN MARY
PRISMATIC LINE, VERTICAL RIBBED

Manufactured by Hocking Glass Company, Lancaster, Ohio, from 1936 to 1948.

Pieces were made in crystal, pink, and royal ruby. Limited production in forest green includes coaster/ashtray, $6.

ITEM	CRYSTAL	PINK	ROYAL RUBY
Ashtray, 2" x 3-3/4" l, oval	4.00	5.50	5.00
Ashtray, 3-1/2" d, round	2.00	—	—
Berry bowl, 4-1/2" d	3.00	6.00	—
Berry bowl, 5" d	5.00	10.00	—
Berry bowl, 8-3/4" d	10.00	17.50	—
Bowl, 4" d, one handle	4.00	12.50	—
Bowl, 5-1/2" d, two handles	6.00	15.00	—
Bowl, 7" d	7.50	35.00	—
Butter dish, cov	42.00	125.00	—
Candlesticks, pr, two lite, 4-1/2" h	24.00	—	70.00

Queen Mary, pink oval open sugar, $12; oval creamer, $14.

ITEM	CRYSTAL	PINK	ROYAL RUBY
Candy dish, cov	25.00	65.00	—
Celery tray, 5" x 10"	10.00	24.00	—
Cereal bowl, 6" d	8.00	20.00	—
Cigarette jar, 2" x 3" oval	6.50	7.50	—
Coaster, 3-1/2" d	3.00	5.00	—
Coaster/ashtray, 4-1/4" sq	2.00	6.00	12.00
Comport, 5-3/4"	15.00	14.00	—
Creamer, ftd	6.00	12.00	—
Creamer, oval	6.00	14.00	—
Cup, large	6.50	10.00	

ITEM	CRYSTAL	PINK	ROYAL RUBY
Cup, small	8.50	12.50	—
Juice tumbler, 5 oz, 3-1/2" h	9.50	15.00	—
Pickle dish, 5" x 10"	10.00	24.00	—
Plate, 6" d, sherbet	4.00	6.00	—
Plate, 6-1/2" d, bread and butter	6.00	—	—
Plate, 8-1/4" d, salad	6.00	—	—
Plate, 9-1/2" d, dinner	15.00	50.00	—
Preserve, cov	30.00	125.00	—
Relish, clover—shape	15.00	17.50	—
Relish, 12" d, three parts	10.00	15.00	—

Queen Mary, crystal 7" d bowl, $7.50; candlesticks, pair, $24.

ITEM	CRYSTAL	PINK	ROYAL RUBY
Relish, 14" d, four parts	15.00	17.50	—
Salt and pepper shakers, pr	25.00	—	—
Sandwich plate, 12" d	15.00	17.50	—
Saucer	3.00	5.00	—
Serving tray, 14" d	15.00	9.00	—
Sherbet, ftd	6.50	12.00	—
Sugar, ftd	—	40.00	—
Sugar, oval	6.00	12.00	—
Tumbler, 9 oz, 4" h	6.00	19.50	—
Tumbler, 10 oz, 5" h, ftd	35.00	70.00	—

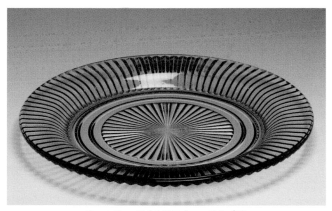

Queen Mary, pink 9-1/2" dinner plate, $50.

RADIANCE

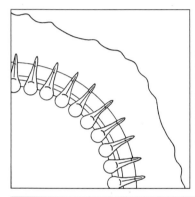

Manufactured by New Martinsville Glass Company, New Martinsville, West Virginia, from 1936 to 1939.

Pieces were made in amber, cobalt blue, crystal, emerald green, ice blue, pink, and red. Some pieces are found with an etched design. This adds slightly to the value.

ITEM	AMBER	COBALT BLUE	CRYSTAL
Bonbon, 6" d	16.00	—	8.00
Bonbon, 6" d, cov	48.00	—	24.00
Bonbon, 6" d, ftd	18.00	—	9.00
Bowl, 6" d, ruffled	—	—	—
Bowl, 6-1/2" d, ftd, metal holder	—	—	—
Bowl, 10" d, crimped	28.00	—	14.00
Bowl, 10" d, flared	22.00	—	11.00
Bowl, 12" d, crimped	30.00	—	15.00
Bowl, 12" d, flared	28.00	—	14.00
Butter dish, cov	200.00	—	100.00
Butter dish, chrome lid	40.00	—	37.50
Cake salver	—	—	—

ITEM	AMBER	COBALT BLUE	CRYSTAL
Candlesticks, pr, two lite	75.00	—	37.50
Candlesticks, pr, 6" h, ruffled	85.00	—	40.00
Candlesticks, pr, 8" h	60.00	—	30.00
Candy dish, cov, three parts	—	125.00	—
Celery tray, 10" l	18.00	—	9.00
Cheese and cracker set, 11" d plate	45.00	—	20.00
Comport, 5" h	18.00	—	9.00
Comport, 6" h	24.00	—	12.00
Condiment set, four pcs, tray	160.00	—	85.00
Cordial, 1 oz	30.00	65.00	20.00
Creamer	15.00	25.00	10.00
Cruet, individual	40.00	—	20.00
Cup, ftd	15.00	18.00	8.00
Decanter, stopper, handle	90.00	195.00	45.00
Lamp, 12" h	60.00	—	30.00
Mayonnaise, three-pc set	37.50	—	19.00
Nut bowl, 5" d, two handles	12.00	—	6.50
Pickle, 7"d	16.00	—	8.00
Pitcher, 64 oz	135.00	350.00	95.00
Pitcher, silver overlay	—	—	—
Plate, 8" d, luncheon	10.00	—	5.00
Punch bowl, 9" d	110.00	—	65.00
Punch bowl liner, 14" d	48.00	—	24.00
Punch cup	8.00	—	5.00
Punch ladle	100.00	—	45.00
Relish, 7" d, two parts	18.00	—	9.00
Relish, 8" d, three parts	28.00	—	14.00
Salt and pepper shakers, pr	50.00	—	25.00
Saucer	6.00	7.50	3.50
Sugar	16.00	—	8.00
Tray, oval	25.00	—	15.00

ITEM	AMBER	COBALT BLUE	CRYSTAL
Tumbler, 9" oz	22.50	35.00	12.00
Vase, 10" h, crimped	48.00	75.00	65.00
Vase, 10" h, flared	48.00	75.00	24.00
Vase, 12" h, crimped	60.00	50.00	30.00
Vase, 12" h, flared	70.00	—	50.00

ITEM	EMERALD GREEN	ICE BLUE	PINK	RED
Bonbon, 6" d	—	32.00	—	32.00
Bonbon, 6" d, cov	—	95.00	—	95.00
Bonbon, 6" d, ftd	—	35.00	—	35.00
Bowl, 6" d, ruffled	—	35.00	—	—
Bowl, 6-1/2" d, ftd, metal holder	—	—	—	45.00
Bowl, 10" d, crimped	—	48.00	—	50.00
Bowl, 10" d, flared	—	48.00	—	55.00
Bowl, 12" d, crimped	—	50.00	—	60.00
Bowl, 12" d, flared	—	50.00	—	65.00
Butter dish, cov	—	450.00	—	450.00
Butter dish, chrome lid	—	—	—	—
Cake salver	—	175.00	—	175.00
Candlesticks, pr, two lite	—	150.00	—	120.00
Candlesticks, pr, 6" h, ruffled	—	175.00	—	175.00
Candlesticks, pr, 8" h	—	110.00	—	110.00
Candy dish, cov, three parts	—	105.00	—	125.00
Celery tray, 10" l	—	32.00	—	32.00
Cheese and cracker set, 11" d plate	—	195.00	—	65.00
Comport, 5" h	—	30.00	—	30.00
Comport, 6" h	—	35.00	—	35.00
Condiment set, four pcs, tray	—	295.00	—	295.00
Cordial, 1 oz	—	60.00	—	45.00
Creamer	—	35.00	32.00	35.00
Cruet, individual	—	26.00	—	27.50

Radiance, ice blue 6" comport with ruffled edge, $35.

ITEM	EMERALD GREEN	ICE BLUE	PINK	RED
Cup, ftd	—	30.00	20.00	20.00
Decanter, stopper, handle	—	225.00	—	225.00
Lamp, 12" h	—	115.00	—	115.00
Mayonnaise, three-pc set	—	85.00	—	85.00
Nut bowl, 5" d, two handles	—	20.00	—	24.00
Pickle, 7" d	—	25.00	—	27.50
Pitcher, 64 oz	—	375.00	—	375.00
Pitcher, silver overlay	—	—	—	125.00
Plate, 8" d, luncheon	—	12.00	—	12.00
Punch bowl, 9" d	165.00	185.00	—	185.00
Punch bowl liner, 14" d	35.00	85.00	—	85.00
Punch cup	—	15.00	—	15.00
Punch ladle	—	120.00	—	120.00

ITEM	EMERALD GREEN	ICE BLUE	PINK	RED
Relish, 7"d, two parts	—	32.00	—	32.00
Relish, 8" d, three parts	—	35.00	—	35.00
Salt and pepper shakers, pr	—	90.00	95.00	95.00
Saucer	—	15.00	8.00	8.00
Sugar	—	30.00	32.00	32.00
Tray, oval	—	32.00	32.00	32.00
Tumbler, 9" oz	—	30.00	—	35.00
Vase, 10" h, crimped	—	60.00	—	70.00
Vase, 10" h, flared	—	60.00	—	70.00
Vase, 12" h, crimped	—	55.00	—	85.00
Vase, 12" h, flared	—	175.00	—	175.00

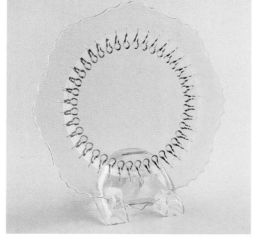

*Radiance,
ice blue
plate, $12.*

RAINDROPS
OPTIC DESIGN

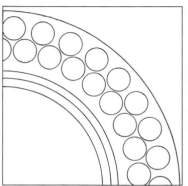

Manufactured by Federal Glass Company, Columbus, Ohio, from 1929 to 1933.

Pieces were made in crystal and green.

Raindrops, green creamer, $10; open sugar, $12.

ITEM	CRYSTAL	GREEN
Berry bowl, 7-1/2" d	30.00	45.00
Cereal bowl, 6" d	10.00	15.00
Creamer	8.00	10.00
Cup	8.50	6.50
Fruit bowl, 4-1/2" d	5.00	11.00
Plate, 6" d, sherbet	1.50	3.00
Plate, 8" d, luncheon	4.00	7.50
Salt and pepper shakers, pr	200.00	350.00
Saucer	3.00	3.50
Sherbet	4.50	7.50
Sugar, cov	7.50	15.00
Tumbler, 2 oz, 2-1/8" h	4.00	7.00
Tumbler, 4 oz, 3" h	4.50	8.50
Tumbler, 5 oz, 3-7/8" h	5.50	9.50
Tumbler, 9-1/2 oz, 4-1/8" h	6.00	12.00
Tumblers, 10 oz, 5" h	6.00	12.00
Tumblers, 14 oz, 5-3/8" h	7.50	15.00
Whiskey, 1 oz, 1-7/8" h	7.50	10.00

Raindrops, green 4-1/2" d fruit bowl, $11.

RIBBON

Manufactured by Hazel Atlas Glass Company, Clarksburg, West Virginia, and Zanesville, Ohio, in the early 1930s.

Pieces were made in black, crystal, green, and pink. Production in pink was limited to salt and pepper shakers, valued at $40

ITEM	BLACK	CRYSTAL	GREEN
Berry bowl, 4" d	—	20.00	22.00
Berry bowl, 8" d	—	27.50	30.00
Bowl, 9" d, wide bands	—	—	35.00
Candy dish, cov	45.00	35.00	45.00
Cereal bowl, 5" d	—	20.00	25.00
Creamer, ftd	—	10.00	15.00
Cup	—	4.50	6.50
Plate, 6-1/4" d, sherbet	—	3.50	47.00
Plate, 8" d, luncheon	15.00	7.00	10.00
Salt and pepper shakers, pr	45.00	22.00	28.00

ITEM	BLACK	CRYSTAL	GREEN
Saucer	—	2.00	3.50
Sherbet	—	6.00	14.00
Sugar, ftd	—	12.00	15.50
Tumbler, 10 oz, 6" h	—	28.00	30.00

Ribbon, green cup, $6.50; creamer, $15.

Ribbon, green covered candy dish, $45.

RING
BANDED RINGS

Manufactured by Hocking Glass Company, Lancaster, Ohio, from 1927 to 1933.

Pieces were made in crystal, crystal with rings of color (black, blue, pink, red, orange, silver, and yellow), green, Mayfair blue, pink, and red. Prices for decorated pieces are quite similar to each other.

ITEM	CRYSTAL	DECORATED	GREEN
Berry bowl, 5" d	4.00	9.00	8.00
Berry bowl, 8" d	7.50	16.00	16.00
Bowl, 5-1/4" d, divided	12.50	—	—
Butter tub	24.00	25.00	20.00
Candy dish, 7" d, ruffled, three applied feet	—	—	30.00
Cereal bowl	—	5.00	8.00
Cocktail shaker, metal top, 10-1/2", 52 oz	24.00	30.00	27.50
Cocktail, 3-1/2 oz, 3-3/4" h	12.00	18.00	18.00
Creamer, ftd	5.00	10.00	10.00
Cup	5.00	8.00	5.00
Decanter, stopper	30.00	35.00	32.00

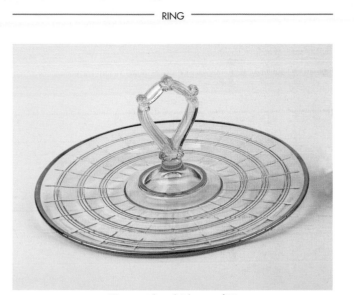

Ring, crystal sandwich server, $15.

ITEM	CRYSTAL	DECORATED	GREEN
Goblet, 9 oz, 7-1/4" h	7.00	14.00	14.00
Ice bucket	24.00	33.00	30.00
Ice tub	20.00	25.00	20.00
Iced tea tumbler, 6-1/2" h	10.00	15.00	15.00
Juice tumbler, 3-1/2" h, ftd	6.50	10.00	15.00
Old fashioned tumbler, 8 oz, 4" h	15.00	17.50	17.50
Pitcher, 60 oz, 8" h	22.00	25.00	25.00
Pitcher, 80 oz, 8-1/2" h	25.00	38.00	36.00

ITEM	CRYSTAL	DECORATED	GREEN
Plate, 6-1/2" d, off-center ring	6.50	8.50	5.00
Plate, 6-1/4" d, sherbet	3.00	3.50	4.00
Plate, 8" d, luncheon	3.00	7.50	9.00
Salt and pepper shakers, pr, 3" h	20.00	40.00	42.00
Sandwich plate, 11-3/4" d	8.00	15.00	15.00
Sandwich server, center handle	15.00	27.50	27.50
Saucer	1.50	4.50	2.50
Sherbet, 4-3/4" h	6.50	10.00	12.00
Sherbet, flat, 6-1/2" d underplate	12.00	18.00	21.00
Soup bowl, 7" d	10.00	9.00	8.00
Sugar, ftd	5.00	10.00	3.00
Tumbler, 4 oz, 3" h	4.00	6.50	6.00
Tumbler, 5-1/2" h, ftd	6.00	10.00	10.00

*Ring, green 8" d master berry bowl with two handles, **$16**;
5" d individual berry bowl with two handles, **$8**.*

ITEM	CRYSTAL	DECORATED	GREEN
Tumbler, 5 oz, 3-1/2" h	6.50	6.50	12.00
Tumbler, 9 oz, 4-1/4" h	7.50	7.50	9.00
Tumbler, 10 oz, 4-3/4" h	8.50	—	9.00
Tumbler, 12 oz, 5-1/8" h, ftd	10.00	12.00	20.00
Vase, 8" h	20.00	35.00	37.50
Whiskey, 1-1/2 oz, 2" h	8.50	9.00	12.00
Wine, 3-1/2 oz, 4-1/2" h	17.50	20.00	24.00

Ring, green cup, $5; saucer, $2.50.

RIPPLE

CRINOLINE, PETTICOAT, PIE CRUST, LASAGNA, NO. 6091, NO. 6040

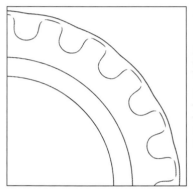

Manufactured by Hazel Atlas Glass Company, Clarksburg, West Virginia, in the early 1950s.

Pieces were made in Platonite white, Jewel Turquoise (white with turquoise trim), and Princess Pink (white with pink trim). All the colors have a similar value.

ITEM	PLATONITE WHITE
Berry bowl, 5" d	12.00
Cereal bowl, 5-5/8" d	9.00
Creamer	7.50
Cup	4.50
Juice tumbler, 5 oz	7.50
Mug	6.00
Plate, 6-7/8" d, salad	5.00
Plate, 8-7/8" d, luncheon	8.00
Sandwich plate, 10-1/2" d	18.00

ITEM	PLATONITE WHITE
Saucer, 5-3/8" d	2.00
Sugar	7.50
Tidbit, three tiers	35.00
Tumbler, 6" h, 16 oz	12.00
Tumbler, 6-3/4" h, 20 oz	15.00

Ripple, Jewel Turquoise luncheon plate, $8.

ROCK CRYSTAL
EARLY AMERICAN ROCK CRYSTAL

Manufactured by McKee Glass Company, Pittsburgh, Pennsylvania, in the 1920s and colors in 1930s.

Pieces were made in amber, amberina red, amethyst, aquamarine, blue frosted, cobalt blue, crystal, crystal with goofus decoration, crystal with gold decoration, dark red, four shades of green, milk glass, pink and frosted pink, red, red slag, vaseline, and yellow.

ITEM	CRYSTAL	COLORS	RED
Banana split dish	75.00	—	—
Bonbon, 7-1/2" d, scalloped edge	22.00	35.00	55.00
Bowl, 4" d, scalloped edge	15.00	24.00	35.00
Bowl, 4-1/2" d, scalloped edge	15.00	24.00	35.00
Bowl, 5" d, plain edge	20.00	26.00	45.00
Bowl, 5" d, scalloped edge	20.00	26.00	45.00
Bowl, 8-1/2" d, center handle	—	—	150.00
Bowl, 12-1/2" d, pedestal	80.00	125.00	300.00
Butter dish, cov	345.00	—	—
Cake stand, 11" d, 2-3/4" h, ftd	40.00	55.00	135.00
Candelabra, pr, two-lite	40.00	110.00	250.00

ITEM	CRYSTAL	COLORS	RED
Candelabra, pr, three-lite	70.00	135.00	350.00
Candlesticks, pr, 5-1/2" h, low	45.00	70.00	175.00
Candlesticks, pr, 8" h	95.00	200.00	400.00
Candy dish, cov, ftd, 9-1/2" d	55.00	95.00	225.00
Candy dish, cov, round	50.00	75.00	175.00
Celery tray, 12" l, oblong	25.00	40.00	85.00
Center bowl, 12-1/2" d, ftd	65.00	135.00	310.00
Champagne, 6 oz, ftd	20.00	25.00	35.00
Claret, 3 oz	—	60.00	—
Cocktail, 3-1/2 oz, ftd	19.50	24.00	45.00
Comport, 7" d	35.00	50.00	90.00
Cordial, 1 oz, ftd	20.00	45.00	65.00
Creamer, 9 oz, ftd	20.00	35.00	75.00
Creamer, flat, scalloped edge	40.00	—	—
Cruet, stopper, 6 oz,	95.00	—	—
Cup, 7 oz	20.00	25.00	70.00
Deviled egg plate	50.00	—	—
Eggcup, 3-1/2 oz, ftd	22.50	20.00	65.00
Finger bowl, 5" d bowl, 7" d plate, piecrust edge	35.00	48.00	70.00
Goblet, 8 oz, ftd	16.00	30.00	60.00
Goblet, 8 oz, 7-1/2" h, low, ftd	18.50	30.00	65.00
Ice dish	35.00	—	—
Iced tea goblet, 11 oz	25.00	35.00	70.00
Jelly, 5" d, ftd, scalloped edge	18.00	30.00	50.00
Juice tumbler, 5 oz	24.00	30.00	50.00
Lamp, electric	225.00	375.00	650.00
Old fashioned tumbler, 5 oz	20.00	30.00	60.00
Parfait, 3-1/2 oz, low, ftd	17.50	35.00	75.00
Pickle, 7" l	37.50	40.00	65.00
Pitcher, covered, 9" h	175.00	350.00	675.00
Pitcher, half gallon, 7-1/2" h	100.00	165.00	—
Pitcher, quart, scalloped edge	150.00	220.00	—

ITEM	CRYSTAL	COLORS	RED
Pitcher, tankard	190.00	650.00	900.00
Plate, 6" d, bread and butter, scalloped edge	6.50	9.50	20.00
Plate, 7-1/2" d, piecrust edge	8.00	12.00	22.00
Plate, 7-1/2" d, scalloped edge	8.00	12.00	22.00
Plate, 8-1/2" d, piecrust edge	9.00	12.00	30.00
Plate, 8-1/2" d, scalloped edge	9.00	15.00	30.00
Plate, 9" d, scalloped edge	18.50	24.00	55.00
Plate, 10-1/2" d, center design, scalloped edge	47.50	75.00	175.00
Plate, 10-1/2" d, scalloped edge	27.50	35.00	65.00

Rock Crystal, amber 8-1/2" d plate, $12.

ITEM	CRYSTAL	COLORS	RED
Plate, 11-1/2″ d, scalloped edge	30.00	40.00	70.00
Punch bowl and stand, 14″	333.00	—	—
Relish, 11-1/2″ d, two parts	30.00	50.00	75.00
Relish, 12-1/2″ d, five parts	35.00	—	—
Relish, 14″ d, six parts	45.00	65.00	—
Roll tray, 13″ d	35.00	60.00	95.00
Salad bowl, 7″ d, scalloped edge	25.00	40.00	65.00
Salad bowl, 8″ d, scalloped edge	32.00	42.00	67.50
Salad bowl, 9″ d, scalloped edge	35.00	50.00	85.00
Salad bowl, 10-1/2″ d, scalloped edge	25.00	50.00	90.00
Salt and pepper shakers, pr	80.00	135.00	—
Salt dip	35.00	—	—
Sandwich server, center handle	32.00	40.00	140.00
Saucer	5.00	6.50	20.00
Sherbet, 3-1/2 oz, ftd	15.00	20.00	25.00
Spoon tray, 7″ l	20.00	40.00	65.00
Spooner	42.00	—	—
Sugar, cov	50.00	95.00	155.00
Sugar, 10 oz, open	18.00	20.00	45.00
Sundae, 6 oz, low, ftd	10.00	15.00	35.00
Syrup, lid	165.00	—	—
Tray, 5-3/8″ x 7-3/8″, 7/8″ h	70.00	—	—
Tumbler, 9 oz, concave	15.00	26.00	30.00
Tumbler, 9 oz, straight	15.00	26.00	30.00
Tumbler, 12 oz, concave	35.00	40.00	70.00
Tumbler, 12 oz, straight	35.00	40.00	70.00
Vase, 11″ h, ftd	75.00	100.00	170.00
Vase, cornucopia	70.00	95.00	—
Whiskey, 2-1/2 oz	25.00	40.00	50.00
Wine, 2 oz	20.00	30.00	50.00
Wine, 3 oz	22.50	30.00	55.00

ROMANESQUE

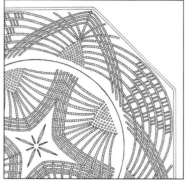

Manufactured by L.E. Smith Glass Company, Mt. Pleasant, Pennsylvania, in the early 1930s.

Pieces were made in amber, black, crystal, green, and yellow.

ITEM	AMBER	BLACK	CRYSTAL	GREEN	YELLOW
Bowl, 10" d, ftd	75.00	80.00	70.00	85.00	75.00
Bowl, 10-1/2" d	42.00	65.00	40.00	42.00	42.00
Cake plate	40.00	45.00	35.00	40.00	40.00
Candlesticks, pr	27.50	35.00	25.00	27.50	27.50
Cup	40.00	48.00	8.00	15.00	18.00
Plate, 5-1/2", octagonal	6.50	10.00	6.00	6.50	6.50
Plate, 7", octagonal	10.00	14.00	8.50	8.50	8.50
Plate, 8", octagonal	12.00	18.00	9.00	15.00	10.00
Plate, 8" d, round	9.00	15.00	8.00	9.00	9.00
Plate, 10", octagonal	20.00	27.50	18.00	20.00	20.00
Sherbet, plain	8.50	14.00	7.50	8.50	8.50
Sherbet, scalloped	10.00	18.00	9.00	10.00	10.00
Snack Tray	15.00	20.00	14.00	15.00	15.00
Vase, 7-1/2" h, fan	50.00	60.00	45.00	50.00	50.00

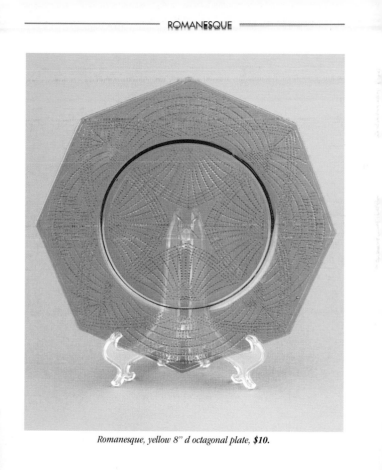

Romanesque, yellow 8" d octagonal plate, $10.

ROSE CAMEO

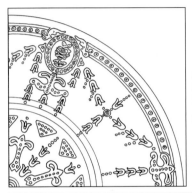

Manufactured by Belmont Tumbler Company, Bellaire, Ohio, in 1931.

Pieces were made in green.

ITEM	GREEN
Berry bowl, 4-1/2" d	14.00
Cereal bowl, 5" d	27.50
Bowl, 6" d, straight sides	30.00
Plate, 7" d, salad	15.00
Sherbet	15.00
Tumbler, 5" h, ftd	28.00
Tumbler, 5" h, ftd, sterling silver trim	30.00

Rose Cameo, green tumbler, $28.

ROSEMARY
DUTCH ROSE

Manufactured by Federal Glass Company, Columbus, Ohio, from 1935 to 1937.

Pieces were made in amber, green, and pink.

Rosemary, amber vegetable bowl, $18; berry bowl, $7.

ITEM	AMBER	GREEN	PINK
Berry bowl, 5" d	7.00	17.50	17.50
Cereal bowl, 6" d	30.00	32.00	35.00
Cream soup, 5" d	18.00	25.00	30.00
Creamer, ftd	10.00	16.00	20.00
Cup	9.00	12.50	10.00
Plate, 6-3/4" d, salad	6.50	12.00	12.50
Plate, 9-1/2" d, dinner	10.00	15.00	25.00
Plate, 9-1/2" d, grill	12.00	15.00	22.00
Platter, 12" l, oval	18.50	24.00	35.00
Saucer	5.00	8.50	9.50
Sugar, ftd	10.00	16.00	20.00
Tumbler, 9 oz, 4-1/4" h	26.00	35.00	45.00
Vegetable bowl, 10" l, oval	18.00	40.00	45.00

Rosemary, green platter, $24.

ROULETTE
MANY WINDOWS

Manufactured by Hocking Glass Company, Lancaster, Ohio, from 1935 to 1939.

Pieces were made in crystal, green, and pink.

ITEM	CRYSTAL	GREEN	PINK
Cup	32.00	8.00	6.50
Fruit bowl, 9" d	12.00	25.00	25.00
Iced tea tumbler, 12 oz, 5-1/8" h	24.00	30.00	35.00
Juice tumbler, 5 oz, 3-1/4" h	15.00	90.00	25.00
Old fashioned tumbler, 7-1/2 oz, 3-1/4" h	24.00	40.00	40.00
Pitcher, 65 oz, 8" h	30.00	35.00	45.00
Plate, 6" d, sherbet	3.50	6.50	5.00
Plate, 8-1/2" d, luncheon	7.00	10.00	6.00
Sandwich plate, 12" d	15.00	18.50	20.00
Saucer	2.50	5.00	3.00

*Roulette, green 4-1/8" flat tumbler, **$20**; 5-1/2"
footed cone-shaped tumbler, **$30**.*

ITEM	CRYSTAL	GREEN	PINK
Sherbet	8.00	10.00	12.00
Tumbler, 9 oz, 4-1/8" h	15.00	20.00	30.00
Tumbler, 10 oz, 5-1/2" h, ftd	18.00	30.00	35.00
Whiskey, 1-1/2 oz, 2-1/2" h	10.00	18.00	25.00

Roulette, green cup, **$8.**

ROXANA

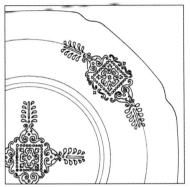

Manufactured by Hazel Atlas Glass Company, Clarksburg, West Virginia, and Zanesville, Ohio, in 1932.

Pieces were made in crystal, golden topaz, and white. Production in white was limited to a 4-1/2-inch bowl valued at $15.

ITEM	CRYSTAL	GOLD TOPAZ
Berry bowl, 5" d	8.50	17.00
Bowl, 4-1/2" x 2-3/8"	8.00	15.00
Cereal bowl, 6" d	9.00	22.00
Plate, 5-1/2" d	5.00	12.00
Plate, 6" d, sherbet	5.00	10.00
Sherbet, ftd	8.00	12.00
Tumbler, 9 oz, 4-1/4" h	12.00	20.00

Roxana, gold topaz plate, $12.

ROYAL LACE

Manufactured by Hazel Atlas Glass Company, Clarksburg, West Virginia, and Zanesville, Ohio, from 1934 to 1941.

Pieces were made in cobalt (Ritz) blue, crystal, green, pink, and some amethyst.

Reproductions: † Reproductions include a 5-ounce, 3-1/2-inch high tumbler found in a darker cobalt blue. A cookie jar has also been reproduced in cobalt blue.

ITEM	COBALT BLUE	CRYSTAL	GREEN	PINK
Berry bowl, 5" d	50.00	18.00	38.00	35.00
Berry bowl, 10" d	100.00	20.00	35.00	45.00
Bowl, 10" d, three legs, rolled edge	650.00	225.00	125.00	100.00
Bowl, 10" d, three legs, ruffled edge	750.00	45.00	125.00	100.00
Bowl, 10" d, three legs, straight edge	—	24.00	75.00	65.00
Butter dish, cov	865.00	90.00	275.00	235.00
Candlesticks, pr, rolled edge	—	45.00	85.00	60.00
Candlesticks, pr, ruffled edge	—	28.00	70.00	60.00
Candlesticks, pr, straight edge	—	35.00	75.00	55.00
Cookie jar, cov †	400.00	45.00	75.00	60.00
Cream soup bowl, 4-3/4" d	55.00	18.00	32.00	30.00
Creamer, ftd	60.00	15.00	25.00	25.00
Cup and saucer	55.00	18.00	28.00	30.00

ITEM	COBALT BLUE	CRYSTAL	GREEN	PINK
Nut bowl	1,500.00	275.00	425.00	425.00
Pitcher, 48 oz, straight sides	190.00	40.00	110.00	85.00
Pitcher, 64 oz, 8" h	295.00	45.00	120.00	120.00
Pitcher, 68 oz, 8" h, ice lip	320.00	60.00	—	115.00
Pitcher, 86 oz, 8" h	—	60.00	135.00	135.00
Pitcher, 96 oz, 9-1/2" h, ice lip	495.00	75.00	160.00	155.00
Plate, 6" d, sherbet	16.50	7.50	12.00	18.00
Plate, 8-1/2" d, luncheon	60.00	12.00	18.00	24.00
Plate, 9-7/8" d, dinner	55.00	24.00	35.00	24.50
Plate, 9-7/8" d, grill	40.00	20.00	25.00	22.50
Platter, 13" l, oval	60.00	42.00	45.00	48.00
Salt and pepper shakers, pr	325.00	45.00	130.00	60.00
Sherbet, ftd	50.00	20.00	25.00	18.00
Sherbet, metal holder	45.00	18.00	—	—
Sugar, cov	155.00	35.00	40.00	50.00
Sugar, open	—	12.50	22.00	25.00
Toddy or cider set	295.00	—	—	—
Tumbler, 5 oz, 3-1/2" h †	65.00	15.00	35.00	35.00
Tumbler, 9 oz, 4-1/8" h †	45.00	20.00	35.00	25.00
Tumbler, 10 oz, 4-7/8" h	245.00	25.00	60.00	60.00
Tumbler, 12 oz, 5-3/8" h	150.00	25.00	50.00	55.00
Vegetable bowl, 11" l, oval	75.00	25.00	35.00	35.00

Royal Lace, crystal dinner plate, $24.

ROYAL RUBY

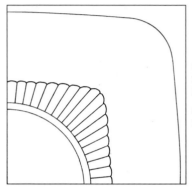

Manufactured by Anchor Hocking Glass Corp., Lancaster, Pennsylvania, from 1938 to 1967.

Pieces were made only in Royal Ruby.

ITEM	ROYAL RUBY
Apothecary jar, 8-1/2" h	22.00
Ashtray, 4-1/2", leaf	5.00
Ashtray, 5-7/8", sq	10.00
Ashtray, 7-3/4"	32.00
Beer bottle, 7 oz	30.00
Beer bottle, 12 oz	32.00
Beer bottle, 16 oz	35.00
Beer bottle, 32 oz	40.00
Berry bowl, 4-5/8" d, small, square	7.50
Berry bowl, 8-1/2" d, round	25.00
Bonbon, 6-1/2" d	20.00
Bowl, 7-3/8" w, sq	18.50

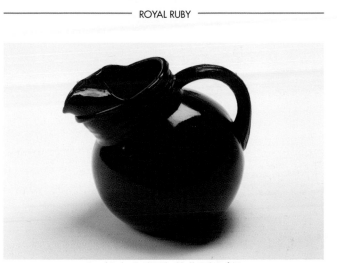

Royal Ruby, 5-1/2" tilted ball pitcher, $45.

ITEM	ROYAL RUBY
Bowl, 11" d, Rachael	50.00
Bowl, 12" l, oval, Rachael	68.00
Cereal bowl, 5-1/4" d	12.00
Cigarette box, card holder, 6-1/8" x 4"	90.00
Cocktail, 3-1/2 oz, Boopie	8.50
Cocktail, 3-1/2 oz, tumbler	10.00
Cordial, ftd	15.00
Creamer, flat	10.00
Creamer, ftd	10.00
Cup, round	6.00
Cup, square	7.50
Dessert bowl, 4-3/4" w, sq	9.00

Royal Ruby, footed sugar, $10; footed creamer (on pedestal), $10; square cup, $7.50; square saucer, $4.

ITEM	ROYAL RUBY
Fruit bowl, 4-1/4" d	5.50
Goblet, 9 oz	9.00
Goblet, 9-1/2 oz	14.00
Goblet, ball stem	12.00
Ice bucket	55.00
Iced tea goblet, 14 oz, Boopie	20.00
Iced tea tumbler, 13 oz, 6" h, ftd	15.00
Ivy ball, 4" h, Wilson	15.00
Juice tumbler, 4 oz	7.00
Juice tumbler, 5-1/2 oz	10.00
Juice tumbler, 5 oz, flat or ftd	12.00
Juice pitcher	39.00
Lamp, Hoover	50.00
Marmalade, ruby top, crystal base	22.00
Pitcher, three-qt, tilted	45.00
Pitcher, three-qt, upright	38.00
Pitcher, 42 oz, tilted	35.00
Pitcher, 42 oz, upright	40.00
Pitcher, 86 oz, 8-1/2"	35.00
Plate, 6-1/4" d, sherbet	6.50
Plate, 7" d, salad	5.50
Plate, 7-3/4" w, sq, salad	7.50
Plate, 8-3/8" w, sq, luncheon	12.00
Plate, 9-1/8" d, dinner	12.00
Plate, 13-3/4" d	35.00
Popcorn bowl, 5-1/4" d	12.50
Popcorn bowl, 10" d, deep	40.00
Puff box, ruby top, crystal base, orig label	28.00
Punch bowl and stand	75.00
Punch set, 14 pieces	125.00
Punch cup	3.50
Relish, 3-3/4" x 8-3/4", tab handle	16.00

Royal Ruby, Coolidge vase with original foil label, $20.

ITEM	ROYAL RUBY
Salad bowl, 8-1/2" d	19.00
Salad bowl, 11-1/2" d	40.00
Saucer, 5-3/8" w, sq	4.00
Saucer, round	5.00
Set, 50 pcs, orig labels, orig box	350.00
Sherbet, 6 oz, flat	8.50
Sherbet, 6-1/2 oz, stemmed	12.00
Shot glass	4.50
Soup bowl, 7-1/2" d	15.00
Sugar, flat	10.00
Sugar, footed	10.00
Sugar lid, notched	11.00
Tray, center handle, ruffled	16.50
Tumbler, 5 oz, 3-1/2" h	6.00
Tumbler, 9 oz, Windsor	9.50
Tumbler, 10 oz, 5" h, ftd	8.00
Tumbler, 14 oz, 5" h	10.00
Tumbler, 15 oz, long boy	15.00
Vase, 3-3/4" h, Roosevelt	7.50
Vase, 4" h, Wilson, fancy edge	12.00
Vase, 6-3/8" h, Harding	15.00
Vase, 6-5/8" h, Coolidge	15.00
Vase, 9" h, Hoover, plain	22.00
Vase, 9" h, Hoover, white birds on branch dec	25.00
Vase, 10" h, fluted, star base	35.00
Vase, 10" h, ftd, Rachael	50.00
Vegetable bowl, 8" l, oval	30.00
Wine, 2-1/2 oz, ftd	12.00

S-PATTERN
STIPPLED ROSE BAND

Manufactured by Macbeth-Evans Glass Company, Charleroi, Pennsylvania, from 1930 to 1933.

Pieces were made in amber, crystal, crystal with amber, blue, green, pink or silver trims, fired-on red, green, light yellow, and Monax.

ITEM	AMBER	CRYSTAL	CRYSTAL WITH TRIMS
Berry bowl, 8-1/2" d	8.50	12.00	—
Cake plate, 11-3/4" d	50.00	48.00	55.00
Cake plate, 13" d	80.00	65.00	75.00
Cereal bowl, 5-1/2" d	6.00	4.00	6.00
Creamer, thick	7.50	6.50	8.00
Creamer, thin	7.50	6.50	8.00
Cup, thick	5.00	4.00	5.50
Cup, thin	5.00	4.00	5.50
Pitcher, 80 oz	—	75.00	—
Plate, 6" d, sherbet	3.50	3.00	4.00
Plate, 8-1/4" d, luncheon	7.00	7.00	9.50

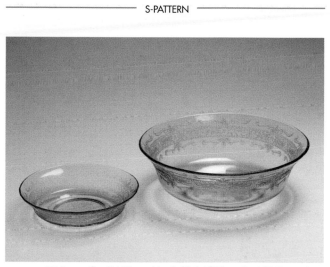

*S-Pattern, yellow 5-1/2" cereal bowl, **$6**; 8-1/2" berry bowl **$8.50**.*

ITEM	FIRED-ON COLORS	YELLOW
Berry bowl, 8-1/2" d	—	8.50
Cake plate, 11-3/4" d	—	50.00
Cake plate, 13" d	—	75.00
Cereal bowl, 5-1/2" d	12.00	6.00
Creamer, thick	15.00	7.50
Creamer, thin	15.00	7.50
Cup, thick	10.00	5.00
Cup, thin	10.00	5.00
Pitcher, 80 oz	—	—
Plate, 6" d, sherbet	—	3.50
Plate, 8-1/4" d, luncheon	—	5.00

S-Pattern, yellow footed sherbet, $8; 4-3/4" flat tumbler, $8.50.

ITEM	AMBER	CRYSTAL	CRYSTAL WITH TRIMS
Plate, 9-1/4" d, dinner	9.50	—	12.50
Plate, grill	8.50	6.50	9.00
Saucer	4.00	3.00	4.00
Sherbet, low, ftd	8.00	5.50	8.50
Sugar, thick	7.50	6.50	8.00
Sugar, thin	7.50	6.50	8.00
Tumbler, 5 oz, 3-1/2" h	6.50	5.00	6.50
Tumbler, 10 oz, 4-3/4" h	8.50	9.00	7.50
Tumbler, 12 oz, 5" h	15.00	10.00	17.50

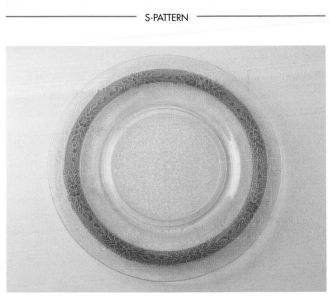

S-Pattern, crystal luncheon plate with yellow trim, $9.50.

ITEM	FIRED-ON COLORS	YELLOW
Plate, 9-1/4" d, dinner	—	9.50
Plate, grill	—	8.50
Saucer	—	4.00
Sherbet, low, ftd	—	8.00
Sugar, thick	15.00	7.50
Sugar, thin	15.00	7.50
Tumbler, 5 oz, 3-1/2" h	—	6.50
Tumbler, 10 oz, 4-3/4" h	—	8.50
Tumbler, 12 oz, 5" h	—	15.00

SANDWICH
HOCKING

Manufactured by Hocking Glass Company, and later Anchor Hocking Corp., from 1939 to 1964.

Pieces were made in crystal, desert gold, 1961-1964; forest green, 1956-1960s; pink, 1939-1940; royal ruby, 1938-1939; and white/ivory (opaque), 1957-1960s.

Reproductions: † The cookie jar has been reproduced in crystal.

ITEM	CRYSTAL	DESERT GOLD	FOREST GREEN
Bowl, 4-5/16" d, smooth	5.50	—	6.00
Bowl, 4-7/8" d, smooth	6.00	6.00	—
Bowl, 4-7/8" d, crimped	20.00	—	—
Bowl, 5-1/4" d, scalloped	5.00	6.00	—
Bowl, 5-1/4" d, smooth	—	—	—
Bowl, 6-1/2" d, scalloped	7.50	12.00	60.00
Bowl, 6-1/2" d, smooth	7.50	9.00	—
Bowl, 7-1/4" d, scalloped	8.00	—	—
Bowl, 8-1/4" d, oval	10.00	—	—
Bowl, 8-1/4" d, scalloped	10.00	—	125.00
Butter dish, cov	45.00	—	—

* No cover is known for the cookie jar in Forest Green.

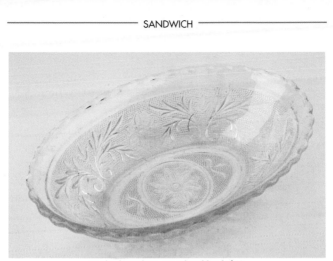

Sandwich, Hocking, crystal oval bowl, $10.

ITEM	CRYSTAL	DESERT GOLD	FOREST GREEN
Cereal bowl, 6-3/4" d	32.00	12.00	—
Cookie jar, cov † *	30.00	45.00	20.00
Creamer	7.50	—	45.00
Cup, coffee	2.00	12.00	25.00
Cup, tea	3.00	14.00	25.00
Custard cup	10.00	—	5.00
Custard cup liner	5.50	—	2.50
Custard cup, crimped	9.50	—	—
Dessert bowl, 5" d, crimped	18.50	—	—
Juice pitcher, 6" h	115.00	—	145.00
Juice tumbler, 3 oz, 3-3/8" h	18.00	—	7.00
Juice tumbler, 5 oz, 3-9/16" h	7.50	—	8.50
Pitcher, half gallon, ice lip	85.00	—	550.00

Sandwich, Hocking, smooth desert gold 6-1/2" d bowl, $9.

ITEM	CRYSTAL	DESERT GOLD	FOREST GREEN
Plate, 6" d	8.00	—	—
Plate, 7" d, dessert	20.00	—	—
Plate, 8" d, luncheon	12.00	—	—
Plate, 9" d, dinner	12.50	10.00	125.00
Plate, 9" d, indent for punch cup	12.00	—	—
Punch bowl, 9-3/4" d	18.00	—	—
Punch bowl and stand	32.00	—	—
Punch bowl set, bowl, base, 12 cups	60.00	—	—
Punch cup	2.50	—	—
Salad bowl, 7" d	8.00	25.00	—
Salad bowl, 7-5/8" d	—	—	60.00
Salad bowl, 9" d	24.00	20.00	—

ITEM	CRYSTAL	DESERT GOLD	FOREST GREEN
Sandwich plate, 12" d	14.00	16.50	—
Saucer	3.50	2.00	25.00
Sherbet, ftd	9.00	8.00	—
Snack set, plate and cup	9.00	—	—
Sugar, cov	30.00	—	—
Sugar, no cover	6.00	—	45.00
Tumbler, 9 oz, ftd	30.00	125.00	—
Tumbler, 9 oz, water	9.00	—	12.00
Vase	—	—	30.00
Vegetable, 8-1/2" l, oval	10.00	—	—

ITEM	PINK	ROYAL RUBY	WHITE
Bowl, 4-5/16" d, smooth	—	—	—
Bowl, 4-7/8" d, smooth	7.00	17.50	—
Bowl, 4-7/8" d, crimped	—	—	—
Bowl, 5-1/4" d, scalloped	—	22.00	—
Bowl, 5-1/4" d, smooth	7.00	25.00	—
Bowl, 6-1/2" d, scalloped	—	35.00	—
Bowl, 6-1/2" d, smooth	—	—	—
Bowl, 7-1/4" d, scalloped	—	—	—
Bowl, 8-1/4" d, oval	—	—	—
Bowl, 8-1/4" d, scalloped	20.00	35.00	—
Butter dish, cov	—	—	—
Cereal bowl, 6-3/4" d	—	—	—
Cookie jar, cov † *	—	—	—
Creamer	—	—	—
Cup, coffee	—	—	—
Cup, tea	—	—	—
Custard cup	—	—	—
Custard cup liner	—	—	—
Custard cup, crimped	—	—	—
Dessert bowl, 5" d, crimped	—	—	—

ITEM	PINK	ROYAL RUBY	WHITE
Juice pitcher, 6" h	—	—	—
Juice tumbler, 3 oz, 3-3/8" h	—	—	—
Juice tumbler, 5 oz, 3-9/16" h	—	—	—
Pitcher, half gallon, ice lip	—	—	—
Plate, 6" d	—	—	—
Plate, 7" d, dessert	—	—	—
Plate, 8" d, luncheon	—	—	—
Plate, 9" d, dinner	10.00	—	—
Plate, 9" d, indent for punch cup	—	—	—
Punch bowl, 9-3/4" d	—	—	15.00
Punch bowl and stand	—	—	30.00
Punch bowl set, bowl, base, 12 cups	—	—	—
Punch cup	—	—	2.00
Salad bowl, 7" d	—	—	—
Salad bowl, 7-5/8" d	—	—	65.00
Salad bowl, 9" d	—	—	—
Sandwich plate, 12" d	—	—	—
Saucer	—	—	—
Sherbet, ftd	—	—	—
Snack set, plate and cup	—	—	—
Sugar, cov	—	—	—
Sugar, no cover	—	—	—
Tumbler, 9 oz, ftd	—	—	—
Tumbler, 9 oz, water	—	—	—
Vase	—	—	—
Vegetable, 8-1/2" l, oval	—	—	—

SANDWICH
INDIANA

Manufactured by Indiana Glass Company, Dunkirk, Indiana, from the 1920s to the 1980s.

Pieces were made in crystal, late 1920s to 1990s; amber, late 1920s to 1980s; milk white, mid-1950s; teal blue, 1950s to 1960s; red, 1933 and early 1970s; smoky blue, 1976 to 1977; and green, late 1960s and 1970s by Tiara.

Reproductions: † Reproductions include a butter dish, decanter, and wine. Reproductions are found in dark amber, crystal, green, and pink.

ITEM	AMBER	CRYSTAL	TEAL BLUE	RED
Ashtray, club	8.25	6.00	—	—
Ashtray, diamond	8.25	6.00	—	—
Ashtray, heart	8.25	6.00	3.00	—
Ashtray, spade	8.25	6.00	—	—
Basket, 10" h	35.00	35.00	—	225.00
Berry bowl, 4-1/4" d	3.50	5.00	—	—
Bowl, 6" w, hexagonal	5.50	6.00	15.00	—
Bowl, 8-1/2" d	10.00	11.00	—	—
Butter dish, cov †	25.00	25.00	150.00	—

ITEM	AMBER	CRYSTAL	TEAL BLUE	RED
Candlesticks, pr, 3-1/2" h	18.00	20.00	—	—
Candlesticks, pr, 7" h	25.00	22.00	—	—
Celery tray, 10-1/2" l	17.50	18.00	—	—
Cereal bowl, 6" d	12.00	6.50	—	—
Cocktail, 3 oz, ftd	7.50	7.50	—	—
Comport, low, ruffled	150.00	—	—	—
Console bowl, 9" d	17.50	17.50	—	—
Console bowl, 11-1/2" d	20.00	20.00	—	—
Creamer	8.00	8.00	—	48.00

Sandwich, Indiana, crystal creamer and sugar with matching tray, $50.

ITEM	AMBER	CRYSTAL	TEAL BLUE	RED
Creamer and sugar, tray	50.00	50.00	65.00	—
Cruet, 6-1/2 oz, stopper	—	—	145.00	—
Cup	4.00	2.00	8.50	30.00
Decanter, stopper †	25.00	25.00	—	90.00
Fairy lamp	15.00	15.00	—	—
Goblet, 9 oz	14.00	25.00	—	45.00
Iced tea tumbler, 12 oz, ftd	10.00	10.00	—	—
Mayonnaise, ftd	14.00	14.00	—	—
Pitcher, 68 oz	24.00	24.00	—	175.00
Plate, 6" d, sherbet	3.50	3.50	7.50	—
Plate, 7" d, bread and butter	4.00	4.00	—	—
Plate, 8" d, oval, indent	—	6.00	6.50	15.00
Plate, 8-3/8" d, luncheon	7.50	8.00	—	20.00
Plate, 10-1/2" d, dinner	24.00	8.50	20.00	35.00
Puff box	18.00	18.00	—	—
Salt and pepper shakers, pr	18.00	18.00	—	—
Sandwich plate, 13" d	14.50	14.50	25.00	35.00
Sandwich server, center handle	40.00	15.00	—	50.00
Saucer	3.50	2.50	7.00	8.50
Sherbet, 3-1/4" h	6.00	9.50	12.00	—
Sugar, cov, large	20.00	20.00	—	48.00
Tumbler, 8 oz, ftd, water	10.00	10.00	—	—
Wine, 3" h, 4 oz †	10.00	12.00	—	15.00

SANDWICH
LINE #41

Manufactured by Duncan & Miller Glass Company, Washington, Pennsylvania, from 1924 to 1955.

Pieces were made in crystal with limited production in amber, cobalt blue, green, pink, and red. The molds were sold to Lancaster Colony, which continues to produce some glass in this pattern, but in newer brighter colors, such as amberina, blue, and green.

ITEM	CRYSTAL
Almond bowl, 2-1/2" d	12.00
Ashtray, 2-1/2" x 3-3/4"	10.00
Ashtray, 2-3/4" sq	5.00
Basket, 6-1/2", loop handle	95.00
Basket 10", loop handle, crimped	165.00
Basket, 10", loop handle, oval	165.00
Basket, 11-1/2", loop handle	225.00
Bonbon, 5" w, heart shape	15.00
Bonbon, 6" w, heart shape, ring handle	20.00
Bonbon, cov, 7-1/2" d, ftd,	45.00
Bowl, 5-1/2" d, handle	15.00
Butter, cov, quarter pound	40.00

ITEM	CRYSTAL
Cake stand, 11-1/2" d, ftd	95.00
Cake stand, 12" d, ftd	90.00
Cake stand, 13" d, ftd	95.00
Candelabra, with bobeche and prisms, 10" h, three-lite	300.00
Candelabra, with bobeche and prisms, 10" h, one-lite	95.00
Candelabra, with bobeche and prisms, 16" h, three-lite	225.00
Candlesticks, pr, 4" h	30.00
Candlesticks, pr, 5" h, three-lite	90.00
Candy box, cov, 5" d, flat	42.00
Candy comport, 3-1/4" d, low, ftd or flared	25.00
Candy dish, 6" sq	375.00
Candy jar, cov, 8-1/2" d, flat	60.00
Celery tray, 10" l, oval	25.00
Champagne, 5 oz	25.00
Cheese comport, 13" d underplate	60.00
Cheese dish, cov	125.00
Cigarette box, cov, 3-1/2"	24.00
Cigarette holder, 3" d, ftd	30.00
Coaster, 5" d	9.00
Cocktail, 3 oz	15.00
Comport, 2-1/4"	17.50
Comport, 4-1/4" d, ftd	20.00
Comport, 5" d, low, ftd	22.00
Comport, 5-1/2" d, ftd, low, crimped	25.00
Comport, 6" d, low, flared	25.00
Condiment set, pr cruets, pr salt and pepper shakers, tray	100.00
Console bowl, 12" d	45.00
Cracker plate, 13" d	32.00
Creamer	10.00
Cup	10.00
Deviled egg plate, 12" d	65.00
Epergne, 9" h	125.00

ITEM	CRYSTAL
Epergne, 12" h, three parts	200.00
Finger bowl, 4" h	18.00
Finger bowl underplate, 6-1/2" d	8.00
Flower bowl, 11-1/2" d, crimped	65.00
Fruit bowl, 5" d	10.00
Fruit bowl, 10" d	65.00
Fruit bowl, 11-1/2" d, crimped, ftd	65.00
Fruit bowl, 12", flared	50.00
Fruit cup, 6 oz	12.00
Fruit salad bowl, 6" d	12.00
Gardenia bowl, 11-1/2" d	48.00
Goblet, 9 oz, 6" h	15.00
Grapefruit bowl, 5-1/2" d or 6" d	17.50
Hostess plate, 16" d	100.00
Ice cream dish 5 oz	8.00
Ice cream plate, rolled edge, 12" d	60.00
Ice cream tray, rolled edge, 12" d	45.00
Iced tea tumbler, 12 or 13 oz, ftd	20.00
Ivy bowl, ftd, crimped	35.00
Jelly, 3" d	8.00
Juice tumbler, 5 oz	12.00
Lazy Susan, 16" d	115.00
Lily bowl, 10" d	55.00
Mayonnaise set, three pcs	35.00
Mint tray, 6" l or 7" l, rolled edge, ring handle	18.00
Nappy, 5" d, two parts	15.00
Nappy, 5" d, ring handle	12.00
Nappy, 6" d, ring handle	18.00
Nut bowl, 3-1/2" d	10.00
Nut bowl, 11" d, cupped	55.00
Oil bottle, orig stopper	38.00
Oil and vinegar tray, 8" l	20.00

Sandwich, crystal salad plate, $10.

ITEM	CRYSTAL
Oyster cocktail, 5 oz	18.00
Parfait, 4 oz, ftd	30.00
Pickle tray, 7″ l, oval	15.00
Pitcher, 13 oz, metal lip	85.00
Pitcher, 64 oz, ice lip	135.00
Plate, 3″ d, jelly	5.00
Plate, 6″ d, bread and butter	6.00
Plate, 7″ d, dessert	7.50
Plate, 8″ d, salad	10.00

ITEM	CRYSTAL
Plate, 9-1/2" d, dinner	35.00
Relish, 5-1/2" d, two parts, ring handle	15.00
Relish, 6" d, two parts, ring handle	18.00
Relish, 7" d, two parts, oval	20.00
Relish, 10" d, three parts, rect	27.50
Relish, 10" d, four parts	45.00
Relish, 10-1/2" l, three parts, rect	27.50
Relish, 12" l, three parts	25.00
Salad bowl, 10" d, deep	75.00
Salad bowl, 12" d, shallow	42.00
Salt and pepper shakers, pr, 2-1/2" h, glass tops	20.00
Salt and pepper shakers, pr, 2-1/2" h, metal tops	20.00
Salt and pepper shakers, set, pr 3-3/4" h, metal tops, 6" tray	35.00
Service plate, 11-1/2" d, handle	50.00
Service plate, 13" d	55.00
Sugar shaker	72.00
Sugar bowl, 5 oz	10.00
Sugar bowl, 9 oz, 3-1/4" h, ftd	12.00
Sundae, 5 oz	15.00
Syrup pitcher, metal lid, 13 oz	70.00
Torte plate, 12" d	48.00
Tray, 8" l	20.00
Urn, cov, 12" h, ftd	150.00
Tumbler, 9 oz, 4-3/4", ftd	15.00
Vase, 3" h, crimped	18.00
Vase, 3" h, flared rim	18.00
Vase, 4" h, hat shape	20.00
Vase, 4-1/2" h, crimped	25.00
Vase, 5" h, fan	40.00
Vase, 5" h, flared or crimped	25.00
Vase, 10" h, ftd	70.00
Wine, 3 oz	12.00

SEVILLE

Manufactured by Fostoria Glass Company, Moundsville, West Virginia, from 1926 to 1931.

Pieces were made in amber and green.

ITEM	AMBER	GREEN
After dinner cup and saucer	32.00	40.00
Ashtray, 4" d	20.00	24.00
Baker, 9" l, oval	27.50	32.00
Baker, 10-1/2" l, oval	37.50	40.00
Bouillon, flat or ftd	15.00	17.50
Bowl, 7" d, low foot	15.50	17.50
Bowl, 10" d, ftd	35.00	40.00
Bowl, 10-1/2" d, flared, ftd	30.00	32.00
Bowl, 12" d, deep, flared	32.00	35.00
Butter dish, cov, round	195.00	250.00
Canapé plate, 8-3/4" d	37.50	42.00
Candlesticks, pr, 2" h	15.00	20.00

Seville, amber 9-1/2" d dinner plate, $12.50.

ITEM	AMBER	GREEN
Candlesticks, pr, 4" h	15.00	22.00
Candlesticks, pr, 9" h	32.00	35.00
Candy jar, cov, flat	70.00	85.00
Candy jar, cov, ftd	90.00	125.00
Celery, 11"	17.50	20.00
Cereal bowl, 6-1/2" d	17.50	20.00
Cheese and cracker	42.00	48.00
Chop plate, 12-3/4" d	32.00	35.00
Cocktail	17.50	20.00
Comport, 7-1/2" d	22.00	30.00
Comport, 8"	30.00	37.50
Console bowl, 11" d, rolled edge	30.00	35.00
Console bowl, 13" d, rolled edge	35.00	40.00
Console bowl, 13" l, oval	40.00	45.00
Cordial	70.00	72.00
Cream soup, ftd	15.00	17.50
Creamer, flat or ftd	15.00	20.00
Cup, flat or ftd	12.00	15.00
Egg cup	30.00	35.00
Finger bowl	10.00	12.50
Fruit bowl, 5-1/2" d	10.00	12.50
Goblet	22.00	25.00
Grapefruit, blown	42.00	48.00
Grapefruit, molded	27.50	35.00
Ice bucket	60.00	65.00
Nappy, 9" d	30.00	35.00
Oyster cocktail	17.50	20.00
Parfait	35.00	37.50
Pickle	15.00	17.50
Pitcher, ftd	250.00	275.00
Plate, 6" d, bread and butter	4.00	6.00
Plate, 7-1/2" d, salad	6.00	7.50

ITEM	AMBER	GREEN
Plate, 8-1/2" d, luncheon	7.50	12.50
Plate, 9-1/2" d, dinner	12.50	17.50
Plate, 10-1/2" d, dinner	30.00	35.00
Platter, 10-1/2" l	24.00	27.50
Platter, 12" l	35.00	40.00
Platter, 15" l	65.00	70.00
Salad bowl, 10" d	35.00	40.00
Salt and pepper shakers, pr	65.00	70.00
Sauce boat and underplate	75.00	95.00
Saucer	3.50	4.00
Serving plate, 15" d	37.50	42.00
Sherbet, high	15.00	17.50
Sherbet, low	12.00	15.00
Soup bowl, 7-3/4" d	24.00	30.00
Sugar bowl lid	75.00	100.00
Sugar bowl, ftd	15.00	15.00
Tray, 11" d, center handle	30.00	32.00
Tumbler, 2 oz, ftd	37.50	42.00
Tumbler, 5 oz, ftd	15.00	17.50
Tumbler, 9 oz, ftd	17.50	20.00
Tumbler, 12 oz, ftd	20.00	24.00
Urn	72.00	95.00
Vase, 8" h	50.00	60.00
Vegetable bowl	24.00	30.00
Wine	24.00	27.50

SHARON

CABBAGE ROSE

Manufactured by Federal Glass Company, Columbus, Ohio, from 1935 to 1939.

Pieces were made in amber, crystal, green, and pink.

Reproductions: † Reproductions include the butter dish, covered candy dish, creamer, covered sugar, and salt and pepper shakers. Reproduction colors include dark amber, blue, green, and pink.

Sharon, pink sherbet, $17.50; 8-1/2" d berry bowl, $40; 5" d berry bowl, $18; creamer, $25.

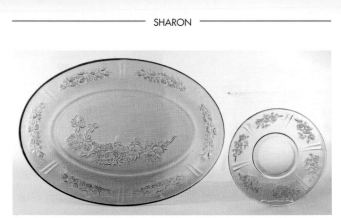

Sharon, amber 12-1/2" l oval platter, $24; 6" d cereal bowl, $24.

ITEM	AMBER	CRYSTAL	GREEN	PINK
Berry bowl, 5" d	9.50	6.00	20.00	18.00
Berry bowl, 8-1/2" d	15.00	12.00	45.00	40.00
Butter dish, cov †	50.00	20.00	85.00	70.00
Cake plate, 11-1/2" d, ftd	30.00	10.00	65.00	50.00
Candy dish, cov †	50.00	20.00	100.00	70.00
Cereal bowl, 6" d	24.00	12.00	32.00	35.00
Champagne, 5" d bowl	—	—	—	12.00
Cheese dish, cov †	225.00	1,500.00	—	950.00
Cream soup bowl, 5" d	27.50	15.00	60.00	50.00
Creamer, ftd †	15.00	14.00	22.00	25.00
Cup	9.00	6.00	18.00	15.00
Fruit bowl, 10-1/2" d	30.00	20.00	45.00	50.00
Iced tea tumbler, ftd	125.00	15.00	—	55.00
Jam dish, 7-1/2" d	40.00	—	48.00	215.00
Pitcher, 80 oz, ice lip	145.00	—	150.00	165.00
Pitcher, 80 oz, without ice lip	140.00	—	150.00	150.00

Sharon, pink 10-1/2" d fruit bowl, $50.

ITEM	AMBER	CRYSTAL	GREEN	PINK
Plate, 6" d, bread and butter	14.00	5.00	9.00	8.00
Plate, 7-1/2" d, salad	16.50	6.50	10.00	30.00
Plate, 9-1/2" d, dinner	17.00	9.50	27.50	24.50
Platter, 12-1/2" l, oval	24.00	—	35.00	40.00
Salt and pepper shakers, pr †	40.00	—	80.00	65.00
Saucer	5.50	4.00	28.00	7.00
Sherbet, ftd	14.00	8.00	35.00	17.50
Soup, flat, 7-3/4" d, 1 7/8" deep	60.00	—	—	50.00
Sugar, cov †	30.00	15.00	50.00	55.00
Tumbler, 9 oz, 4-1/8" h, thick	30.00	—	65.00	45.00
Tumbler, 9 oz, 4-1/8" h, thin	30.00	—	65.00	42.00
Tumbler, 12 oz, 5-1/4" h, thick	70.00	—	95.00	50.00
Tumbler, 12 oz, 5-1/4" h, thin	55.00	—	95.00	52.50
Tumbler, 15 oz, 6-1/2" h, thick	125.00	18.00	—	63.00
Vegetable bowl, 9-1/2" l, oval	25.00	—	35.00	42.50

SIERRA
PINWHEEL

Manufactured by Jeannette Glass Company, Jeannette, Pennsylvania, from 1931 to 1933.

Pieces were made in green and pink. A few forms are known in ultramarine.

ITEM	GREEN	PINK
Berry, small	25.00	25.00
Berry bowl, 8-1/2" d	40.00	40.00
Butter dish, cov	80.00	85.00
Cereal bowl, 5-1/2" d	25.00	20.00
Creamer	25.00	25.00
Cup	14.50	17.50
Pitcher, 32 oz, 6-1/2" h	160.00	135.00
Plate, 9" d, dinner	25.00	22.00
Platter, 11" l, oval	70.00	65.00
Salt and pepper shakers, pr	40.00	50.00
Saucer	10.00	10.00

Sierra Pinwheel, green butter dish, $80; pink cup, $17.50; pink saucer, $10.

ITEM	GREEN	PINK
Serving tray, 10-1/4" l, two handles	25.00	30.00
Sugar, cov	48.00	48.00
Tumbler, 9 oz, 4-1/2" h, ftd	90.00	80.00
Vegetable bowl, 9-1/4" l, oval	135.00	90.00

SPIRAL

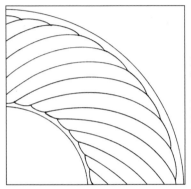

Manufactured by Hocking Glass Company, Lancaster, Ohio, from 1928 to 1930.

Pieces were made in crystal, green, and pink. Collector interest is strongest in green.

ITEM	GREEN
Berry bowl, 4-3/4" d	8.00
Berry bowl, 8" d	16.50
Bowl, low, 8-1/2" d	17.50
Butter tub	27.50
Creamer, flat	8.00
Creamer, footed	8.00
Cup	5.00
Ice tub	25.00
Juice tumbler, 5 oz, 3" h	5.00
Mixing bowl, 7" d	9.00
Pitcher, three styles	35.00
Plate, 6" d, sherbet	5.00

*Spiral, green 5-7/8" h footed cone tumbler, **$24**; pitcher with bulbous base, **$35**; pitcher with straighter sides, **$35**.*

ITEM	GREEN
Plate, 8" d, luncheon	6.50
Platter, 12" l	32.00
Preserve, cov	35.00
Salt and pepper shakers, pr	37.50
Sandwich server, center handle	30.00
Saucer	4.00
Sherbet	5.00
Sugar, flat	8.00
Sugar, footed	8.00
Tumbler, 5-7/8" h, ftd	24.00
Tumbler, 9 oz, 5" h	12.00

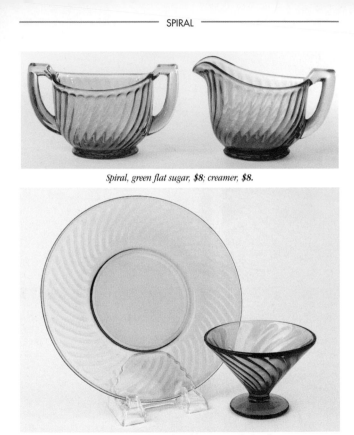

Spiral, green flat sugar, $8; creamer, $8.

Spiral, green luncheon plate, $6.50; green sherbet, $5.

STARLIGHT

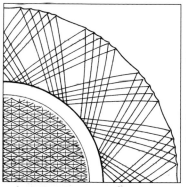

Manufactured by Hazel Atlas Glass Company, Clarksburg, West Virginia, and Zanesville, Ohio, from 1938 to 1940.

Pieces were made in cobalt blue, crystal, pink and white. Production in cobalt blue was limited to a 8-1/2" diameter bowl valued at $30.

ITEM	CRYSTAL	PINK	WHITE
Berry bowl, 4" d	9.50	—	—
Bowl, 8-1/2" d, two handles	18.00	20.00	18.00
Bowl, 11-1/2" d, deep	25.00	—	25.00
Bowl, 12" d, 2-3/4" deep	25.00	—	25.00
Cereal bowl, 5-1/2" d, two handles	7.00	12.00	7.00
Creamer, oval	10.00	—	5.00
Cup	6.00	—	5.00
Plate, 6" d, sherbet	4.50	—	4.00
Plate, 7-1/2" d, salad	5.00	—	4.50
Plate, 8-1/2" d, luncheon	5.00	—	5.00
Plate, 9" d, dinner	8.50	—	8.50
Relish dish	15.00	—	15.00

ITEM	CRYSTAL	PINK	WHITE
Salad bowl, 11-1/2" d, deep	25.00	—	25.00
Salt and pepper shakers, pr	30.00	—	30.00
Sandwich plate, 13" d	25.00	20.00	—
Saucer	4.00	—	2.50
Sherbet	15.00	—	12.00
Sugar, oval	10.00	—	10.00

Starlight, crystal cup, $6; creamer, $10.

Starlight, crystal 11-1/2" bowl, $25; crystal 4" two-handled berry bowl, $9.50.

STRAWBERRY

Manufactured by U. S. Glass Company, Pittsburgh, Pennsylvania, in the early 1930s.

Pieces were made in crystal, green, pink, and some iridescent.

ITEM	CRYSTAL	GREEN	IRIDESCENT	PINK
Berry bowl, 4" d	7.50	12.00	7.50	12.00
Berry bowl, 7-1/2" d	16.00	20.00	16.00	20.00
Bowl, 6-1/4" d, 2" deep	40.00	60.00	40.00	60.00
Butter dish, cov	125.00	185.00	135.00	195.00
Comport, 5-3/4" d	55.00	60.00	55.00	60.00
Creamer, large, 4-5/8" h	24.00	35.00	24.00	35.00
Creamer, small	12.00	18.50	12.00	18.50
Olive dish, 5" l, one handle	8.50	14.00	8.50	14.00
Pickle dish, 8-1/4" l, oval	8.00	14.00	8.00	14.00
Pitcher, 7-3/4" h	150.00	200.00	150.00	195.00
Plate, 6" d, sherbet	5.00	10.00	5.00	8.00
Plate, 7-1/2" d, salad	10.00	14.00	10.00	18.00

ITEM	CRYSTAL	GREEN	IRIDESCENT	PINK
Salad bowl, 6-1/2" d	15.00	20.00	15.00	20.00
Sherbet	6.00	9.00	6.50	14.50
Sugar, large, cov	60.00	45.00	60.00	45.00
Sugar, small, open	12.00	32.00	12.00	32.00
Tumbler, 8 oz, 3-5/8" h	20.00	32.00	20.00	60.00

*Strawberry, pink sherbet, **$14.50**; 5" one-handled olive dish, **$14**.*

*Strawberry, pink 5-3/4" footed comport, **$60**.*

SUNBURST
HERRINGBONE

Manufactured by Jeannette Glass Company, Jeannette, Pennsylvania, in the late 1930s.

Pieces were made in crystal.

ITEM	CRYSTAL
Berry bowl, 4-3/4" d	12.00
Berry bowl, 8-1/2" d	18.00
Bowl, 10-1/2" d	30.00
Candelabra, pr, double	30.00
Creamer, ftd	16.00
Creamer and sugar underplate, oval	18.00
Cup	8.50
Plate, 5-1/2" d	12.00
Plate, 9-1/4" d, dinner	15.00
Platter, oval	18.00
Relish, two parts	14.50

ITEM	CRYSTAL
Sandwich plate, 11-3/4" d	25.00
Saucer	4.50
Sherbet	12.00
Sugar	16.00
Tumbler, 4" h, 9 oz, flat	18.50

Sunburst, crystal sugar, $16; creamer, $16; oval underplate, $18.

Sunburst, crystal sandwich plate, **$25.**

SUNFLOWER

Manufactured by Jeannette Glass Company, Jeannette, Pennsylvania, in the 1930s.

Pieces were made in Delphite, green, pink, and some opaque colors. Look for a creamer in Delphite that is valued at $85.

ITEM	DELPHITE	GREEN	PINK	OPAQUE
Ashtray, 5" d	—	12.00	10.00	—
Cake plate, 10" d, three legs	—	22.00	20.00	—
Creamer	90.00	20.00	20.00	85.00
Cup	—	15.00	15.00	75.00
Plate, 9" d, dinner	—	22.00	24.00	—
Saucer	—	17.50	12.00	85.00
Sugar	—	25.00	22.00	—
Trivet, 7" d, three legs, turned up edge	—	325.00	315.00	—
Tumbler, 8 oz, 4-3/8" h, ftd	—	35.00	32.00	—

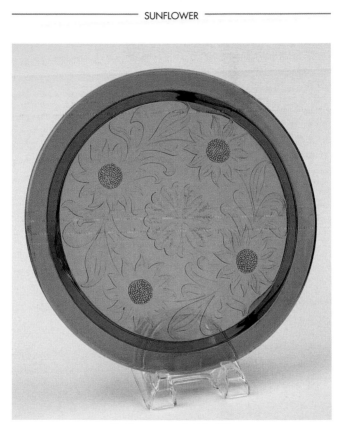

Sunflower, green cake plate, $22.

SWIRL

PETAL SWIRL

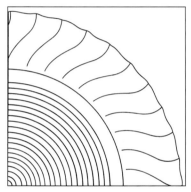

Manufactured by Jeannette Glass Company, Jeannette, Pennsylvania, from 1937 to 1938.

Pieces were made in amber, Delphite, ice blue, pink, and ultramarine. Production was limited in amber and ice blue.

ITEM	DELPHITE	PINK	ULTRAMARINE
Berry bowl, 9" d	15.00	—	18.00
Bowl, 10" d, ftd, closed handles	—	25.00	35.00
Butter dish, cov	—	175.00	245.00
Candleholders, pr, double branch	—	40.00	60.00
Candleholders, pr, single branch	115.00	—	—
Candy dish, cov	—	95.00	125.00
Candy dish, open, three feet	—	20.00	25.00
Cereal bowl, 5-1/4" d	15.00	9.00	15.00
Coaster, 1" x 3-1/4"	—	15.00	14.00
Console bowl, 10-1/2" d, ftd	—	20.00	35.00
Creamer	12.00	9.50	12.00

Swirl, ultramarine sugar, $15; creamer, $12.

ITEM	DELPHITE	PINK	ULTRAMARINE
Cup and saucer	17.50	14.00	22.50
Plate, 6-1/2" d, sherbet	6.50	7.00	8.00
Plate, 7-1/4" d, luncheon	—	6.50	12.00
Plate, 8" d, salad	9.00	8.50	18.00
Plate, 9-1/4" d, dinner	12.00	16.00	24.50
Plate, 10-1/2" d, dinner	18.00	—	30.00
Platter, 12" l, oval	35.00	—	—
Salad bowl, 9" d	30.00	18.00	35.00
Salad bowl, 9" d, rimmed	—	20.00	35.00
Salt and pepper shakers, pr	—	—	50.00
Sandwich plate, 12-1/2" d	—	20.00	30.00
Sherbet, low, ftd	—	13.00	18.00
Soup, tab handles, lug	—	25.00	35.00
Sugar, ftd	—	12.00	15.00
Tray, 10-1/2" l, two handles	25.00	—	—

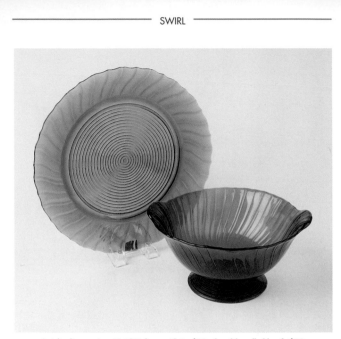

Swirl, ultramarine 10-1/2" dinner plate, $30; closed-handled bowl, $35.

ITEM	DELPHITE	PINK	ULTRAMARINE
Tumbler, 9 oz, 4" h	—	18.00	35.00
Tumbler, 9 oz, 4-5/8" h	—	18.00	—
Tumbler, 13 oz, 5-1/8" h	—	45.00	90.00
Vase, 6-1/2" h, ftd, ruffled	—	28.00	—
Vase, 8-1/2" h, ftd	—	—	40.00

TEA ROOM

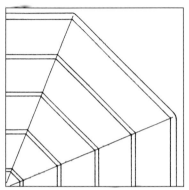

Manufactured by Indiana Glass Company, Dunkirk, Indiana, from 1926 to 1931.

Pieces were made in amber, crystal, green, and pink.

ITEM	AMBER	CRYSTAL	GREEN	PINK
Banana split bowl, 7-1/2" l	—	85.00	200.00	210.00
Candlesticks, pr, low	—	—	80.00	85.00
Celery bowl, 8-1/2"d	—	—	35.00	27.50
Creamer, 3-1/4" h	—	—	30.00	28.00
Creamer, 4-1/2" h, ftd	80.00	—	24.00	20.00
Creamer and sugar on tray	—	—	125.00	85.00
Cup	—	—	65.00	60.00
Finger bowl	—	80.00	50.00	40.00
Goblet, 9 oz.	—	—	75.00	65.00
Ice bucket	—	—	95.00	80.00
Lamp, electric	—	140.00	175.00	145.00
Mustard, cov	—	—	160.00	140.00

Tea Room, pink footed sugar, $60 (without lid); footed creamer, $28.

ITEM	AMBER	CRYSTAL	GREEN	PINK
Parfait	—	—	72.00	65.00
Pitcher, 64 oz	425.00	400.00	150.00	135.00
Plate, 6-1/2" d, sherbet	—	—	35.00	32.00
Plate, 8-1/4" d, luncheon	—	—	37.50	35.00
Plates, 10-1/2" d, two handles	—	—	50.00	60.00
Relish, divided	—	—	30.00	25.00
Salad bowl, 8-3/4" d, deep	—	—	150.00	135.00
Salt and pepper shakers, pr, ftd	—	—	85.00	70.00
Saucer	—	—	30.00	25.00
Sherbet	—	—	40.00	35.00
Sugar, 3" h, cov	—	—	115.00	100.00
Sugar, 4-1/2" h, ftd	80.00	—	24.00	35.00
Sugar, cov, flat	—	—	200.00	170.00

Tea Room, green ruffled footed sundae, $75; 12 oz footed tumbler, $60; and crystal 9-1/2" h ruffled vase, $50.

ITEM	AMBER	CRYSTAL	GREEN	PINK
Sundae, ftd, ruffled	—	—	75.00	70.00
Tumbler, 6 oz., ftd	—	—	30.00	40.00
Tumbler, 8 oz, 5-1/4" h, ftd	75.00	—	35.00	32.00
Tumbler, 11 oz., ftd	—	—	45.00	40.00
Tumbler, 12 oz., ftd	—	—	60.00	55.00
Vase, 6-1/2" h, ruffled edge	—	—	145.00	125.00
Vase, 9-1/2" h, ruffled	—	50.00	175.00	100.00
Vase, 9-1/2"h, straight	—	175.00	95.00	225.00
Vase, 11" h, ruffled edge	—	—	350.00	395.00
Vase, 11" h, straight	—	—	200.00	395.00
Vegetable bowl, 9-1/2" l, oval	—	—	65.00	65.00

TEARDROP
LINE #301

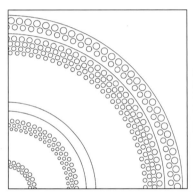

Manufactured by Duncan and Miller Glass Company, Washington, Pennsylvania, from 1936 until 1955.

Pieces were made only in crystal.

ITEM	CRYSTAL
Ale, 8 oz	18.50
Ashtray, 3" d	6.50
Ashtray, 5" d	9.00
Bonbon	12.00
Butter dish, cov, two handles	25.00
Cake salver, 13" d, ftd	50.00
Canapé set	30.00
Candlesticks, pr, 4" h	40.00
Candlesticks, pr, 7" h, two lite	40.00
Candlesticks, pr, 7" h, bobeches, prisms	125.00
Candy basket, 5-1/2" x 7-1/2"	80.00

ITEM	CRYSTAL
Candy box, cov, 7", two parts	60.00
Candy box, cov, 8" d, three parts	65.00
Candy dish, 7-1/2" w, heart shape	30.00
Celery tray, 11" l, two handles	30.00
Celery tray, 11" l, two handles, two parts	24.00
Celery tray, 12" l, three parts	28.50
Champagne, 5 oz	12.00
Cheese and cracker	48.00
Claret, 4 oz	20.00
Coaster, 3" d	6.50
Cocktail, 3-1/2 oz	17.50
Comport, 4-3/4", ftd	15.00
Comport, 6"	18.00
Condiment set, salt and pepper shakers, two cruets, 9" tray	120.00
Cordial, 1 oz	32.00
Creamer and sugar tray, two handles, 8" or 10"	10.00
Creamer, 3 oz	6.50
Creamer, 5 oz	9.00
Creamer, 8 oz	12.00
Cruets tray	12.50
Cup	8.50
Demitasse cup and saucer	12.00
Dessert bowl, 6" d	6.50
Finger bowl, 4-1/4" d	7.50
Flower basket	125.00
Flower bowl, 12" d, ftd	48.00
Flower bowl, 8" x 12"	48.00
Fruit bowl, 6" d	7.00
Gardenia bowl, 13" d	40.00
Goblet, 5-3/4" h	12.00
Goblet, 7"	15.00
Highball, 10 oz	12.00

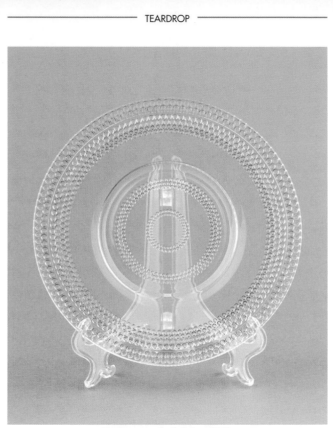

Teardrop, crystal salad plate, $6.50.

ITEM	CRYSTAL
Ice bucket	70.00
Iced tea tumbler, 12 oz or 14 oz	20.00
Juice tumbler, 3-1/2 oz, flat or ftd	7.50
Juice tumbler, 4-1/2 oz, ftd	10.00
Lazy Susan, 18" d	75.00
Lemon plate, 7" d, two handles	15.00
Marmalade, cov	37.50
Mayonnaise, ladle, underplate	35.00
Milk pitcher, 5"	20.00
Mustard jar, cov	30.00
Nappy, 5" d	6.50
Nappy, 7" d	12.00
Nappy, 9", two handles	25.00
Nut dish, 6"	12.00
Oil bottle, 3 oz	22.00
Old fashioned tumbler, 7 oz	7.50
Olive dish	15.00
Oyster cocktail, 3-1/2 oz, ftd	9.00
Pickle dish	15.00
Pitcher, 64 oz, ice lip	120.00
Plate, 6" d, bread and butter	6.00
Plate, 7-1/2" d, salad	6.50
Plate, 8-1/2" d, luncheon	9.00
Plate, 10-1/2" d, dinner	32.50
Punch bowl, 15-1/2"	115.00
Punch bowl underplate, 18" d, rolled edge	65.00
Relish, 7" l, two parts, two handles	12.50
Relish, 7-1/2" d, two parts, heart shape	22.00
Relish, 9" l, three parts, three handles	32.00
Relish, 11" l, three parts, two handles	32.00
Relish, 12" d, five parts	37.50
Relish, 12" d, six parts	37.50

ITEM	CRYSTAL
Relish, 12" l, three parts	35.00
Salad bowl, 9" d	30.00
Salt and pepper shakers, pr	25.00
Salt and pepper shakers tray	12.00
Saucer	1.50
Sherbet, 5 oz	8.50
Sherry, 1-3/4" oz	32.00
Sugar, 3 oz	6.00
Sugar, 6 oz	7.50
Sugar, 8 oz	10.00
Sweetmeat, center handle, 6-1/2"	36.00
Sweetmeat, star shape, two handles, 5-1/2" or 7"	40.00
Torte plate, 13" d, rolled edge	32.00
Torte plate, 14" d, rolled or plain edge	37.50
Torte plate, 16" d, rolled edge	40.00
Tumbler, 8 oz, ftd	10.00
Tumbler, 9 oz, flat or ftd	10.00
Urn, cov, 9" h, ftd	125.00
Vase, 9" h, ftd, fan	32.00
Vase, 9" h, ftd, round	40.00
Whiskey, 2 oz, flat or ftd	15.00
Wine, 3 oz	20.00

THISTLE

Manufactured by MacBeth-Evans, Charleroi, Pennsylvania, about 1929-1930.

Pieces were made in crystal, green, pink, and yellow. Production was limited in crystal and yellow.

Reproductions: † Recent reproductions have been found in pink, a darker emerald green, and wisteria. Several of the reproductions have a scalloped edge. Reproductions include the cake plate, fruit bowl, pitcher, salt and pepper shakers, and small tumbler.

ITEM	GREEN	PINK
Cake plate, 13" d, heavy †	195.00	225.00
Cereal bowl, 5-1/2" d	38.00	60.00
Cup, thin	32.00	24.00
Fruit bowl, 10-1/4" d †	250.00	450.00
Plate, 8" d, luncheon	22.00	20.00
Plate, 10-1/4" d, grill	35.00	30.00
Saucer	12.00	12.00

Thistle, green luncheon plate, $22.

THUMBPRINT

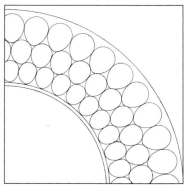

Manufactured by Federal Glass Company, Columbus, Ohio, from 1927 to 1930.

Pieces were made in green.

ITEM	GREEN
Berry bowl, 4-3/4" d	10.00
Berry bowl, 8" d	25.00
Cereal bowl, 5" d	10.00
Creamer, ftd	12.00
Cup	8.00
Fruit bowl, 5" d	10.00
Juice tumbler, 4" h	6.00
Iced tea tumbler	12.00
Milk pitcher	25.00
Pitcher, 7-1/4" h	65.00
Plate, 6" d, sherbet	4.50
Plate, 8" d, luncheon	7.00
Plate, 9-1/4" d, dinner	24.00

ITEM	GREEN
Salt and pepper shakers, pr.	65.00
Saucer	4.00
Sherbet	9.00
Sugar, ftd	10.00
Vase, 9" h	65.00
Tumbler, 5" h	6.50
Tumbler, 5-1/2" h	10.00
Whiskey, 2-1/4" h	6.50

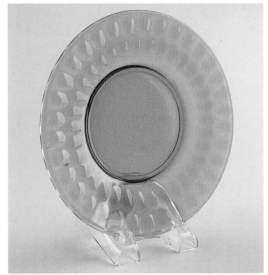

Thumbprint, green luncheon plate, $7.

Thumbprint, green vase, $65.

TULIP

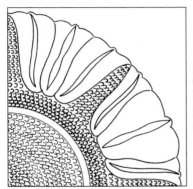

Manufactured by Dell Glass Company, Millville, New Jersey, in the early 1930s.

Pieces were made in amber, amethyst, blue, crystal, and green.

ITEM	AMBER	AMETHYST	BLUE	CRYSTAL	GREEN
Bowl, 6" d	20.00	18.00	18.00	20.00	20.00
Bowl, 13-1/4" l, oblong oval	940.00	100.00	100.00	80.00	90.00
Candleholders, pr, 3-3/4" h	24.50	30.00	30.00	24.50	24.50
Candy, cov	175.00	195.00	195.00	150.00	165.00
Creamer	20.00	25.00	25.00	20.00	25.00
Cup	15.00	20.00	20.00	15.00	15.00
Decanter, orig stopper	—	500.00	500.00	—	350.00
Ice tub, 4-7/8" wide, 3" deep	70.00	95.00	95.00	65.00	65.00
Juice tumbler	15.00	40.00	40.00	15.00	15.00
Plate, 6" d	10.00	12.00	22.00	9.50	10.00
Plate, 7-1/4" d	12.00	10.00	24.00	13.50	24.00
Plate, 10-1/4" d	35.00	40.00	40.00	20.00	32.00
Saucer	10.00	8.50	10.00	5.00	7.50

ITEM	AMBER	AMETHYST	BLUE	CRYSTAL	GREEN
Sherbet, 3-3/4" h, flat	20.00	24.00	24.00	18.00	20.00
Sugar	20.00	25.00	25.00	20.00	20.00
Tumbler, 4-5/8" h, 3-3/8" d	—	—	—	—	150.00
Whiskey	22.00	28.00	30.00	20.00	25.00

Tulip, green creamer, $25.

TWIGGY

Manufactured by Indiana Glass Company, Dunkirk, Indiana, in the 1950s and early 1960s.

Pieces were made in crystal, some green and pink, and rarely in light blue with an opalescent edge. Collector interest is highest in the crystal.

ITEMS	CRYSTAL
Jelly, 8" d	8.00
Nappy, 4-1/2" d	5.00
Nappy, 8" d	8.00
Plate, 8" d	8.00
Punch bowl	35.00
Punch cup	5.00
Relish, 10" d, divided	12.00
Relish, 8" d	10.00
Snack plate, 10" d	8.00

Twiggy, crystal 4-1/2" d nappy, $5.

*Twiggy, green 8" d nappy, **$12**.*

TWISTED OPTIC

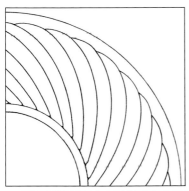

Manufactured by Imperial Glass Company, Bellaire, Ohio, from 1927 to 1930.

Pieces were made in amber, blue, canary, green, and pink.

ITEM	AMBER	BLUE	CANARY	GREEN	PINK
Basket, 10" h	55.00	95.00	75.00	60.00	60.00
Bowl, 7" d, ruffled	—	—	—	—	18.00
Bowl, 9" d	18.50	28.50	28.50	18.50	35.00
Bowl, 11-1/2" d, 4-1/4" h	24.00	48.00	48.00	24.00	24.00
Candlesticks, pr, 3" h	22.00	40.00	40.00	35.00	22.00
Candlesticks, pr, 8" h	30.00	50.00	50.00	30.00	30.00
Candy jar, cov, flat	25.00	50.00	50.00	40.00	25.00
Candy jar, cov, flat, flange edge	50.00	90.00	90.00	55.00	55.00
Candy jar, cov, ftd, flange edge	50.00	90.00	90.00	55.00	55.00
Candy jar, cov, ftd, short	55.00	100.00	100.00	60.00	60.00
Candy jar, cov, ftd, tall	55.00	100.00	100.00	35.00	60.00
Cereal bowl, 5"d	8.50	15.00	15.00	10.00	10.00
Cologne bottle, stopper	60.00	85.00	85.00	60.00	60.00

ITEM	AMBER	BLUE	CANARY	GREEN	PINK
Console bowl, 10-1/2" d	25.00	45.00	45.00	25.00	35.00
Cream soup bowl, 4-3/4" d	12.00	25.00	25.00	15.00	15.00
Creamer	8.00	14.00	14.00	8.00	8.00
Cup	7.50	12.50	12.50	5.00	6.00
Mayonnaise	20.00	50.00	55.00	30.00	30.00
Pitcher, 64 oz.	45.00	—	—	40.00	42.00
Plate, 6" d, sherbet	3.00	6.50	7.50	3.00	3.00

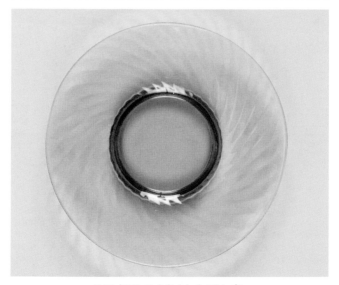

Twisted Optic, pink 6" d sherbet plate, $3.

Twisted Optic, green tall footed covered candy dish, $35.

ITEM	AMBER	BLUE	CANARY	GREEN	PINK
Plate, 7" d, salad	4.00	8.00	800	4.00	4.00
Plate, 7-1/2 x 9" l, oval	6.00	12.00	12.00	6.00	6.00
Plate, 8" d, luncheon	6.00	12.00	12.00	6.00	5.00
Powder jar, cov	38.00	65.00	65.00	38.00	60.00
Preserve jar	30.00	—	—	30.00	30.00
Salad bowl, 7"d	12.00	25.00	25.00	15.00	15.00
Sandwich plate, 10" d	12.00	20.00	20.00	15.00	15.00
Sandwich server, center handle	22.00	35.00	35.00	22.00	22.00
Sandwich server, two handles, flat	15.00	20.00	20.00	15.00	15.00
Saucer	2.50	4.50	4.50	2.50	2.50
Sherbet	7.50	12.00	15.00	7.00	7.50
Sugar	8.00	14.00	14.00	8.00	8.00
Tumbler, 4-1/2" h, 9 oz	6.50	—	—	6.50	7.00
Tumbler, 5-1/4" h, 12 oz	9.50	—	—	9.50	10.00
Vase, 7-1/4" h, two handles, rolled edge	35.00	65.00	65.00	40.00	40.00
Vase, 8" h, two handles, fan	45.00	95.00	95.00	50.00	50.00
Vase, 8" h, two handles, straight edge	45.00	95.00	95.00	50.00	50.00

*Twisted Optic, two green covered preserve jars,
covers notched for spoon, $30 each.*

U.S. SWIRL

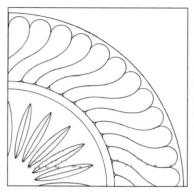

Manufactured by U.S. Glass Company in the late 1920s.

Pieces were made in crystal, green, iridescent, and pink. Production in crystal and iridescent was limited.

ITEM	GREEN	PINK
Berry bowl, 4-3/8" d	8.00	10.00
Berry bowl, 7-7/8" d	15.00	17.00
Bowl, 5-1/2" d, handle	10.00	12.00
Bowl, 8-1/4" l, 2-3/4" h, oval	40.00	40.00
Bowl, 8-3/8" l, 1-3/4" h, oval	50.00	50.00
Butter dish, cov	115.00	115.00
Candy, cov, two handles	30.00	32.00
Comport, 4-3/4" h	40.00	45.00
Creamer	15.00	17.50
Pitcher, 48 oz, 8" h	55.00	50.00
Plate, 6-1/8" d, sherbet	3.00	2.50
Plate, 7-7/8" d, salad	6.00	6.50

ITEM	GREEN	PINK
Salt and pepper shakers, pr	48.00	45.00
Sherbet, 3-1/4" h	5.00	6.00
Sugar, cov	35.00	32.00
Tumbler, 8 oz, 3-5/8" h	12.00	12.00
Tumbler, 12 oz, 4-3/4" h	15.00	17.50
Vase, 6-1/2" h	25.00	25.00

U.S. Swirl, green comport, $40; 8-3/8" l x 1-3/4" d oval bowl, $50.

U.S. Swirl, green pitcher, $55.

VERNON

NO. 616

Manufactured by Indiana Glass Company, Dunkirk, Indiana, from 1930 to 1932.

Pieces were made in crystal, green, and yellow.

ITEM	CRYSTAL	GREEN	YELLOW
Creamer, ftd	10.00	25.00	30.00
Cup	10.00	15.00	18.00
Plate, 8" d, luncheon	6.00	10.00	12.00
Sandwich plate, 11-1/2" d	14.00	25.00	30.00
Saucer	4.00	6.00	6.00
Sugar, ftd	10.00	25.00	30.00
Tumbler, 5" h, ftd	16.00	40.00	45.00

Vernon, yellow tumbler, $45.

VICTORY

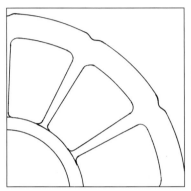

Manufactured by Diamond Glass-Ware Company, Indiana, Pennsylvania, from 1929 to 1932.

Pieces were made in amber, black, cobalt blue, green, and pink.

ITEM	AMBER	BLACK	COBALT BLUE	GREEN	PINK
Bonbon, 7" d	15.00	20.00	20.00	15.00	15.00
Bowl, 11" d, rolled edge	30.00	50.00	50.00	30.00	30.00
Bowl, 12-1/2" d, flat edge	30.00	60.00	60.00	30.00	30.00
Candlesticks, pr, 3" h	35.00	100.00	100.00	35.00	35.00
Cereal bowl, 6-1/2" d	15.00	30.00	30.00	15.00	12.00
Cheese and cracker set, 12" d indented plate and comport	45.00	—	—	45.00	45.00
Comport, 6" h, 6-1/4" d	18.00	—	—	18.00	18.00
Console bowl, 12" d	35.00	65.00	65.00	35.00	35.00
Creamer	17.50	45.00	45.00	15.00	15.00
Cup	12.00	35.00	40.00	10.00	10.00
Goblet, 7 oz, 5" h	20.00	—	—	20.00	20.00

ITEM	AMBER	BLACK	COBALT BLUE	GREEN	PINK
Gravy boat, underplate	185.00	325.00	325.00	185.00	185.00
Mayonnaise set, 3-1/2" h, 5-1/2" d bowl, 8-1/2" d indented plate, ladle	55.00	100.00	100.00	55.00	55.00
Plate, 6" d, bread and butter	6.50	17.50	17.50	6.50	6.50
Plate, 7" d, salad	7.50	20.00	20.00	8.00	7.00
Plate, 8" d, luncheon	10.00	32.00	36.00	8.00	10.00
Plate, 9" d, dinner	20.00	40.00	40.00	22.00	20.00
Platter, 12" l, oval	30.00	70.00	70.00	32.00	32.00
Sandwich server, center handle	30.00	65.00	65.00	32.00	30.00
Saucer	5.00	12.50	12.50	5.00	5.00
Sherbet, ftd	15.00	27.50	27.50	15.00	15.00
Soup bowl, 8-1/2" d, flat	20.00	45.00	45.00	20.00	20.00
Sugar	15.00	45.00	45.00	15.00	15.00
Vegetable bowl, 9" l, oval	35.00	85.00	85.00	35.00	35.00

Victory, pink creamer, $15; sugar, $15.

Victory, green with gold edge cheese and cracker plate, $25.

WATERFORD
WAFFLE

Manufactured by Hocking Glass Company, Lancaster, Ohio, from 1938 to 1944.

Pieces were made in crystal, forest green (1950s), pink, white, and yellow. Forest green production was limited; currently an ashtray is valued at $5 and a 13-3/4" diameter sandwich plate is $45. Yellow was also limited. Collector interest is low in white.

ITEM	CRYSTAL	PINK
Ashtray, 4" d	7.50	—
Berry bowl, 4-3/4" d	8.50	18.00
Berry bowl, 8-1/4" d	12.00	36.00
Bonbon, cov	45.00	
Butter dish, cov	30.00	250.00
Cake plate, 10-1/4" d, handles	15.00	30.00
Cereal bowl, 5-1/2" d	18.50	32.00
Coaster, 4" d	3.50	—
Creamer, Miss America style	35.00	—
Creamer, oval	5.00	15.00
Cup	7.50	18.00
Cup, Miss America style	—	45.00
Goblet, 5-1/2" h, Miss America style	35.00	85.00

Waterford, crystal 7-1/8" d salad plate, $6; 5-1/4" h goblet, $12.

ITEM	CRYSTAL	PINK
Goblet, 5-1/4" h	12.00	—
Goblet, 5-5/8" h	20.00	—
Juice pitcher, 42 oz, tilted	30.00	—
Juice tumbler, 5 oz, 3-1/2" h, Miss America style	—	65.00
Lamp, 4" spherical base	45.00	—
Pitcher, 80 oz, tilted, ice lip	50.00	165.00
Plate, 6" d, sherbet	4.50	9.50
Plate, 7-1/8" d, salad	6.00	15.00
Plate, 9-5/8" d, dinner	12.00	35.00
Platter, 14" l	14.00	—
Relish, 13-3/4" d, five parts	20.00	—
Salt and pepper shakers, pr	12.00	—
Sandwich plate, 13-3/4" d	15.00	40.00
Saucer	3.00	5.00
Sherbet, ftd	5.00	15.00
Sherbet, ftd, scalloped base	8.00	—
Sugar, cov	12.50	35.00
Sugar, Miss America style	35.00	—
Tray, 10-1/4" l, handles	10.00	—
Tumbler, 10 oz, 4-7/8" h, ftd	18.00	30.00

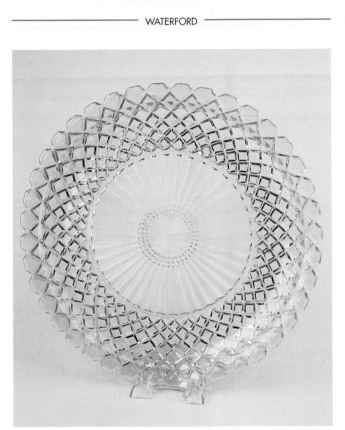

Waterford, crystal dinner plate, $12.

WEXFORD

Manufactured by Anchor Hocking Glass Corp.

Pieces were made in crystal.

ITEM	CRYSTAL
Bowl, 7-3/4" d, ftd	30.00
Bud vase, 9" h	8.00
Butter dish, cov	30.00
Candlestick	9.00
Candy dish, cov, 7-3/4" d	15.00
Canister, cov, coffee, 5-3/8" h	15.00
Canister, cov, flour, 9-1/4" h	22.00
Canister, cov, sugar, 6-3/8" h	18.00
Centerpiece bowl	18.00
Champagne, 3-5/8" h	8.00
Chip and dip set	20.00
Claret, 5-3/8" h	10.00
Creamer, 4-1/4" h	10.00

Wexford, crystal goblet, $12.

ITEM	CRYSTAL
Cruet, 7-1/2" h	15.00
Cup, ftd, 3" h	6.00
Decanter, 11-3/4" h	30.00
Decanter, 14-1/2" h	35.00
Dessert bowl, 5-1/2" d	4.00
Fruit bowl, 10" d, ftd	30.00
Goblet, 6-5/8" h	12.00
Iced tea tumbler, 5-1/2" h, 12 oz	12.00
Juice tumbler	9.00
Old fashioned tumbler, 3-3/4" h	9.00
Pitcher, 5-1/4" h, pint	20.00
Pitcher, 9-3/4" h, two-quart	25.00
Plate, luncheon	9.00
Plate, salad	6.00
Punch bowl	10.00
Punch cup, 3" d	3.00
Relish	20.00
Relish, three parts, 8-5/8" l	18.00
Salad bowl, 9-3/4" d	15.00
Serving plate	20.00
Sherbet, low	6.50
Sugar, cov, 5-1/4" h, ftd	15.00
Toothpick holder	12.00
Torte plate, 14" d	24.00
Tumbler, 5-1/2" h, flat	6.00
Vase, ftd	20.00
Wine, 4-1/2" h	10.00

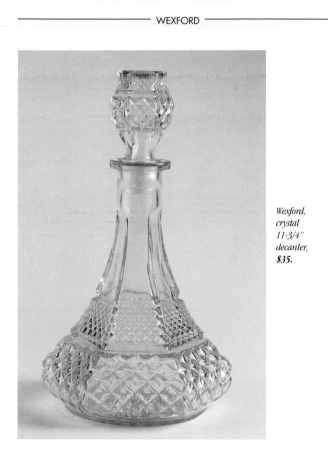

Wexford, crystal 11-3/4" decanter, $35.

WILD ROSE WITH LEAVES & BERRIES

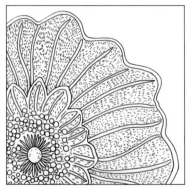

Manufactured by Indiana Glass Company, Dunkirk, Indiana, from the early 1950s to 1980s.

Pieces were made in crystal, iridescent, milk glass, multicolored blue, green, pink, and yellow, satinized crystal, satinized green, pink, and yellow, sprayed green lavender, and pink.

ITEM	CRYSTAL, MILK GLASS, SATINIZED CRYSTAL	IRIDESCENT, SATINIZED COLORS, SPRAYED COLORS	MULTICOLORED
Bowl, large	10.00	15.00	40.00
Candleholder	5.00	8.00	20.00
Relish, handle	6.50	10.00	25.00
Relish, handle, divided	7.50	12.00	25.00
Sauce bowl, handle	4.00	7.00	12.00
Sherbet	5.00	6.50	15.00
Sherbet plate	2.50	3.50	9.00
Tray, two handles	15.00	20.00	35.00

Wild Rose with Leaves & Berries, crystal bowl, **$10.**

WINDSOR

WINDSOR DIAMOND

Manufactured by Jeannette Glass Company, Jeannette, Pennsylvania, from 1936 to 1946.

Pieces were made in crystal, green, and pink with limited production in amberina red, delphite, and ice blue.

ITEM	CRYSTAL	GREEN	PINK
Ashtray, 5-3/4" d	15.00	75.00	55.00
Berry bowl, 4-3/4" d	5.00	12.00	11.50
Berry bowl, 8-1/2" d	18.00	18.50	30.00
Bowl, 5" l, pointed edge	10.00	—	25.00
Bowl, 7 x 11-3/4", boat shape	18.00	45.00	45.00
Bowl, 7-1/2" d, three legs	8.00	—	24.00
Bowl, 8" d, two handles	9.00	24.00	20.00
Bowl, 8" l, pointed edge	10.00	—	48.00
Bowl, 10-1/2" l, pointed edge	25.00	—	32.00
Butter dish, cov	40.00	95.00	65.00
Cake plate, 10-3/4" d, ftd	12.00	24.00	35.00

ITEM	CRYSTAL	GREEN	PINK
Candlesticks, pr, 3" h	25.00	—	85.00
Candy jar, cov	18.00	—	—
Cereal bowl, 5-3/8" d	10.00	30.00	35.00
Chop plate, 13-5/8" d	25.00	42.00	40.00
Coaster, 3-1/4" d	8.50	18.00	25.00
Comport	9.00	—	—
Cream soup plate, 5" d	6.00	32.00	25.00
Creamer	5.00	15.00	15.00
Creamer, Holiday shape	7.50	—	—
Cup	5.00	22.00	12.00
Fruit console, 12-1/2" d	45.00	—	135.00
Pitcher, 16 oz, 4-1/2" h	20.00	—	115.00
Pitcher, 52 oz, 6-3/4" h	15.00	65.00	45.00
Plate, 6" d, sherbet	3.75	12.00	6.00
Plate, 7" d, salad	4.50	20.00	25.00
Plate, 9" d, dinner	8.00	25.00	25.00
Plate, 10-1/4" d	15.00	30.00	25.00
Platter, 11-1/2" l, oval	8.00	25.00	35.00
Powder jar	15.00	—	55.00
Relish platter, 11-1/2" l, divided	15.00	—	200.00
Salad bowl, 10-1/2" d	12.00	—	—
Salt and pepper shakers, pr	20.00	50.00	48.00
Sandwich plate, 10" d, closed handles	10.00	—	24.00
Sandwich plate, 10" d, open handles	12.50	18.00	24.00
Saucer	2.50	5.00	4.50
Sherbet, ftd	3.50	15.00	14.50
Sugar, cov	10.00	35.00	45.00
Sugar, cov, Holiday shape	12.00	—	100.00
Tray, 4" sq	5.00	12.00	10.00
Tray, 4" sq, handles	6.00	—	40.00
Tray, 4-1/8" x 9"	5.00	16.00	10.00
Tray, 4-1/8" x 9", handles	9.00	—	50.00

ITEM	CRYSTAL	GREEN	PINK
Tray, 8-1/2" x 9-3/4"	7.00	35.00	25.00
Tray, 8-1/2" x 9-3/4", handles	14.00	45.00	85.00
Tumbler, 4" h, ftd	7.00	—	—
Tumbler, 5 oz, 3-1/4" h	9.00	35.00	28.00
Tumbler, 7-1/4" h, ftd	19.00	—	—
Tumbler, 9 oz, 4" h	7.50	30.00	22.00
Tumbler, 11 oz, 4-5/8" h	8.00	—	—

*Windsor, pink 11-1/2" oval platter, $35, in back; 10-1/2" oval
bowl with pointed ends, $32; 8-1/2" l oval bowl, $30.*

ITEM	CRYSTAL	GREEN	PINK
Tumbler, 12 oz, 5" h	10.00	55.00	37.50
Tumbler, 11 oz, 5" h, ftd	10.00	—	—
Vegetable bowl, 9-1/2" l, oval	7.50	30.00	25.00

Windsor, crystal covered butter with steeple type finial, $40; green covered butter, $95; green 10-1/4" d cake plate with three legs, $24.

*Windsor, crystal chop plate, **$25**; pink pitcher, 16 oz, **$115**.*

YORKTOWN

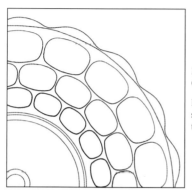

Manufactured by Federal Glass Company in the mid 1950s.

Pieces were made in crystal, iridescent, smoke, white, and yellow. Values for all the colors are about the same.

ITEMS	CRYSTAL
Berry bowl, 5-1/2" d	3.50
Berry bowl, 9-1/2" d	10.00
Celery tray, 10" l	10.00
Creamer	6.00
Cup	5.50
Fruit bowl, 10" d, ftd	18.00
Iced tea tumbler, 5-1/4" h, 13 oz	7.50
Juice tumbler, 3-7/8" h, 6 oz	4.00
Mug	15.00
Plate, 8-1/4" d	4.50
Plates, 11-1/2" d	8.50
Punch bowl set	40.00

ITEMS	CRYSTAL
Punch cup	2.50
Saucer	1.00
Sherbet, 7 oz	3.50
Snack cup	2.50
Snack plate with indent	3.50
Sugar	6.00
Tumbler, 4-3/4" h, 10 oz	6.00
Vase, 8" h	15.00

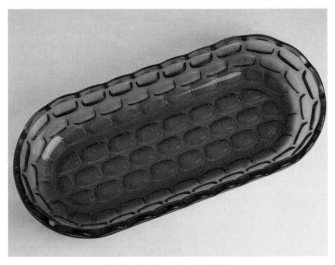

Yorktown, yellow celery tray, $10.

Yorktown, crystal fruit bowl, $18.

RESOURCES

COLLECTORS' CLUBS

INTERNATIONAL ASSOCIATIONS

Akro Agate Club, Inc.
236 Brinker St.
Bellevue, OH 44811
Website: http://club.akroagate.us

**Canadian Depression
Glass Association**
PO Box 41564
HLRPO, 230 Sandalwood Pkwy
Brampton, Ontario L6Z 4R1 Canada
Website: http://www.CDGA.com

**Fenton Art Glass
Collectors of America, Inc.**
PO Box 384
Williamstown, WV 26187
Website: users.wirefire.com/faglassinc.

**Fostoria Glass Society
of America, Inc.**
PO Box 826
Moundsville, WV 26041
Website: www.fostoriaglass.org

H.C. Fry Glass Society
PO Box 41
Beaver, PA 15009
Website: thenostalgialeague.com/fryglass/

**Heisey Collectors
of America, Inc.**
169 N. Church St.
Newark, OH 43055
Website: www.heiseymuseum.org

Indiana Glass Society
PO Box 444
Hampstead, MD 21074

**National Cambridge
Collectors Inc.**
PO Box 416
Cambridge, OH 43725
Website: www.cambridgeglass.org

National Depression Glass Association
PO Box 8264
Wichita, KS 67208-0264
Website: www.ndga.org

National Duncan Glass Society, Inc.
525 Jefferson Ave.
Washington, PA 15301
Website: www.duncanmiller.net

**National Imperial Glass
Collectors Society**
PO Box 534
Bellaire, OH 43906
Website: www.imperialglass.org

**National Westmoreland Glass
Collectors Club**
PO Box 372
Westmoreland City, PA 15692
Website: www.westmorelandglassclub.org

**Old Morgantown Glass
Collectors Guild Inc.**
PO Box 894
Morgantown, WV 26507-0894
Website: www.oldmorgantown.org

**Pacific Northwest
Fenton Association**
PO Box 881
Tillamook, OR 97141
Website: www.pnwfa.com

**Paden City
Glass Society, Inc.**
PO Box 139
Paden City, WV 26159
Website: www.padencityglasssociety.com

**Tiffin Glass
Collectors' Club**
PO Box 554
Tiffin, OH 44883
Website: www.tiffinglass.org

REGIONAL

There are many regional clubs where people gather to discuss Depression-era glassware. Many hold wonderful Depression glass shows that are open to collectors as well as the general public. Check with the National Depression Glass Association for a club in your region if none is listed below. The Internet has also changed the face of collector clubs. Many no longer have a "bricks and mortar address" but can be found online with the location of meeting places, dates, show schedules, etc.

Big "D" Pression Glass Club
10 Windling Creek Trail
Garland, TX 75043

Buckeye Dee Geer's
2501 Campbell St.
Sandusky, OH 44870

Central Florida Glassaholics
421 E Park St.
Lakeland, FL 33803
Website: www.GLASSaholics.com

Central Jersey Depression Glass Club
181 Riviera Dr.
Brick Town, NJ 08723

Charter Oak Depression Glass Club
PO Box 604
Chester, CT 06412

Cigar City Depression Glass Club
PO Box 17322
Tampa, FL 33612

Crescent City Depression Glass Club
PO Box 55981
Metairie, LA 70055
Website: crescentcitydglass.org

Depression Era Glass Society of Wisconsin
1534 S. Wisconsin Ave.
Racine, WI 53403

Depression Glass Club of Greater Rochester
PO Box 10362
Rochester, NY 14610
Website: dgcrochester.org

Evergreen Depression Era Collectors
312 Golden Gate
Fircrest, WA 98466

Fire King Collectors Club
1406 E. 14th St.
Des Moines, IA 50316

**Greater Tulsa Depression
Era Glass Club**
PO Box 470763
Tulsa, OK 74147-0763

**Great Lakes Depression
Glass Club**
Website: www.depressionglassclub.com

**Hazelnut Depression
Glass Club**
129 Southcliff Dr.
Findlay, OH 45840

Heart of America Glass Collectors
14404 E. 36th Terrace
Independence, MO 64055
Website: hoagc.org

Houston Glass Club
PO Box 1254
Rosenberg, TX 77471-1254
Website: www.houstonglassclub.org

Hudson Valley Depression Club
129 Southcliff Dr.
Findlay, OH 45840

**Kansas City Depression
Glass Club**
12950 East 51st Terrace
Independence, MO 64055

**Illinois Valley Depression
Glass Club**
RR 1, Box 52
Rushville, IL 62681

Iowa Depression Glass Club
1517 SE Delaware Ave, Unit #1
Ankeny, IA 50021
Website: home.earthlink.net/~idgc

**Land of Sunshine Depression
Glass Club**
PO Box 560275
Orlando, FL 32856-0275

Liberty Bell Glass Club
30 Lee Lane
Audobon, PA 19403-2044

Lincoln Land Depression Glass Club
1625 Dial Court
Springfield, IL 62704

Long Island Depression Glass Society
PO Box 147
West Sayville, NY 11796

Low Country Depression Glass Club
209 Trestle Wood Dr.
Summersville, SC 29483

Michigan Depression Glass Club
Website: michigandepressionglass.com

Montclair Depression Glass Club
1254 Karesh Ave.
Pomona, CA 91767

Mountain Laurel Depression Glass Club
942 Main St.
Hartford, CT 06103

**Northeast Florida
Depression Glass Club**
PO Box 338
Whitehouse, FL 32220

North Jersey Dee Geer's
82 High St.
Butler, NJ 07405

Nutmeg Depression Glass Club
230 Hillside Ave.
Naugatuck, CT 06770

Old Dominion Depression Glass Club
8415 W. Rugby Rd.
Manassas, VA 22111

Pikes Peak Depression Glass Club
2029 Devon
Colorado Springs, CO 80909
Website: ppdgc.com

Portland's Rain of Glass, Inc.
PO Box 819
Portland, OR 97207-0819

**Rocky Mountain Depression
Glass Society**
Website: www.rmdgs.com

Sandlapper Depression Glass Club
503 Leyswood Dr.
Greenville, SC 29615

South Bay Depression Glass Society
PO Box 7400
Torrance, CA 90504-7400

South Florida Depression Glass Club
PO Box 845
Boca Raton, FL 33429
Website: www.sfdgc.com

**Sparkling Clearwater Depression
Glass Club**
405 Seminole St
Clearwater, FL

Spokane Falls Depression Glass Etc.
PO Box 113
Veradale, WA 99037

**Three Rivers Depression Era
Glass Society**
3275 Sylvan Rd.
Bethel Park, PA 15102
Website: pghdepressionglass.org

**Top of Texas Depression Era
Glass Club**
42149 1st St.
Lubbock, TX 79424

Tri-State Depression Era Glass Club
RD #6, Box 560D
Washington, PA 15301

20-30-40 Society, Inc.
PO Box 856
LaGrange, IL 60525

Western North Carolina
PO Box 116
Mars Hill, NC 28743

Western Reserve Depression Glass Club
8669 Courtland Dr.
Strongsville, OH 44136.

INTERNET SITES

Many Internet websites offer information about Depression-era glassware in the form of online articles, references, chats, dates for shows, etc. Be sure to check out the National Depression Glass Association website (www.ndga.org) for links to several great Depression glass websites. There are hundreds of websites from which to purchase Depression-era glassware as well as numerous e-auctions.

INDEX OF PATTERNS